A
SHORT
HISTORY
OF ISLAMIC
THOUGHT

A
SHORT
HISTORY
OF ISLAMIC
THOUGHT

FITZROY
MORRISSEY

OXFORD
UNIVERSITY PRESS

OXFORD
UNIVERSITY PRESS

Oxford University Press is a department of the University of Oxford. It furthers
the University's objective of excellence in research, scholarship, and education
by publishing worldwide. Oxford is a registered trade mark of Oxford University
Press in the UK and certain other countries.

Published in the United States of America by Oxford University Press
198 Madison Avenue, New York, NY 10016, United States of America.

CIP data is on file at the Library of Congress.

ISBN 9780197522011

1 3 5 7 9 8 6 4 2

Printed by Sheridan Books, United States of America

TABLE OF CONTENTS

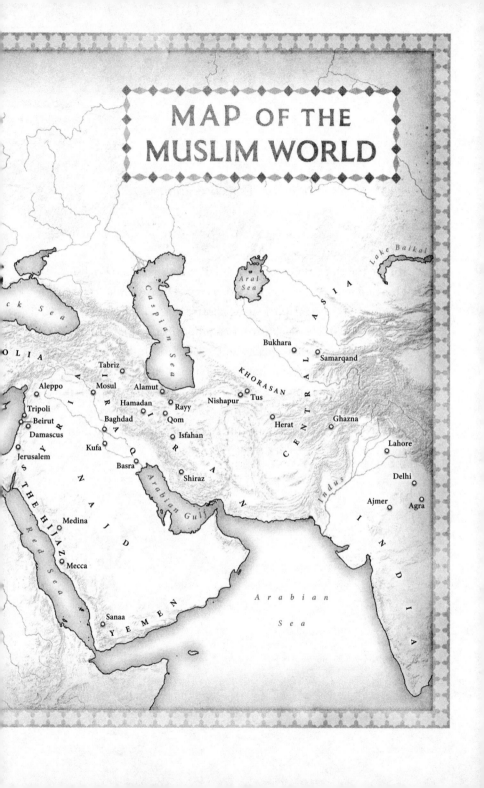

Note on Transliteration

For the transliteration of Arabic and Persian terms into English, I have adopted a highly simplified system. The Arabic letter *'ayn* is represented as a forward-facing apostrophe ('), while the *hamza* is represented as a backward-facing apostrophe ('). No other special characters have been used, except for in the endnotes where books or articles that use them are cited. Arabic and Persian terms that appear in one or more of the standard English dictionaries (e.g. ulema), and proper names that are in wide use in English (e.g. Nasser, Khomeini), are written according to their common English spelling.

PREFACE

In a book published in 1959, the Egyptian religious leader Mahmud Shaltut (1893–1963) attempted to define the basic elements of Islam: 'Islam,' he wrote, 'is the religion of God (*din Allah*), who entrusted His teachings concerning His fundamental principles and His laws to the Prophet Muhammad and gave him the task of calling all people to it.'[1]

As Shaltut's definition indicates, Islam is first and foremost a religion, or what in Arabic is called a *din*: a way of believing in God and of organizing life around obedience to Him. The very word *islam*, an Arabic word literally meaning 'submission', originally denoted the act of giving oneself entirely and exclusively to God.[2] Muslims, those who practise Islam, call this deity Allah, another Arabic word, which simply means 'God'.

More specifically, Islam, like Judaism and Christianity, is a monotheistic religion. Allah, it teaches, is the one and only deity. The first half of the *shahada*, the Islamic testimony of faith, is *la ilaha illa Allah*, 'There is no god but Allah'. The first and fundamental principle of Islamic belief is *tawhid*, the act of declaring God's unity.

Islam is also, again like Judaism and Christianity, a scriptural religion. Its adherents revere a sacred and authoritative book

1

called the Qur'an (literally, 'the recitation').[3] Muslims believe that Allah revealed the Qur'an, through the angel Gabriel, to a prophet (*nabi*) or messenger (*rasul*) named Muhammad, in the first decades of the seventh century AD. *Wa-Muhammad rasul Allah*, 'and Muhammad is the messenger of Allah', runs the second half of the *shahada*. In the Islamic view, the Qur'an is the very word of Allah. While Christians believe that God's word became flesh, Muslims believe that it became a book; like a Christian receiving holy communion, a Muslim reciting the Qur'an believes him- or herself to be partaking in the eternal word of God.[4]

Islam is also an Arabic religion. Muhammad was a native of Mecca, in the Hijaz region of the Arabian Peninsula, and the scripture he received was in Arabic. Muslims regard Arabic as the language of Allah, pray in Arabic, and, for the first five centuries or so of Islamic history, used Arabic almost exclusively as the language of their religious writings, whatever their ethnic or linguistic background.[5] Though other languages – like Persian, Turkish, and Urdu – would later become key languages of Islamic thought, a special, almost mystical attachment to the Arabic language is still discernible among Muslims today.[6]

Despite the centrality of the Arabic language, however, Islam is also a universal religion, meaning that, like Christians, Muslims believe their religion to be valid for all times, peoples, and places. This idea is rooted in the notion that the Qur'an is perfect and complete, and Muhammad the best and final prophet sent to mankind, the implication being that only by following Muhammad and his message can a person fully serve the one God.

Islam is also (to borrow a phrase from the sociologist Max Weber) a 'this-worldly' religion, concerned with giving order to the lives of individuals and communities in this world.[7] The framework for this ordering of life is supplied by the Shariʿa, an Arabic word originally meaning the 'path to water', but used in Islamic thought to denote the law decreed by Allah. As we shall see, like the Halakha or Jewish law, this divine law is thought to extend to areas of life that a modern secular law wouldn't normally cover, like how to pray or what foods to avoid.

At the same time, Islam is also a salvific religion, concerned with the fate of human beings in the world-to-come. After belief in God's unity and prophecy, the third fundamental principle of Islamic faith is the belief in the 'return' (maʿad) to Allah after death.[8] As well as being a guide to life on earth, then, the Shariʿa is also, as the Ottoman scholar Katib Çelebi (1609–57) put it, playing on the original meaning of the word, 'a path to the cooling streams of God's mercy for those who thirst'.[9]

Muslims have tended to read all of these ideas about their religion out of their scripture. As the Egyptian Qur'an scholar Nasr Hamid Abu Zayd (1943–2010) has written, 'Whatever issue emerges in the life of Muslim communities, the Qur'an is the first source to be consulted for a solution.'[10] Yet, though the monotheistic message of the Qur'an is the foundation of Islam, Islam is not just the Qur'an, nor should Islam be reduced to these basic principles. Alongside the Islamic scripture, other sources, most notably the sayings (hadith) and customs (sunna) of Muhammad, have been recognized as sacred and authoritative by the adherents of Islam. Just as importantly, like all religions, Islam has been subject to a process of historical development and contestation. As Muslims have wrestled with the teachings of the Qur'an and come under the influence of peoples of other faiths and traditions, they have developed new ideas – or, as they might see it, new ways of understanding the message of Muhammad – and founded new intellectual traditions that have often competed with one another for the right to claim the inheritance of their prophet.[11]

In the medieval (*c.*600–1500) and early modern (*c.*1500–1800) periods, four such traditions – legal theory (*fiqh*), Sufi mysticism (*tasawwuf*), revealed theology (*kalam*), and philosophy (*falsafa*) – and two major denominations, Sunnism and Shi'ism, dominated Islamic thought.[12] In modern times (*c.*1800–present), other traditions – like Islamic revivalism, modernism, and Salafism – have come to the foreground. As we shall see, the interaction and competition between these traditions has helped set the course for the development of Islam. To understand Islam properly, we have to understand this history.

Yet why should we care about Islamic thought and its history? In a world where politics, power, and privilege are often thought to explain everything, studying the intellectual history of a religious faith may seem like something of a luxury. Nevertheless, we *should* care about Islamic thought. Here are three reasons why.

First and most fundamentally, Islamic thought, as the present book aims to show, is intrinsically fascinating. 'What serious and intelligent persons over many generations ... have held to be significant,' the historian Marshall Hodgson once observed, 'rarely turns out, on close investigation, to be trivial'.[13] This is as true of serious and intelligent Muslims as of those of other faiths. Anyone interested in the history of ideas – in the story of human responses to the big questions about God, man, and the world – ought to take into account the Muslim contribution to that history.

Second, while the world may appear increasingly 'post-religious' from the vantage point of Western Europe and North America, religion nevertheless remains a key fact of life – for many, *the* key fact of life – for countless people everywhere. This seems particularly true for those whose religion is Islam. Adherents of Islam number some 1.8 billion people – about a quarter of the world's population – and can be found everywhere from Los Angeles to Jakarta. Whatever our own beliefs, engaging with our fellow human beings in a thoughtful way requires us to know something about the ideas that make them tick.

Third, as the historian of Islam Michael Cook has written, while most of the major world faiths are politically relevant, 'it is hard to miss the fact that Islam today has a higher political profile than any of its competitors.'[14] From Afghanistan to the Abraham Accords, the persecution of the Uyghurs in China to the reconversion of the Hagia Sophia in Istanbul, Islam and Muslims have long since become major and regular talking points in the political news cycle. An engaged and informed perspective on these phenomena is impossible without an understanding of Islam.

Studying the history of Islamic thought requires us to get inside the heads of people who, in many cases, may have held views very different from our own. It also necessitates thinking about a living faith that is embraced and cherished by hundreds of millions of people the world over. For these reasons and others, the history of Islamic thought is bound to take us into difficult and often controversial territory. This book does not court controversy, however, but understanding. Its agenda is strictly historical, rather than polemical or apologetic. Texts and ideas are analysed within their own historical contexts, rather than through the prism of modern values. This is not to deny the contemporary relevance of Islamic intellectual history, but rather to recognize that, as Noel Malcolm has put it, 'to understand the present we must understand the past, and we cannot do that properly if we try to force the past to conform to the standards of the present.'[15] By telling the story of one of the world's major faiths, this book aims to help us better understand both the present and the past.

Chapter One

THE WORD OF ALLAH

Recite in the name of your Lord who created, Who created
man from a clot of blood. Recite, your Lord is the Most
Generous. It was He who taught by the pen, Who taught man
what he did not know (Qur'an 96:1–5).[1]

With these words, Islam began.[2]

The man who heard them was Muhammad, a man born
around AD 570 in Mecca. Located in a mountain valley in the
Hijaz, in the west of the Arabian Peninsula, Mecca's climate is
notoriously harsh. A tenth-century Muslim geographer would
note the city's 'suffocating heat, deadly winds, [and] clouds of
flies', while the mountains that surround the city have been
described as 'unbelievably bare, rocky crags with no scrap of
soil, sharp, jagged, broken edges, sheer from top to bottom'.[3]

Yet, by Muhammad's time, Mecca was a thriving centre of
pilgrimage and trade. Under the leadership of the Quraysh,
the tribe into which Muhammad had been born, the city had
established itself as a key staging post on the south–north trading

route running from India to the Mediterranean, and the east–
west route that went from Iran to eastern Arabia. It was also the
site of the Ka'ba, the ancient cube-like shrine that stood at the
city's heart, to which pilgrims came from across the peninsula.

The religion of the pre-Islamic Arabs was a form of idol-
worship, a polytheism in which a multitude of deities and angels
were worshipped. Their conception of the world, recorded in the
Arabic poems of which they and their descendants were justly
proud, was of a universe ruled by chance, and of life as a game
in which fate (*al-dahr*) was the perennial winner and posthumous
justice inconceivable.[4]

Yet monotheism, the belief in a single god who created
and ruled over all, was by no means unknown to the Arabs.
On the peripheries of the Arabian Peninsula – in Yemen in
the south, and western Syria and Iraq to the north – Judaism
and Christianity had won many adherents over the preceding
centuries. Christians could be found travelling the well-trodden
trading routes across the peninsula or secluded away in their
monasteries, the lonely monk in his cell becoming a well-worn
trope of ancient Arabic poetry.[5] Within the Hijaz itself, the city
of Yathrib, about two hundred miles to the north of Mecca, had
a notable Jewish presence.[6] As his earliest Muslim biographers
recognized, Muhammad's cultural world was as much the world
of the prophets and patriarchs of the Hebrew Bible and the
monks and monasteries of Syria and Egypt as that of Arabian
sorcery and paganism.[7]

Under the influence of these monotheistic communities, the
pagans of Mecca had come to believe in a high god – called
al-ilah ('the deity') or Allah – who stood above the other, lesser
deities as the creator of the universe, the giver of rain, the

sanctifier of oaths, and the lord of the Ka'ba.[8] As a young man, the Islamic tradition informs us, Muhammad became devoted to this high god. Every year in the month of Ramadan he would seclude himself in a cave on Mount Hira – in that desolate mountain range on the outskirts of Mecca – and practise what the historical sources call *tahannuth*, a series of pious devotions, inspired by reverence for Allah, which concluded with the circumambulation of the Ka'ba.[9] In his fortieth year, around 610 of the Christian calendar, he did the same. That year, however, would be very different. One 'blessed night' (*layla mubaraka*) (44:3) – 'the night of power' (*laylat al-qadr*) (97:1), as the Qur'an describes it – he suddenly encountered a presence that commanded him to 'recite' (*iqra'*). Muhammad was initially resistant: 'But I cannot read!' he is said to have cried out.[10] Feeling that he was being visited by death itself, Muhammad finally did as he was told, and uttered that first revelation:

'Recite in the name of your Lord who created…'

Yet still Muhammad was disturbed. Fearing that he had gone mad, he contemplated hurling himself off the mountain, only to hear the voice again: 'O Muhammad, you are the Messenger of Allah, and I am Gabriel.'

When Muhammad told his wife Khadija what had happened, she went and sought the counsel of her cousin, Waraqa. A Christian who had studied the Bible, Waraqa interpreted Muhammad's experience in the light of Biblical sacred history: 'Holy, holy!' he cried, 'By God, if you speak the truth, Khadija, then he is truly the prophet of this people, and that great messenger who came to Moses has come to him.'[11]

★

The revelation that Muhammad received on Mount Hira was to be the first of many over the next two and a half decades. The more he received, the more he learnt what it was that he was receiving. The revelations announced themselves as a *qur'an*, or recitation, and a *kitab*, or book. The Qur'an, he was told, was a reminder and an admonition, a lesson and a distinction between truth and falsehood, a blessing and a cure. None but Allah could have produced it (10:37). As the word of Allah, it was clear and flawless; those who denigrated it were dared to produce something of equal eloquence – the ultimate challenge to a people who believed that their genius lay in the poetic word.

The Qur'an describes itself, too, as a confirmation of the previous scriptures – of the Torah (*al-Tawrah*) of Moses, the Psalms (*al-Zabur*) of David, and the Gospel (*al-Injil*) of Jesus. All had come from Allah: 'Nothing is said to you that has not been said to other messengers before you' (41:43). Yet there was also something different about Muhammad's revelation. While most earlier prophets had been sent to the Israelites, the Qur'an had been revealed to Muhammad 'in a clear Arabic tongue' (*bi-lisan 'arabi mubin*) (26:195). His mission was to the Arabs, a people who, though they may have been visited by a prophet or two in earlier times, had never received a written scripture.

Yet Muhammad's mission was not to be confined to the Arabian Peninsula. He heard how he had been sent to all mankind (7:158), how the Qur'an was the best of scriptures (39:23), and how he himself was 'the seal of prophets' (*khatam al-nabiyyin*) (33:40) and a 'token of mercy' for all beings (21:107). Far from being a parochial prophet, he was, as a saying or Hadith ascribed to him put it, the messenger of 'the red and the black', that is, of all peoples and races.[12] As his followers saw it, he was the perfect prophet bringing the perfect book in the perfect language, in order to establish the perfect faith throughout the world.

Muhammad continued to receive revelations until he died in 632. Following his death – the Islamic tradition says during the reign of the third caliph 'Uthman (r. 644–56) – the scattered revelatory utterances, previously written down on palm leaves, bits of wood and stone, or animal bones, were collected into a single, definitive volume. This canonical Qur'an was a book (*kitab*) made up of 114 chapters (called *suras* or 'enclosures' in Arabic), spanning 6,236 verses (*ayas* or 'signs'), and containing roughly 77,400 words, making it just over half the size of the Greek New Testament.[13] It was arranged not chronologically, but by chapter-length, with the longest chapters coming towards the beginning of the book, and the shortest chapters appearing at the end – an arrangement perhaps intended to underline the idea that the Qur'an was not, like the books of the Old Testament, a book of historical narrative, but rather the timeless word of God.[14]

In 622, finding his message rejected by his clansmen the Quraysh, Muhammad and his followers fled Mecca for the agricultural oasis of Yathrib. There, in the town that would come simply to be known as Medina – the City – they founded the first Islamic polity. This *hijra* or Emigration would be seen as a crucial moment in Muhammad's mission. The year 622 would become the year zero of the Islamic calendar, and later interpreters would divide the Qur'an into Meccan and Medinan *suras*, depending on whether they were revealed before or after the Emigration.

The different conditions of these two cities were believed to have resulted, too, in different kinds of revelation. In Mecca, Muhammad's primary task had been to call his pagan townsmen to the path of monotheism; hence the Meccan revelations abound in polemic, alongside vivid descriptions of the End Times, as advertisements for Muhammad's cause. They are also shorter and more poetic, like the Psalms of the Hebrew Bible.[15] Medina, by contrast, was home to a sizeable Jewish community, and where before the Muslims had been a pious community in a pagan environment, now they had their own proto-state, with Muhammad as its ruler, and were engaged in open warfare with the unbelievers of Mecca. The Medinan revelations therefore focus more on the relationship between Muhammad's community and the Jews and Christians, and tend to deal with ethical, legal, and military matters. They are also longer, and so are generally to be found at the beginning of the Qur'an.

Muhammad's mission was above all to call people to Allah, a deity whose principal attribute was His unity. 'Say: "He is Allah, One, Eternal",' runs Surat al-Ikhlas (The Chapter of Sincerity), the third-to-last chapter of the Qur'an. 'He begot none, nor was He begotten. And none is equal to Him' (112:1–4). According to one Hadith or prophetic saying, Muhammad once said that anyone who recited this chapter was guaranteed salvation. According to another, the chapter's four verses contained one-third of the whole Qur'anic message.[16]

The chapter's uncompromising emphasis on *tawhid*, Allah's absolute oneness, is directed against two alternative views.

First, there is the Christian Trinity. 'He begot none, nor was He begotten' seems to be a backhanded swipe at the 'begotten, not created' formula of the Nicene Creed, the basic statement of Christianity adopted at the Council of Nicaea in 325.[17] Second, there is the pagan idol-worship of the Arabs, which the Qur'an describes as polytheism or *shirk* – literally, the practice of 'ascribing partners' to Allah by worshipping deities alongside Him. In the Qur'anic view, this is an unforgiveable sin (4:48), and those who persist in it are heading straight for hell (17:39).

Alongside 'the One', the Qur'anic God has many other 'most beautiful names' (7:180). These are traditionally numbered at ninety-nine, 1,001, or said to be innumerable. One of the most significant is *al-khallaq*, 'the Creator' (15:86). Allah, the Qur'an announces, has created everything, and everything in the heavens and on earth belongs to Him. Although the Qur'an contains no extended creation account like those found in Genesis, the first book of the Hebrew Bible, it does repeatedly say that God 'created the heavens and the earth in six days and then settled upon the Throne' (7:54, 10:3, 32:4, etc.). In distinction from the Biblical tradition, however, where God rests on the seventh day, the Qur'an elsewhere makes the point that the act of creation did not tire Allah (46:33; 50:38), for creation is an easy task for an omnipotent deity.[18] When Allah wishes to create something, we are told, 'He need only say "Be!" and it will be' (2:117, 36:82, etc.).

The Qur'an insists that Allah created the world not for 'idle sport' (21:16), but a specific purpose. Again and again it calls on its listeners to reflect on the *ayat* or 'signs' of Allah in creation

− the alternation of night and day, the sun, moon, and stars, the wind, rain, and lightning, animals and vegetation, the milk of cattle and the honey produced by bees, wakefulness and sleep, the diversity of languages and skin colours − and encourages them to see these things as 'traces of Allah's mercy' (30:50), and so to give thanks and render obedience to the divine being who created them.

Among the things created by Allah, the Qur'an, like the Bible, puts special emphasis on the creation of human beings. It approaches this subject from two angles, one that ennobles mankind and one that humbles him. In several instances − seven to be precise − the Qur'an tells the story of the creation of Adam, the first human being.[19] In one of the seven accounts, it is announced that Allah has made man His 'deputy' (*khalifa*) on earth and taught him the names of all things. In another, Allah, like the God of Genesis (2:7), is said to have 'breathed His spirit' into Adam (15:29, 32:9). In all of them, in contrast to the Biblical book of Psalms (8:5), man is said to be higher than the angels, whom Allah commanded to bow down before Adam. All did so, we are told, except Iblis, a character identified with the Biblical Satan. (The Arabic word comes from the Greek *diabolos*.)

In this way, humanity is put on a lofty pedestal. Nevertheless, in the Qur'anic view, humans undoubtedly remain inferior to Allah, their creator. This comes out forcefully in the other, 'humbling' type of creation account − those passages in which the Qur'an describes the stages of the creation of man:

We [Allah] created man from an extract of clay. Then We placed him, a drop of [seminal] fluid, in a secure place. Then We turned the drop of fluid into a clot of blood, then the clot into a lump of flesh. We turned the flesh into bones, and then clothed the bones in flesh, thus creating another creature. Blessed be Allah, the best of creators (23:12–15).

Such passages stress the omnipotence of Allah and the utter fragility of human beings, who depend entirely on Him for their existence: 'You people! You are the ones who need Allah, while Allah needs no one' (35:15).

Allah's knowledge, the Qur'an likewise insists, is total, while human knowledge is limited. 'Allah knows,' it declares, 'and you know not' (2:216). 'Do you not see that Allah knows everything in the heavens and the earth? If three people confer in secret, He is their fourth; if five, He is their sixth; if they are fewer or more numerous, He is with them wherever they may be … Allah has knowledge of all things' (58:7). His power, too, is said to be incomparable. The phrase 'Allah has power over all things' is repeated over thirty times. Allah is called 'the Sovereign of all Sovereignty' (3:26) and 'the All-Powerful King' (54:55).[20] Just as He has the power to create, so too, we are told, can He bring the dead to life (22:6).

The purpose of bringing back the dead was to judge them. Like the God of the Hebrew Bible, Allah can be a harsh and imposing figure, particularly when dealing with those who reject Him. Fourteen times the Qur'an describes Allah as 'severe in punishment' and eight times as 'quick to hold to account', while those who threaten Muhammad are warned that Allah is 'mighty and vengeful' (39:37).

Yet just as the Old Testament also describes God as 'merciful and gracious, longsuffering, and abounding in goodness and truth' (Exodus 34:6), so too does the Qur'an present its audience at other times with the image of a kind and forgiving deity. The name *al-Rahman* – 'the Merciful' – is used almost interchangeably with Allah (55:1). The prophet Joseph is quoted as calling Allah 'the most merciful of the merciful' (12:92). Allah 'has decreed mercy for Himself' (6:12, 6:54), Muhammad informs his listeners, and His 'mercy encompasses all things' (7:156). Except for chapter nine, every *sura* of the Qur'anic text opens with the formula, *Bismillah al-rahman al-rahim*, 'In the name of Allah, the Merciful, the Compassionate'.

While Allah's mercy is open to all, however, it is conditional on those who have rejected Him mending their ways (5:39). Allah, it constantly reminds us, loves the gooddoers, the penitent, the pure, and the pious, but not the evildoers and those who sow corruption on earth.

The Qur'an is a scripture immersed in sacred history: stories about the great prophets and patriarchs of the Bible, of whom it mentions twenty-five by name, are repeated or alluded to again and again. Like the 'signs' in nature, the Qur'an refers to these stories as 'signs' (*ayat*) or 'parables' (*amthal*). The purpose in telling them was to put courage into the hearts of Muhammad and his followers as they faced the faithlessness, mockery, and persecution of their opponents in Mecca (11:120): every prophet, the Qur'an reminded Muhammad, had met with resistance and persecution. Abraham was cast into a furnace for preaching against idol-worship. Moses, whose struggle to liberate the Israelites from slavery in Egypt the Qur'an tells many times, was accused of peddling 'evident sorcery' (10:76), while the ancient Arabian prophet Hud – who was believed to have been sent to the tribe of 'Ad soon after the time of Noah – had been charged with telling a mere 'tale of the ancients' (26:137), both accusations that would later be hurled at Muhammad too. Noah, Abraham, and Moses had all been threatened with stoning. Yet these earlier messengers, the Qur'an notes, 'patiently endured unbelief and persecution, until Our help came to them' (6:34). So too, then, should Muhammad and his followers. Despite the best efforts of the evildoers, the truth of monotheism would always triumph over the falsehood of unbelief.

Monotheism is a theological position that defines itself against an alternative view. True to this, the Qur'anic revelations are as interested in the erroneous beliefs of the polytheists and other non-believers as in the positive message that Muhammad is to convey.

The archetypal 'others' in the Qur'an are 'the unbelievers' (al-kafirun), those pagans of Mecca who have rejected Muhammad's call to monotheism. Kufr, the Arabic word for unbelief, has the root meaning of 'covering up': the kafirun are those who cover up the benefits given to them by Allah by wilfully rejecting His signs.[21] They deny the message of the Qur'an – which they dismiss as a 'medley of dreams', an invention of Muhammad, or the incantations of a bewitched poet (21:5) – and mock and persecute Muhammad and his followers. They refuse to believe in the truth of Muhammad's mission unless he performs spectacular miracles, deny the resurrection and the life to come, and show no gratitude for Allah's blessings.

Consistent with this, the kafirun are also accused of indulging in various kinds of misguided beliefs and actions. 'They ascribe daughters to Allah' (16:57) – among whom are female deities called al-Lat, al-ʿUzza, and al-Manat (53:19-20) – and worship Allah's signs in creation, like the sun and moon, instead of Allah Himself (41:37). Such actions are classic *shirk*, the one unpardonable sin. More generally, they are said to treat life as a mere game devoid of inner meaning. They gamble, drink, obsess over money and lineage, and practise inhumane customs like infanticide. In short, they are living in *jahiliyya*, that state of barbarism that is the very opposite of Islam.[22]

A subset of unbelievers is 'the hypocrites' (*al-munafiqun*), a group traditionally identified with the secret opponents of Muhammad in Medina. The hypocrites are in a sense worse than out-and-out unbelievers because they 'say with their mouths, "We believe," but do not have faith in their hearts' (5:41). They are a fifth column within the monotheistic community, undermining the cause from within. They come up with lame excuses for why they have to stay behind when the Muslims go into battle against the pagans of Mecca. They are greedy for their share of charity even while giving only with reluctance (9:54–8), and they 'command evil and forbid good' (9:67), inverting the Qur'anic commandment to 'command good and forbid evil' (3:110).

If the *kafirun* and *munafiqun* are unambiguously opposed to the truth, the Qur'an's attitude towards the Jews and Christians is much less clear-cut. As we've seen, the Qur'an presents Biblical figures loved and revered by Jews and Christians as models for Muhammad and his followers to emulate. It adopts from the Biblical tradition ideas like monotheism and the creation of the world in six days, characters such as Satan and the angels, and stories like the Exodus from Egypt and the miracles of Jesus. And it acknowledges that the Jews and Christians, like the followers of Muhammad, are monotheists in possession of a scripture; hence it calls them 'People of the Book' (*ahl al-kitab*) (e.g. 2:109, 3:69–71), a moniker that indicates not just that Judaism and Christianity are scriptural religions like Islam, but more fundamentally that the Jews and Christians have received a form of the same eternal 'Book' as has been given to Muhammad.[23]

In light of these affinities, the Qur'an has many positive things to say about the Jews and Christians. It tells us that they have been chosen, blessed, and guided by Allah, and that they were the only two religious communities to have previously been given the Book (6:156). 'And when you debate with the People of the Book,' Muhammad and his followers are told, 'be courteous, except with those among them who do wrong. Say: "We believe in what has been revealed to us and in what was revealed to you. Our God and your God is one, and to him we submit"' (29:46). Those who doubt the truth of Muhammad's message are advised to consult the People of the Book, for they know what a true prophet and scripture looks like; indeed, they know Allah 'like they know their own children' (6:20).

This spirit of ecumenism extends to both of the earlier monotheistic communities. Repeating the central message of the Hebrew Bible, the Qur'an announces that Allah had made a covenant with the Jews, exalted them above the nations, assigned them the Holy Land, and bestowed on them a scripture, the Torah, which was a source of 'guidance and light' (5:44, 6:91). As for the Christians, the Qur'an echoes their belief in the Virgin Birth and that Jesus was the Messiah and the 'Word' of God (3:45, 4:171; cf. John 1:1–14), commends the humility of their priests and monks, and describes them as 'nearest in love to the believers' (5:82). Such is the positive regard for the older communities, in fact, that the historian of Islam Fred Donner has suggested that at this early stage the movement led by Muhammad may have included those who identified as Jews and Christians in an ecumenical 'Believers' movement.[24]

And yet, while the Qur'an acknowledges the Torah and the Gospel as true scriptures and affirms the chosenness of the earlier monotheistic communities, it also proclaims that the Jews and Christians have distorted (*tahrif*) the true meaning of their scriptures, either by tampering with their words, or else by misinterpreting, disagreeing over, or simply ignoring them. This in fact is one of several charges levelled against the two earlier religious communities. The Jews, the Qur'an declares, killed some of their prophets (2:61) (an idea taken from Christian anti-Jewish polemic), libelled the Virgin Mary (4:156), and practised usury (*riba*) though it was forbidden in their law (4:161).[25] After welcoming Muhammad and his followers to their city, the Jews of Medina refused to accept him as a prophet, leading to a Qur'anic revelation (2:142–5) that was understood as an order to the Muslims to no longer pray towards Jerusalem, and to turn instead towards Mecca in a decisive rupture with the older faith. Worse, one Jewish tribe of Yathrib, the Banu Qurayza, was believed to have conspired with the unbelievers in their efforts to destroy the nascent Islamic polity. As punishment, the Islamic tradition tells us, their men were sentenced to death and their women and children taken into slavery.[26] Nor do the Christians escape the Qur'an's censure. They are accused of committing several doctrinal errors, chief among them their belief in the

Trinity (4:171; 5:73), their claim that Jesus was the incarnation of God (5:17, 5:116–17) (both of which the Qur'an deems little better than polytheism), and their insistence that Jesus was crucified and resurrected from the dead (4:157–8). Elsewhere the Christians are condemned for taking their clerics and monks as 'lords' (9:31) and for inventing monasticism (57:27), which is cast as a misguided and extreme form of world-denial.

The Qur'an's view of the People of the Book, then, is an ambivalent one. On the one hand, Muhammad's followers are encouraged to feel a sense of kinship with the Jews and Christians as fellow scriptural monotheists. On the other, there is a profound sense that the Jews and Christians have gone astray, and that this is why Allah has sent Muhammad: to cut through the confusion sown by the People of the Book and return mankind to the simple monotheism taught by the prophets of old.

The aim of the Qur'an is not simply to inculcate belief in the one God, but also to guide its hearers and readers towards a pious and moral way of life, to lead them to what it calls 'the straight path' (*al-sirat al-mustaqim*) (1:6). An ethical life, it teaches, is founded on submission to Allah in worship and obedience. This includes praying to Allah before dawn, before dusk, and during the night and day, praising Him morning and evening (33:42), fasting in Ramadan (the month in which Muhammad received his first revelation) (2:183–5), and going on pilgrimage (*hajj*) to the 'sacred mosque' (*al-masjid al-haram*) at Mecca (2:196). From these injunctions Muslim jurists would derive the five pillars of Islam: the testimony of faith (*shahada*) in Allah and His messenger, ritual prayer (*salat*) five times a day (and communally on Fridays), almsgiving (*zakat*), the Ramadan fast (*sawm*), and the pilgrimage (*hajj*) to the Ka'ba. Again, these rites testify to the fact that Islam is similar yet different to Judaism and Christianity, which have their own daily prayers, fasts, and pilgrimages.[27]

As well as these ritual acts, the Qur'an also commends a number of virtues dictating how people should relate to the deity. The true believers are those who fear and worship their Lord – the virtues of *taqwa* ('Godwariness') and *'ibada* ('service') – who put their trust in Him, who are loyal to the covenant they have made with Him, who give thanks to Him for His blessings and reflect upon His signs, who adhere to His laws, and who strive to obtain salvation in the life to come. The Qur'an also tells Muslims how to behave towards their fellow men. The believers are enjoined to be charitable towards orphans and the poor – charity being the supreme virtue (35:32) – to honour their father and mother, to love their relatives, and to endure persecution with fortitude.

Yet forbearance (*sabr*), the Qur'an suggests, should not preclude armed struggle when necessary. The Qur'an makes repeated reference to those who fight or 'struggle' – the Arabic term is *jihad* – 'in the cause of Allah', and offers a range of views on the legitimacy of violence. The most militant statements come in the Medinan revelations – a reflection of the new circumstances facing the Muslim proto-state in Medina. The so-called Verse of the Sword (*ayat al-sayf*) instructs the believers to 'kill the polytheists wherever you find them', to 'seize them, surround them, and lie in wait for them everywhere' (9:5). Another, similarly violent verse from the same *sura* seems to legitimize warfare against the People of the Book: 'Fight those who do not believe in Allah or the Last Day, who do not forbid what Allah and His messenger have forbidden, and do not profess the religion of truth – even if they are those who have been given the Book – until they render the tribute (*jizya*), by hand, subdued' (9:29). Aggressive warfare, it is elsewhere proclaimed, is justified when its aim is to root out dissension and establish the supremacy of Allah's religion (8:39).

Yet the Medinan revelations also enjoin peacemaking with those who wish to make peace (8:61), and the more militant verses tend to contain so-called 'escape clauses' placing limits on the exercise of violence. Verse 9:29, as we've just seen, announces that the Jews and Christians should not be subject to attack if they agree to pay a special tax as tribute – the origin of the *jizya* poll tax, a central pillar of the *dhimmi* system in which Jews and Christians living under Muslim rule would be given protected yet subordinate status in Islamic law.[28] The Verse of the Sword, similarly, continues: 'If they repent and perform the prayer and pay the alms tax, allow them to go their way; Allah is forgiving and compassionate.'[29]

Like its teachings on jihad, the Qur'an's views on gender relations would stoke controversy, especially in modern times. Undeniably, the Qur'an puts forward a hierarchical distinction between men and women. A woman's testimony in court, it declares, is worth half that of a man (2:282), while a male heir, it instructs, shall inherit twice as much as a female heir (4:11). In the context of marriage, men are permitted to take four wives, on the condition that they can provide for each of them equally (4:3), while an often-discussed verse announces:

> Men have authority over women insofar as Allah has made some superior to others, and insofar as they spend their wealth

[in support of them]. Righteous women are obedient. They are
protective of their unseen parts insofar as Allah has protected
them. As for those from whom you fear disloyalty, admonish
them, [then] refuse to share their beds, [and finally] beat them.
If they then obey you, do not wrong them (4:34).

Many Qur'an commentators, medieval and modern, would
seek to mitigate the violently patriarchal dimension of this
verse. For the contemporary Qur'an scholar Muhammad Abdel
Haleem, the beginning of the verse ought to be understood as
a reference to the husband's 'maintenance and stewardship of
the family', rather than to male superiority in general,[30] while
the broader exegetical tradition would insist that the Qur'an
had meant that unfaithful wives should be 'lightly' beaten – for
instance, with a toothpick.[31] In support of this, the commentators
could point out that the Prophet was said to have never beaten
his wives, and to the fact that other Qur'anic verses seek to
protect the rights of women and to give a sense of equality
between the sexes.[32] Thus the Qur'an insists that when it comes
to divorce, women should have 'rights similar to the rights
against them' (2:228), and elsewhere forcefully condemns the
female infanticide practised by the pre-Islamic Arabs (16:59,
81:8–9). And while Muhammad's revelation may afford men a
status above women in the family and social sphere, the Qur'an
is clear that it is piety – not gender – that ultimately determines
a person's reward in the life-to-come:

Muslim men and Muslim women, believing men and believing
women, devout men and devout women, sincere men and
sincere women, patient men and patient women, humble men

and humble women, charitable men and charitable women, men who fast and women who fast, men who are chaste and women who are chaste, and men who remember Allah and women who remember Allah – they will find forgiveness and a great reward (33:35).

These verses dealing with inheritance, marital relations and divorce are not merely ethical guidance, but legal rulings. Coming almost exclusively in Medinan *suras*, such laws were apparently a response to the early Muslims' encounter with Jewish law. In keeping with the Qur'an's generally ambivalent view of the People of the Book, legal rulings that clearly emulate Jewish practice – such as the prohibitions on usury and eating pork – sit uneasily alongside the declaration that Allah has made Jewish law burdensome as a punishment for the errors of the Jews.[33]

The Qur'an, however, is not primarily a book of law. The 'straight path' is essentially an ethical rather than a legal code. This ethical vision is summed up in a verse that would come to be known as *ayat al-birr*, 'the Verse of Piety':

Piety is not turning your faces to the east or to the west [in prayer]. Piety is [exemplified in] those who believe in Allah, the Last Day, the angels, the book, and the prophets; who, though they love it, give their wealth to relatives, orphans, the poor, the traveller in need, and beggars, and for the ransom of slaves; who perform the prayer and give the alms tax; who stay true to their covenants and are steadfast in trial, adversity, and times of war. Those are the people of truth; those are the Godwary (2:177).

★

The goal of leading a moral and pious life is the attainment of Allah's mercy in the life-to-come. By this the Qur'an seems to mean not just the life of a human being after death, but more fundamentally the end of time itself. This is said to be imminent: 'People ask you about the Hour (*al-sa'a*) [of the End Times]. Say, "None but Allah knows it. What do you know, the Hour may well be near"' (33:63).

This was a frightening prospect, for when 'the Hour' came all human beings would be brought back from the dead and held to account for their actions. It was 'the Day of Judgement' (*yawm al-din*), 'the Day of Reckoning' (*yawm al-hisab*) on which all humans would either be admitted to the garden of paradise or condemned to the fires of hell. Those who believe in Allah and walk along the straight path, the Qur'an declares, could expect to be made 'glad' (*sa'id*), while those who reject the message of monotheism and live sinful lives will be 'wretched' (*shaqiy*) (11:105).

This simple formula – heaven for the believers and the righteous, hell for the unbelievers and the evildoers – is held up as a sign of the justice of Allah, 'the most just of judges' (11:45). At the same time, some verses seem to suggest that the errors of the evildoers have been willed by Allah: 'Those whose hearts Allah does not wish to purify will have shame in this world and a grave punishment in the life to come' (5:41). To thoughtful listeners, this paradox would suggest that divine justice was ultimately inscrutable.

Nevertheless, those who heard the Qur'an would still come away with a strong sense of the importance and urgency of choosing the path that led to salvation. In vivid portraits of the wonders of paradise and the torments of hell, the saved are promised an eternal life in gardens watered by rivers – a particularly appealing prospect for an audience living in the Arabian Peninsula, where there could be no rain for as much as four years. Wearing bracelets of gold and fine silk, they would lie on soft couches, eating sweet fruits and fresh meats and drinking the purest wine, with 'big-eyed, white-skinned women, chaste like pearls' for company (56:22–3). As for the damned, they would be dragged into hell by their forelocks and their feet. They would be made to 'taste' their punishment, forced to eat the bitter fruit – shaped liked demons' heads – of the cursed Zaqqum tree, and to gulp down scalding water like thirsty camels (e.g. 37:62–8; 56:55).

The Qur'an presents its audience with a clear and consistent message. There is one God, Allah. He has revealed His message to a series of prophets, culminating in Muhammad, to whom He has delivered a revelation that is perfect and complete. The Jews and Christians, to whom earlier prophets were sent, have gone astray, misinterpreting or neglecting the basic message of monotheism. Those who believe in multiple gods have strayed even further from the straight path. Those who believe in Allah and behave accordingly will be rewarded with entry to paradise, while those who reject Allah and his Prophet and live immorally will be consigned to the hellfire.

Imprinted on the hearts of the believers, these ideas, the basic teachings of the Qur'an, are the foundation of Islamic thought.

Chapter Two

HEIRS TO
THE PROPHETS

For the first Muslims, Muhammad's death in 632 was – as a common inscription on early Muslim gravestones put it – 'the greatest of calamities'.[1] 'Umar, one of Muhammad's closest companions, initially refused to accept it, insisting that the Prophet would return just as Moses had from Mount Sinai.[2] The vivid eschatology of the Qur'anic revelations had led many to think that Muhammad would lead them into the final judgement. Now that he was gone, and 'the Hour' (*al-sa'a*) of the End Times had not arrived, the question was how his community was to be guided. How, now that prophecy had been 'sealed' (33:40), were the believers to be kept to the straight path? Certainly, they had the Qur'an and the example of the Prophet to fall back on. But, like all texts, the Qur'an needed to be interpreted. So, too, did the example of the Prophet. What was needed, therefore, was a living guide.

The first to lay claim to the role of living guide were the caliphs or 'deputies (s. *khalifa*, pl. *khulafa'*) of Allah'. This was the term that the Qur'an had used for Adam, and came to be used for the political leaders of the community in the post-prophetic era. The history of the early caliphate is traditionally divided into three stages. From the death of Muhammad until 661, the Muslim community was led successively by four men, Abu Bakr, 'Umar, 'Uthman, and 'Ali, who had all been close to the Prophet during his lifetime. In time, the majority Sunni tradition would revere them as the *Rashidun* ('rightly guided') caliphs and look back on the years of their rule as a veritable golden age. The period witnessed some notable achievements, like Abu Bakr's (r. 632–4) pacification of the tribes of Arabia in the so-called 'apostasy (*ridda*) wars'; the conquest under 'Umar (r. 634–44) of Syria and Egypt, Iraq and Iran; and the finalization of the definitive text of the Qur'an under 'Uthman (r. 644–56). But it also ended with the First Fitna or civil war (656–61), a struggle, bookended by the murders of 'Uthman and 'Ali (r. 656–61), which pitted the nearest and dearest companions of the Prophet against one another in a brutal contest for the caliphate.

In the aftermath of the First Fitna, Mu'awiya (r. 661–80), 'Ali's bitter enemy, came to power. He was the leader of the Umayyads, an old and powerful clan of Muhammad's tribe the Quraysh, who claimed the caliphate in the name of their murdered kinsman 'Uthman. They shifted the centre of the caliphate to *al-Sham*, or geographical Syria, oversaw the expansion of Muslim rule into North Africa and Spain in the west and Central Asia and India in the east, and transformed the nascent Islamic state into a centralized empire. Yet, with the exception of the devout caliph 'Umar II (r. 717–20), they would be remembered as impious rulers, known mainly for their nepotism, their discriminatory treatment of non-Arab Muslims, and their moral laxity.

In the middle of the eighth century, amid widespread discontent, the Umayyads were overthrown by the 'Abbasids.

Descendants of the Prophet's great-grandfather Hashim, they launched a revolution in the provinces of Iran and Iraq in the name of an unspecified 'chosen one' (*al-rida*) from Muhammad's family.[3] Shifting the centre of the empire to the east, from 762 they ruled as caliphs from their new capital at Baghdad, which – with a population by the mid-ninth century of around half a million – would become the largest, wealthiest, and most cosmopolitan city in the world. Though the 'Abbasids' power would soon be usurped by local dynasties and foreign invaders and challenged by other claimants to the caliphate, Baghdad would remain the political centre of the Muslim world until the Mongols sacked the city and killed the caliph in 1258.[4]

Though these early caliphs were undoubtedly political figures, they did not present themselves as kings. 'Kingship' (*mulk*) was a pejorative term in the Islamic lexicon, associated with the Byzantine Emperor, the Sasanian Shah of Iran, and the Egyptian Pharaoh – all historic enemies of Islam.[5] Where kings were simply secular rulers, the caliphs, as Allah's deputies, claimed religious as well as political authority, the right to interpret Islam as well as to rule an empire. As the Umayyad caliph al-Walid II (r. 743–4) proclaimed – and as the caliphs' court poets, the journalists of the time, constantly repeated – the caliphs were the successors of the prophets, tasked by Allah with ensuring the fulfilment of His commandments and the salvation of His servants.[6]

As Allah's representatives, the early caliphs were responsible for leading the communal prayer, the Hajj caravan to Mecca, and the jihad against the Christian Byzantines, the principal rivals of the early Islamic state.[7] Notably, they also regarded themselves as interpreters of the sacred law, responsible for working out Allah's will when obvious guidance from the Qur'an was not forthcoming; hence another name for the caliph was *imam*, a word denoting a model of religious conduct.[8]

To work out the divine law, the caliphs relied on the past practice or *sunna* of the prophets and earlier caliphs, and their own supposedly inspired reasoning.[9] Asked to determine the punishment for drunkenness, for instance, the Rashidun caliphs 'Umar and 'Ali decreed that the penalty should be set at eighty lashes, reasoning that this was the penalty set by the Qur'an for the crime of falsely accusing someone of adultery (*qadhf*), and someone who got drunk was more likely to start making false accusations.[10]

Occasionally, too, the caliphs manifested their religious authority by wading into theological controversies, as they did, most notoriously, in the Mihna. From an Arabic word meaning 'trial', the Mihna is often described as an 'inquisition', though unlike the inquisitions in medieval Christendom it was short-lived, touched relatively few people, and resulted in few, if any, deaths. It was, however, deeply traumatic and controversial. Initiated by the 'Abbasid caliph al-Ma'mun (r. 813–33) just before his death in 833, and continued by his successors al-Mu'tasim (r. 833–42) and al-Wathiq (r. 842–7), the Mihna was concerned with the complex question of the relationship between Allah and the Qur'an.

A key distinction in Islamic theology is the dichotomy between the eternal and the created: Allah, it is said, is eternal (*qadim*), while the world has been created in time (*hadith*). What, though, of the Qur'an? The sacred book, after all, is thought to be Allah's 'speech' (*kalam*). As such, it is identical with one of Allah's attributes. Since these divine attributes are eternal, so too, it can be said, is the Qur'an. The mainstream Muslim view, both in this early period and afterwards, therefore, was that the Qur'an was 'uncreated' (*ghayr makhluq*), that is, that it had always existed in Allah's knowledge, even before its revelation to Muhammad and codification in book form, the words of Allah bearing no resemblance to human speech.[11]

In 833, however, al-Ma'mun issued an edict instructing the judges and religious scholars of his realm to testify that the Qur'an had in fact been 'created' by Allah in time. Allah, the caliph reasoned, had declared, 'We have made it an Arabic Qur'an' (43:3), and anything that was 'made' was, by definition, 'created'. In intervening in this way, al-Ma'mun was seeking to assert his religious authority – the right to define and interpret the holy book – as caliph. 'Allah,' he wrote, justifying the policy, 'has a right to expect from His deputies on earth … the putting into effect of His ordinance and His laws'.[12]

To many, the decree seemed to relegate the sacred book to a status that was less than divine. Yet the pressure applied by the caliph was great: those who did not comply were barred from employment in government service and from testifying in court, and one dissenting religious scholar even had his marriage forcibly annulled on the grounds that in dissenting he'd become an unbeliever, and an unbeliever couldn't legally be married to a Muslim woman.[13] Yet a brave few – led, as we'll see, by the scholar Ahmad ibn Hanbal (780–855) – refused to give in. Eventually, faced with widespread discontent and wearied by the fractiousness of the dispute, the caliph al-Mutawakkil (r. 847–61) revoked the Mihna. The doctrine of the 'uncreated Qur'an' had won out, and the caliphs were forced to accept the limitations on their religious authority.[14]

★

If al-Ma'mun had launched the Mihna to assert the caliph's authority in religious matters, then this was perhaps because, by 'Abbasid times, an alternative source of religious guidance had arisen. The conquests had brought wealth to the Muslim community, and with wealth came the time and leisure to sit in the mosque and reflect on life's big questions. In this way, there emerged a group of pious individuals who, when they were not earning their living as traders or artisans, devoted their lives to the collection and transmission of *'ilm*, that is, religious knowledge based on the Qur'an and the example of the first Muslims.[15] Gradually these men and women came to be known as the ulema, 'those who possess *'ilm*', or simply, 'the scholars'. It was they who would prove the greatest challenger – and ultimately, the successor – to the religious authority of the caliphs.

Not a priesthood, but a loose network of learned individuals, their closest model was the rabbis of Judaism, whose own centre, after all, was Iraq. Like the rabbis, the ulema saw their primary task as the interpretation and teaching of the divine law, or what they called *fiqh* – literally, the 'understanding' of the law. Just as in Judaism the sacred law or Halakha was thought to apply to all areas of life, however apparently trivial, so too did the ulema view the Shari'a, the sacred law of Islam, as a guide for everything – from how to brush one's teeth to how to settle questions of life and death, the rules of buying and selling to how to sit in the mosque.[16]

A law so universal, however, could not be built on the Qur'an alone, for the practical legal content of the sacred scripture was relatively minimal. Of the Qur'an's 6,236 verses, Muslim scholars would traditionally count five or six hundred specifically legal verses, mostly dealing with family law, dietary regulations, and the appropriate punishments – called the *hudud* or the 'limits' of Allah – for crimes like theft (cutting off the hand) and adultery (one hundred lashes).[17] Qur'anic law, therefore, needed supplementing. While the caliphs could do this in an *ad hoc* way, responding to issues like the penalty for drunkenness as and when they arose, only the scholars had the time and ability to think about how to extend the spirit of the Qur'an to all areas of life.

The two main centres of religious scholarship in this early period were Medina and Kufa. Medina, the city of the Prophet, had been the capital of the nascent Islamic state from the Emigration in 622 until 656. Though its political importance had subsequently diminished, the city nevertheless enjoyed the wealth that flowed from the conquests, becoming renowned in Umayyad times for its female singers, its poets, and especially its scholars. The spiritual heart of the city was its mosque, where the Prophet had led the first Muslims in prayer and directed the political affairs of the community. It was there, in a spot once occupied by the caliph 'Umar I and his counsil of advisors, that Malik (*c*.711–95), the scholar known in his day as 'the legal authority of the Hijaz', would teach his interpretation of the law.[18]

During his long life, it was said, Malik only ever left Medina to perform the pilgrimage to Mecca, and this attachment to the city of the Prophet determined his legal views. These were recorded in his book *The Well-Trodden Path* (*al-Muwatta'*), the oldest surviving book on Islamic law.[19] In Malik's view, the most important source of law other than the Qur'an was the so-called 'practice' (*'amal*) or 'custom' (*sunna*) of the people of Medina. It was the Medinans, he argued, who had best preserved the Islam of the Prophet and his companions, and it was Medina that most fully embodied the spirit of the Qur'an. '[This is] the custom (*sunna*) here and what I found the people of knowledge in our city doing', Malik would say when discussing a point of law.[20]

Kufa, the other great centre of early Islamic scholarship, had been founded in 638 in the wake of the Arab conquest of Iraq from the Sasanian Persians. Like Basra and Fustat (Old Cairo), it was a garrison town purpose-built for Arab Muslim troops and their families. The fourth caliph 'Ali had made the city his capital in 656, and over the ensuing century it would play an important political role, serving as the source of several anti-Umayyad rebellions, and as the site where the 'Abbasids first declared their caliphate.

Though originally founded as a city for Arab Muslim soldiers, Kufa was increasingly becoming home to non-Arabs – particularly those from the lower classes of the conquered peoples of Iran and Iraq – who were moving to the city, converting to Islam, and attaching themselves to one or other of the Arab tribes as *mawali* or 'clients', a legal status that, in theory at least, gave converts and their descendants the same rights as Arab Muslims. It was these clients who led the way in the field of religious scholarship. Though ethnically non-Arab, they pioneered the study of Arabic grammar – which, since Arabic was the language of the Qur'an, was indispensable for the religious scholar – and took the lead in developing the other branches of Islamic learning, including the study of the law.[21]

In Kufa, the most outstanding of these client-scholars was Abu Hanifa (699–767). A successful trader in silk, his grandfather, a Persian from Kabul, had been brought to Kufa as a slave, and had subsequently become a client of the Arab tribe that had set him free. Abu Hanifa's approach to the law was a rationalist one. In addition to the practice of the people of Kufa and the sayings of Muhammad and his companions, he made the *ra'y* or independent judgement of the legal scholar a source of law; hence he was identified as one of the preeminent *ashab al-ra'y* or 'partisans of reasoning'.[22] Such reasoning could take several forms. The most reliable was thought to be *qiyas*, or analogy, a basic form of which we've already encountered being used by the caliphs. This was the method of deriving laws by seeking out the underlying rationale (*'illa*) of comparable rulings found in the Qur'an: because the Qur'an had forbidden wine made from grapes, for instance, it was generally agreed that date wine was also forbidden, the underlying rationale in both cases being that drunkenness was sinful. Abu Hanifa and his associates, however, also adopted other, more flexible forms of reasoning, including what was called *istihsan* or 'seeking the good', where the jurist took into account the benefit to the public good, and *hiyal*, legal stratagems that allowed scholars to get around the letter of the law while still adhering to its spirit – a utilitarian approach that may have been guided by Abu Hanifa's experience as a trader.[23]

By the late eighth century, then, religious scholars in Medina and Kufa had come up with several ways of supplementing the legal material of the Qur'an. Yet some worried that these various sources – from the practice of Medina to the individual reasoning of the Kufan jurists – were unlikely to produce unanimity on questions of law.[24] This was a problem, for Muslims were supposed to be a single community united around a single divine law.

The solution to the problem was provided by al-Shafi'i (767–820). Born in the same year – some said on the very same day – that Abu Hanifa died, al-Shafi'i had lost his father in infancy, and had been taken by his mother to Mecca, where he grew up in poverty, yet still managed to excel at the local Qur'an school. Legend has it that by the age of fifteen he was already issuing fatwas, that is, legal opinions given in response to a question posed by a member of the public, the stock in trade of the religious scholar.[25]

While in Mecca, al-Shafi'i had heard of the reputation of Malik in neighbouring Medina, and, after memorizing *The Well-Trodden Path*, made the trip to Medina to study with the master, remaining there for some ten years until Malik's death in 795. Yet like Aristotle, the student of Plato, it was said, al-Shafi'i prioritized the truth over slavish adherence to his teacher.[26] Specifically, he felt that the 'practice of Medina' was not a sufficient or reliable basis for working out Allah's law. Since Muslims in Medina had disagreed on important issues from the beginning, there was, he thought, no such common Medinan practice. 'We still have not grasped what you mean by *'amal* [practice],' he wrote, addressing Malik, 'and without doubt we shall not know for as long as we live.'[27] What was more, he explained in *The Compendium (al-Umm)*, his summary of the law, Malik and his followers had 'put the opinion of the inhabitants of Medina ahead of that of the Prophet, and this was impermissible'.[28]

That last statement was an indication of what al-Shafi'i thought *was* the most valid source of law after the Qur'an, namely, the Hadith (sayings) or Sunna (custom) of the Prophet. Allah, he wrote in *The Compendium*, 'made it [the Muslims'] duty to follow what He had revealed to them', i.e. the Qur'an, 'and what His messenger had made customary (*sanna*) for them' – the Sunna.[29] When the Qur'an had announced, 'Allah has sent down to you the Book and the wisdom' (4:113), this, he asserted in his *Epistle on Legal Theory* (*al-Risala*), meant that the Qur'an ('the Book') and the sayings and customs of Muhammad ('the wisdom') were to be their guides.[30]

Al-Shafi'i was here making two important innovations. First, he was equating *sunna* or 'custom' not with the usual practice of a particular place like Medina or Kufa, but with the recorded sayings and actions of the Prophet himself. Second, he was putting the Hadith of the Prophet on a level with the Qur'an. While the sayings of Muhammad were not scripture, he argued, they were nonetheless divinely inspired, and as such had just as much legal weight as the Qur'an. Indeed, in those places where the Qur'an was ambiguous, the Hadith could help interpret it, similar to how, in Judaism, the Oral Torah (a body of unwritten tradition believed to have been revealed to Moses on Mount Sinai) was used to interpret the written Torah (the first five books of the Hebrew Bible).[31]

After Medina and a spell in Yemen, al-Shafi'i moved to Iraq, where he met and debated with the students of Abu Hanifa. They too fell short of al-Shafi'i's standards. Methods like *istihsan*, working out the law based on the potential public benefit, al-Shafi'i argued, were purely arbitrary. 'Judge between them according to what Allah has revealed,' he recited from the Qur'an to the Kufans, 'and do not follow their whims' (5:49).[32]

Al-Shafi'i did, however, grant some scope for juristic reasoning. Analogy (*qiyas*), he acknowledged, could be a useful and valid way of working out the law, on the condition that those who used it were, like Malik, 'careful and cautious' in their approach, as could the agreement of those who devoted their lives to scriptural knowledge.[33] In this way, he laid the foundation for the later, definitive Sunni legal theory, in which, as we'll see, four sources of law would come to be accepted: the Qur'an, the Hadith or Sunna, the consensus (*ijma*) of the community, and analogy (*qiyas*).

The significance of al-Shafi'i's contribution to Islamic legal thinking would quickly be recognized. Following a Hadith report that Allah would send a *mujaddid* or 'renewer' of the faith every hundred years, most Sunnis would see him as the renewer of the second Islamic century, following the pious Umayyad caliph 'Umar II in the previous century. His influence on Islamic legal thinking, it was said, was equivalent to Aristotle's on logic.[34] This exalted reputation was largely due to the fact that, by elevating the status of the Hadith of the Prophet, he had helped secure the triumph of the ulema in the struggle to be the interpreters of the law. If the sayings of the Prophet were to be the most important source of Islamic law, then it followed that the scholars – whose careers were devoted to collecting, transmitting, and interpreting those sayings – were best placed to guide Muslims in their quest to understand and live out the Shari'a.

This triumph was sealed by the failure of the Mihna. Just as the caliph al-Ma'mun had launched the inquisition as an assertion of his religious authority, so too was the steadfast refusal of some religious scholars to relent an assertion of their authority. The most famous example of steadfastness in the face of caliphal persecution was that of Ahmad ibn Hanbal. Like al-Shafi'i, Ahmad (as he was known) had lost his father when he was small, and had been raised in Baghdad by his mother. From a young age, his heart had been set on a career as a religious scholar. The affairs of the world did not much interest him; like many scholars, he lived off the rent from a property he had inherited, and, occupied by his religious studies, didn't marry until he was forty.[35]

While in Mecca Ahmad had met al-Shafi'i, whom he held in high esteem.[36] Like al-Shafi'i, he believed that, besides the Qur'an, the Hadith of the Prophet was the only reliable guide to the truth; hence he was identified as the leader of *ashab al-hadith*, the 'partisans of Hadith'.[37] From the age of sixteen, he devoted himself to the collection of Hadith, travelling to Kufa and Basra, Mecca and Yemen, Tarsus in south-eastern Anatolia, Homs, and Damascus in search of reliable transmitters of the sayings of the Prophet – for, as one much-cited Hadith advised, a true scholar should 'seek knowledge even as far as China'.[38] When asked how many prophetic sayings a scholar had to know in order to be qualified to give legal opinions, Ahmad indicated that even half a million might not be enough. His own collection of Hadith, the product of a lifetime's study, contained some 30,000 reports.[39]

When the 'Abbasids instituted the Mihna, Ahmad insisted that it was Hadith, not the opinion of the caliph, that should determine the status of the Qur'an – and there was no Hadith that indicated that the Qur'an was 'created'.[40] For clinging to the principle of the uncreated Qur'an, he was flung into prison and flogged. For this he earned the love and respect of the people of Baghdad. According to legend, when Ahmad died in 855, one to two million people attended his funeral, and 20,000 Christians, Jews, and Zoroastrians converted to Islam on the spot.[41] More to the point, his opposition to the Mihna had exposed the limitations of the caliph's religious authority. From now on, it was the religious scholars, confident in their position as guardians and interpreters of the Prophet's words and example, who would be – as the Hadith put it – 'the heirs of the prophets'.

For many early Muslims, the law was a sufficient guide to life. Yet though it claimed to be all-encompassing, there were some areas, some thought, that it did not fully cover. The Prophet, in addition to being a statesman and a lawgiver, had been a model of spiritual devotion and communion with Allah. Islam had set a pattern for personal piety and spirituality as well as individual and communal rectitude.

This was the domain of the Sufis, those believers who, when they reflected on the Qur'an, discovered an emphasis on the individual believer's personal relationship with his or her Lord. Taking Muhammad as their model, they stressed the believer's experience of the 'numinous', the term used by the German theologian Rudolf Otto for that intermingled sense of awe, fascination, and attraction felt by the lowly human being when confronted by the might of God.[42] Eventually, this would develop into mysticism, the kind of religion that sought what in the thirteenth century the Christian theologian Thomas Aquinas would call *cognitio dei experimentalis*, 'the knowledge of God through experience'.[43]

The first to be called Sufis appeared in the late eighth century, in Basra, the other great Iraqi garrison town alongside Kufa; people spoke proverbially of 'the legal scholarship of Kufa and the pious worship of Basra'.[44] As medieval Muslim authors pointed out, the Sufis got their name because they wore cloaks of wool – in Arabic, *suf* – as a mark of their asceticism or abandonment of the world.[45] This may have been a form of protest at what they saw as the neglect of the simple piety of Muhammad and his companions in the wealthy post-conquest society of Iraq.[46] In an attempt to recover the humble spirit of original Islam, they rejected worldly wealth and its trappings, and, inspired by Christian monks, would head out into the desert or into caves in order to be alone with Allah.[47]

The attitude of the early Sufis and their ascetic forbears was characterized above all by fear of Allah and His judgement.[48] Soon, however, they began to speak, as mystics tend to do, of their love for Him. 'I do not worship God out of fear of God,' the female ascetic Rabi'a of Basra (c.714–801) – later described as a 'second Virgin Mary'[49] – was quoted as saying, 'for then I would be like a wretched slave girl who only works out of fear. Nor do I worship Him out of love for Paradise, for then I would be like a wretched slave girl who only works when she is given something in return. No, I worship Him out of love for Him, and out of desire for Him.'[50]

By the middle of the ninth century Sufis in the north-eastern Iranian province of Khorasan and the imperial capital of Baghdad were teaching the mystical doctrine that the divine was present within the world. One such was the Khorasanian mystic Abu Yazid al-Bistami (c.804–75), to whom several *shatahat* or scandalous 'outpourings' of mystical ecstasy were attributed. 'Glory be to me!' Abu Yazid is said to have cried out, in a deeply provocative twist on the pious expression 'Glory be to Allah!' – the idea being that in the state of mystical union there was no difference between the mystic and God.[51] In Baghdad, similarly, Sufis began to talk of the 'annihilation' (*fana'*) of the human self in Allah and their 'unveiling' (*kashf*) of the divine presence in themselves and in the world. One Baghdadi Sufi is said to have cried out 'At your service, my Lord!' when he heard a dog bark; another would do the same when he heard the wind blow or a bird squawk.[52]

The Sufis claimed that these ideas could be read out of the Qur'an and Hadith: one Qur'anic verse declared that Allah was 'nearer to man than his jugular vein' (50:16), while an often-cited prophetic tradition indicated that, through extra acts of worship, humans could draw closer to Allah and enhance His love for them to the point where the distinction between the human and divine was blurred.[53] But although, like the ulema, the Sufis depended on the Qur'an and Sunna, the lessons they drew from the holy texts were rather different. The Sufis' disregard for worldly riches stood in direct contrast to the attitude of most religious scholars, many of whom, as we've seen, earned their livelihoods as merchants or artisans. The ulema saw in Sufi ideas about mystical union and renunciation dangerous echoes of Christianity. 'Poverty is almost like apostasy,' announced al-Shaybani (750–805), one of the leading students of Abu Hanifa in Kufa.[54] 'There is no monasticism in Islam,' declared a popular Hadith.[55] Perhaps most dangerously of all, in claiming to understand the inner meaning of the Qur'an, the Sufis were offering themselves as an alternative source of religious authority; indeed, they, too, claimed to be 'the heirs of the prophets' predicted in the Hadith.[56]

All this had practical consequences. In 877 a follower of Ahmad ibn Hanbal launched an 'inquisition' – a *mihna* – against the Sufis of Baghdad, and succeeded in having around seventy mystics arrested on the orders of the caliph.[57] One who escaped was al-Junayd (d. 910), the leader of the Baghdad Sufis. Al-Junayd recognized the dangers of going to extremes: unlike some

Sufis, he was known for dressing well and living comfortably.[58] He taught a sober kind of Sufism, and developed sophisticated ways of conveying mystical truths to fellow initiates so that the suspicions of outsiders weren't aroused.

Where his predecessors had spoken simply of mystical union or the annihilation of their selves, al-Junayd taught a three-stage process that preserved the distinction between the mystic and Allah: first there was 'separation' (farq), then 'joining' (jam') with God, and then, when the Sufi returned to a state of consciousness, 'separation' (farq) once again.[59] 'In their absence, they are entirely present,' he wrote of those Sufis who had achieved the 'second separation'. 'They are non-existent in their existence, existent in their non-existence. They are where they are not, and they are not where they are.'[60]

Utterances such as these were difficult to understand, let alone condemn. More straightforward statements of Junayd's like 'the path to Allah is blocked to His creatures, except for those who follow in the footsteps of the Messenger of God',[61] could have been uttered by al-Shafi'i – whose legal teachings Junayd followed – or Ahmad ibn Hanbal. Though it would continue to be controversial, Junayd's more intellectual approach helped to make mysticism more acceptable to the ulema, and Sufism an increasingly central part of Islamic thought – a status, as we shall see, that would only be enhanced over the ensuing centuries.

Chapter Three

DEFENDERS
OF ISLAM

Islam grew up in a multi-confessional environment. For several centuries after the death of Muhammad, in Syria and Egypt, Iraq and Iran, Muslims were a minority, and interaction with Jews and Zoroastrians, Christians and Manichaeans (dualists who sought the triumph of the 'light' of the soul over the 'darkness' of matter) was an everyday fact of life.[1] Though attempts were seldom made to convert these 'People of Book', it was still thought important to demonstrate that the older faiths had been superseded by the revelation of Muhammad.

A very public way of doing this was to build monuments testifying to the glory of Islam. The Dome of the Rock in Jerusalem, built by the Umayyad caliph 'Abd al-Malik (r. 685– 705) in 692, stood on the site of the Jewish Temple and looked down across the Holy City on the Church of the Holy Sepulchre. Inside, a 240-metre-long inscription, an amalgamation of Qur'anic verses, advised the People of the Book not to go to 'extremes' in their religion, asserted that Jesus was only a messenger of Allah, and warned Christians not to speak of three gods, for 'the true religion with Allah is Islam' (3:19).[2] In the

Umayyad capital Damascus, a city that teemed with Christian sights and sounds, the caliph al-Walid I (r. 705–15) built the great Umayyad Mosque on the site of the Cathedral of John the Baptist, reportedly taking a pickaxe and commencing the razing of the church himself. 'Our Lord is Allah, we worship none other than Him', ran the inscription on the mosque's inner walls. 'Our master is Allah alone, our religion is Islam, and Muhammad is our Prophet.'[3]

Another way of asserting Muslim supremacy was through the law. Legal restrictions imposed on non-Muslims by the Umayyad caliph 'Umar II were codified by the religious scholars into the so-called 'Pact of 'Umar', according to which Christians, in exchange for safe conduct, were forbidden from speaking 'improperly' about Muhammad, displaying crosses or building churches in Muslim cities, striking the *naqus* (a wooden gong used to summon worshippers to prayer), or 'proclaiming [their] polytheistic beliefs about Jesus, son of Mary'. They were also obliged, among other burdens, to wear a special belt, to avoid occupying the middle of the road, and to pay the *jizya* poll tax mentioned in the Qur'an. Such rules provided the basis for the *dhimmi* system by which Jews and Christians were given the 'protection' (*dhimma*) of their Muslim overlords in exchange for their recognition of their second-class status.[4]

The People of the Book, for their part, did not shy away from meeting the intellectual challenge presented by the new faith. Within a few years of Muhammad's death, Eastern Christian writers could be found mocking the claim of the 'Saracen prophet' to possess the keys of paradise and dismissing him as a mere 'man of war whom they call a prophet'.[5] By the early eighth century, Christian writers were engaging more closely with the teachings of the Qur'an. The theologian John of Damascus (*c*.675–750) – an employee in the Umayyad administration like his father and grandfather before him – devoted a chapter of his book on heresies to the 'superstition of the Ishmaelites'. There he denied that the Qur'an was a genuine revelation, rejected the Islamic charge that Christians were idol-worshippers who venerated the cross, and criticized, among other things, the Qur'an's permitting of polygamy and divorce.[6]

From an Islamic perspective, criticisms like these required a response, and this was provided by the practitioners of *kalam*. This Arabic term literally means 'talk' or 'speech': as the historian of Islamic theology Josef van Ess has explained, the word originally denoted the act of 'holding conversations' about religious topics with non-Muslims or Muslims who were thought to have gone astray in their beliefs.[7] Yet the term soon came to be used more specifically for what in the Latin West was called 'revealed theology', the act of thinking rationally about God and His creation on the basis of scripture.

The most important group of theologians in early Islam were known as the Mu'tazila – literally, 'those who withdraw' – perhaps because they started out as neutrals who 'withdrew' from politics, or maybe because they were ascetics who, like the early Sufis, withdrew from a society luxuriating in ever greater wealth.[8] The traditional explanation for the name of the Mu'tazila, however, connected it to their position on the controversial question of the 'status of the sinner'. During the First Fitna, the bloody civil war between Muhammad's early followers, there had emerged a group of pious militants known as the Kharijites – 'seceders' from the party of 'Ali – who held that sin made someone an unbeliever deserving of death.[9] Against them, the Murji'a or 'deferrers' argued that a person's actions could only tell you so much about their belief. To know whether they were truly a believer, they thought, you had to look into their heart, and this was something only Allah could do; hence the question should be 'deferred' until the Day of Judgement.[10]

The Mu'tazila, it was said, cut a middle path between these two extremes. One day, the story went, the scholar and ascetic Hasan al-Basri (c.642–728) was asked his opinion on the status of the sinner while teaching in the mosque of Basra. Before he could answer, one of his students, Wasil ibn 'Ata', (d. 748), jumped in, asserting that the sinner was 'neither an unqualified believer nor an unqualified unbeliever' but rather 'in a station between two stations', before getting up and withdrawing to a corner of the mosque. 'Wasil has withdrawn (i'tazala) from us,' Hasan said, so Wasil and his disciples became known as the Mu'tazila.[11]

Wasil would go on to debate Buddhists and the dualist Manichaeans as well as his fellow Muslims. From Basra, his movement spread to Kufa and then to Baghdad, where, in the early ninth century, the Mu'tazila became prominent at the 'Abbasid court, representing Islam in interreligious debates.[12] Though they held a variety of views, these early Mu'tazila were united by a commitment to reasoned debate and certain fundamental theological doctrines. Above all, they strove to articulate a rational basis for the key Qur'anic doctrine of *tawhid* or monotheism, and in so doing to show that competing doctrines like Manichaean dualism or Christian Trinitarianism were irrational. To say that Allah was 'one', the Mu'tazila argued, was to say that He was utterly unique; any notion that Allah was comparable to His creatures (*tashbih*) was to be rejected. The names and attributes that the Qur'an had ascribed to Allah were therefore not to be understood as being like human attributes. Allah did not 'know' or 'live' in the same way that humans did; rather, His attributes were indistinguishable from His unique essence. Nor did Allah have a body: when the Qur'an said things like 'the Merciful sat upon the throne' (20:5), this was simply a metaphor for Allah's majesty and power, not an invitation for the kind of anthropomorphism that Christians and others had fallen into.[13]

Alongside His unity, the Mu'tazila emphasized Allah's justice ('adl). This divine attribute was closely connected to the question of free will and determinism, a key issue in interreligious polemic. John of Damascus had divided the world into two groups – Muslim determinists and Christian libertarians – while Christians in their turn had faced Muslim mockery for attributing their sufferings to 'destiny'.[14] A range of views on the issue could be found in the Qur'an and early Islam. Many Muslims, perhaps under the influence of the fatalism of the pre-Islamic Arabs, stressed the deterministic side of the Qur'anic message.[15] The most insistent determinists were known as Jabrites, because they thought that human beings were driven by 'compulsion' (jabr) to do what they did and believe what they believed. At the other end of the spectrum were the Qadarites, who – in the words of the theologian al-Ash'ari (874–940) – 'affirmed that their fate (qadar) was their own and not their Lord's, and that they themselves determine (yuqaddir) their acts and not their Creator'.[16] Hasan al-Basri, the teacher of Wasil, had held this view, and the Mu'tazila would likewise argue for human free will.[17] The Qur'an, they noted, had promised paradise for the righteous and hell for the sinners. Since a just deity would not punish evildoers who were compelled to do evil, humans, they concluded, must be free to

49

choose and perform their actions, and to be able to know, using their unaided reason, what good and evil meant.[18]

Like the Mu'tazila, the 'Abbasid caliph al-Ma'mun was keen to assert the truth of Islam in the face of Christian polemic. This, in fact, may have been one of the reasons for his insistence during the Mihna that the Qur'an was 'created'. The Christians, as we've seen, held that Jesus was 'begotten, not created', and that, as the divine 'Word' or *logos*, Christ had existed with God 'in the beginning' (John 1:1). To say that the Qur'an was uncreated, al-Ma'mun declared, was therefore to 'talk just like the Christians when they claim that Jesus son of Mary was not created, because he was the Word of God', which could only undermine attempts to prove the irrationality of the Christian doctrine.[19] The Mu'tazila, in their capacity as court theologians and defenders of Islam, agreed with the caliph. When al-Ma'mun instituted the Mihna, 'the theologians', as van Ess has put it, 'were on the side of the persecutors'.[20] This decision would ultimately be their undoing. When the Mihna failed and the official policy was reversed, the Mu'tazila fell out of favour at court. Worse, cast as instigators of the whole sorry affair, they had been tainted in the eyes of the majority.[21]

After the Mihna, the Mu'tazila would never again represent the mainstream Muslim view, which condemned the doctrine of the created Qur'an as a *bid'a*, that is, an illegitimate 'innovation' or deviation from the Sunna of the Prophet.[22] It was the ulema, the interpreters of the law, not the rationalist theologians, who would speak for the majority of Muslims. Yet both the Mu'tazili movement and *kalam* would survive. The early Mu'tazila had been evangelists for their cause: outside Baghdad, their ideas and approach had won adherents in Damascus, Baalbek, western

Iran, and even North Africa and India, and over the ensuing centuries, Mu'tazili thinkers, divided into schools named after the Iraqi cities of Basra and Baghdad, would develop Mu'tazilism into an elaborate theological system.[23] Far from dying out, this system, and revealed theology more generally, would continue to influence Islamic thought throughout its subsequent history.

Those who practised *kalam* were rationalists, but only in a limited sense. They were, as we've seen, engaged in revealed theology, using their reason not so much to discover the true nature of things as to explain and defend the truths of scripture. Yet there was also a tradition of strictly rational Islamic thought, comparable to what in medieval Europe was called natural theology, which sought truths not so much in scripture as through the use of unaided human reason.

This was philosophy, or as it was known in Arabic, *falsafa*. The word *falsafa* was obviously of foreign origin, and, even more so than *kalam*, *falsafa* was a product of the early Muslims' interaction with non-Muslims. At the moment of the Arab conquests, philosophy was on the rise in both the eastern Byzantine Empire and Sasanian Iran, the very regions that would soon become the heartlands of the Muslim world. In Syria, where since the mid-fifth century Eastern Christians had been making translations from ancient Greek into Syriac (a branch of the ancient Semitic language Aramaic widely used by Eastern Christians), the first half of the seventh century had seen a boom in the translation of Greek works on logic, ethics, and medicine.[24] In Iran, a similar culture of translation – in this case from Greek into Pahlavi (Middle Persian) – had grown up, promoted by the Sasanian

Shahs, whose imperial ideology made them responsible for the collection and preservation of the sciences of the ancient world. When the 'Abbasids seized the caliphate and shifted the political centre of the Islamic empire from Syria to formerly Sasanian Iraq, they inherited this idea. From their new capital, Baghdad – built near the site of the old Sasanian capital Ctesiphon on the banks of the river Tigris – they launched one of the great cultural projects of the medieval world: the translation movement.[25]

Between roughly 750 and 950, with the financial support of the caliphs and their courtiers, almost all the extant major works of the ancient world were translated into Arabic. Among the translated books were works on astrology – which seems to have particularly fascinated the caliphs – geometry, and medicine. Yet it was books of philosophy that were prized above all.

The philosophical tradition of late antiquity (*c*.200–800) encountered by the translators was made up of two interlocking strands. These two strands went back to the two greatest names in the history of philosophy, Aristotle and his teacher Plato, and are known today as Aristotelianism and Neoplatonism. Originating in a division made by Aristotle himself, Aristotelian philosophy is typically divided into three types of sciences: theoretical sciences such as physics (the science of the nature of things) and metaphysics (the science of existence itself); practical sciences like ethics and politics; and productive sciences such as rhetoric and poetics. In all these fields and others, the Aristotelian approach is to subject the relevant phenomena to rational enquiry; indeed, Aristotle is credited with developing the first systematic logic, or way of arguing rationally from premises to conclusions.[26] Neoplatonism is primarily concerned with metaphysics. Its characteristic teaching, elaborated by the late antique philosophers Plotinus (205–70) and Proclus (412–85), is the theory of emanation, the idea that the existence of the phenomenal world is the result of a process by which existence overflows or 'emanates' from 'the One' – a perfect deity about which almost nothing can be known or said – and through a series of secondary causes called 'the Intellect' and 'the Soul'. Salvation, for the Neoplatonist, consists in escaping this world and returning to the One, and is achieved by casting off all bodily desires and developing the rational part of the soul through philosophical activity.[27]

By the time of the Arab conquests, philosophers in the Greek-speaking world generally sought to harmonize the Aristotelian and Neoplatonic traditions, arguing for the essential agreement of Aristotle and Plato on the fundamental questions of philosophy. With the translation movement, both strands, and the idea of the essential harmony between them, were carried into Islam.

That said, in the Islamic tradition, philosophy was associated above all with the name of Aristotle. According to legend, the translation movement was begun after the caliph al-Ma'mun – the same caliph who initiated the Mihna – had a dream in which Aristotle informed him that human reason, rather than revealed law or public opinion, was the best guide to 'the good'.[28] Legend though this was – the translation movement had in fact already begun under al-Ma'mun's predecessor al-Mansur (r. 754–75) – in making Aristotle central it contained a kernel of truth. Over the course of the ninth century, the vast majority of Aristotle's works would be translated into Arabic, and his influence on the Islamic philosophical tradition was such that he would become known as 'the First Teacher' (al-mu'allim al-awwal).[29]

This did not mean, however, that the Neoplatonic writings were rejected, only that they came into Islam under Aristotle's name: books IV to VI of *The Enneads* of the Neoplatonist Plotinus were translated – or rather, paraphrased – into Arabic as *The Theology of Aristotle*, while the Arabic version of Proclus's *The Elements of Theology* was given the title *Aristotle on the Pure Good*.[30] The paraphrase of Plotinus, in particular, would leave a deep imprint on philosophy in Islam into the early modern period, ensuring that *falsafa*, like philosophy in the late antique Near East and medieval Europe, would be an amalgamation of Aristotelianism and Neoplatonism.[31]

Several things made the translation movement possible. Supporting the sciences requires money, and the 'Abbasids and their courtiers were fabulously wealthy. The 'Abbasid vizier or chief minister Ibn al-Zayyat (d. 847), whose family had amassed a fortune as suppliers of olive oil, tents, and parasols to the caliphal court, reportedly spent the colossal sum of two thousand dinars a month on funding translations. (By comparison, foot soldiers in the 'Abbasid army received a salary of six dinars a month.[32]) Another prerequisite was paper, said to have been introduced to the Islamic world by Chinese prisoners of war captured at the Battle of Talas, in Central Asia, in 751.[33] Just as important were skilled translators, and here the caliphs were fortunate to be able to call on the learning of Christian scholars. The Christian translator Hunayn ibn Ishaq (808–73) – whose Greek was said to be so perfect that he could recite Homer – claimed to have translated 129 works of the Greek philosopher-physician Galen into Arabic and Syriac.[34] 'Were it not for this,' wrote the historian of Islamic scholarship Ibn Khallikan (1211–82), 'persons unacquainted with

Greek could have derived no benefit from such works.'[35]

The work of translators like Hunayn enabled Muslims not only to read Aristotle, Galen, and Plotinus, but also to develop a philosophical tradition of their own. The first major exponent of this tradition was al-Kindi (c.801–70). A member of the aristocratic Arab tribe of Kinda, al-Kindi's father had been governor of Kufa, and he himself was tutor to the caliph's son. Reputedly a miser, he used most of his inherited wealth to fund translations for his own work: the circle of translators working under him produced the paraphrase of Plotinus's *Enneads* as well as Arabic renderings of important works by Aristotle.[36] He became known as 'the Philosopher of the Arabs' (*faylasuf al-'arab*) because, as the Spanish historian of the sciences Sa'id al-Andalusi (1029–70) put it, 'there was no one in Islam who was so well-known among the people for being interested in the philosophical sciences.'[37]

As one of the first Muslim philosophers, al-Kindi had to contend with the charge that philosophy was inconsistent with Islam. The ancient Greeks, after all, were pagans whose wisdom was based on reason rather than revelation. In the first chapter of his major work, *On Metaphysics*, al-Kindi met the charge head on. 'The goal of philosophy,' he declared, 'is, in its theoretical dimension, to correctly identify the truth, and, in its practical dimension, to act according to the truth.' Even if the truth came 'from far-away peoples or from nations that are different to us', the philosopher insisted, it was still the truth, and should be embraced as such.[38] *Al-haqq*, the Arabic word for 'the truth' used here, was also one of the 'most beautiful names' of Allah. In its highest form, philosophy was a quest to know God. 'The most noble and most exalted form of philosophy,' al-Kindi wrote, 'is metaphysics, by which I mean knowledge of the First Truth (*al-haqq al-awwal*), who is the cause of all truth.'[39] In line with this, the stated goal of *On Metaphysics* was 'to establish a proof of [Allah's] lordship, make apparent His unity, and repel those who stubbornly oppose Him and disbelieve in Him through proofs that destroy their unbelief' – in other words, to provide a philosophical demonstration of the truth of Islam.[40]

Given this, however, al-Kindi was not prepared to go along with the views of the ancients where they directly contradicted fundamental Islamic teachings. In his work on physics, for instance, Aristotle had taught that the world had always existed, a position that clearly went against the Qur'an's assertion that Allah had created the world in six days. Making use of philosophical arguments for creationism first put forward by the Christian philosopher John Philoponus (*c*.490–570), al-Kindi attempted to demonstrate the internal inconsistency of the Aristotelian view. Far from being eternal, he insisted, the world had been created out of nothing by God, just as the Qur'an said.[41]

For the Philosopher of the Arabs, then, *falsafa* was not a pagan alternative to Islam, nor was it merely justifiable from an Islamic perspective; it was in fact the best way to understand Islam and defend it from its detractors, that is, a more rigorously rationalistic form of *kalam*. As we shall see, not all philosophers would share this view. And many non-philosophers would not accept it. Yet, in making the argument, al-Kindi helped make *falsafa* part of Islamic thought. Alongside the legal scholarship of the ulema, the mysticism of the Sufis, and the revealed theology of the theologians, philosophy had become – and would remain – one of the major intellectual traditions in Islam.

Chapter Four

THE SUNNI COMPROMISE

The Qur'an had willed its listeners to become a single *umma*, a community united in its devotion to Allah. Yet the unity established by Muhammad was not to survive his death. 'Whoever among you outlives me shall see a vast dispute,' the Prophet was remembered to have said.[1] The flashpoint was the caliphate. As al-Ash'ari, the most influential of Sunni theologians, would recall, 'The first disagreement among the Muslims after the death of their Prophet concerned the leadership of the community.'[2] This was no mere academic disagreement. 'The greatest dispute within the Muslim community is the dispute over the Imamate [the caliphate],' wrote al-Shahrastani (1086–1158), a historian of Islamic sects, 'for, in Islam, the sword has not been drawn over a religious matter like it has been drawn over the Imamate in every era.'[3]

The dispute went back to the very day Muhammad died. The Qur'an had apparently given no guidance as to who should lead the community after the Prophet's death; nor, according to the Sunni tradition, had Muhammad nominated a successor. On his death, Abu Bakr, one of the Prophet's closest friends and advisors, and the father of his beloved wife 'A'isha, had received the acclamation of the Muslims of Medina. Before his own death two years later, he had nominated 'Umar, another of the Prophet's most reputable companions, to succeed him. When 'Umar was murdered in 644, a committee of six of the leading men of the community – a *shura* or 'consultative body' – had elected 'Uthman, an early convert and the father of two of Muhammad's wives, as his replacement. When 'Uthman was himself killed, 'Ali, the cousin of the Prophet and husband of his daughter Fatima, had been acclaimed caliph.

These events, and the Fitna or civil war which followed the murder of 'Uthman, laid the foundation for the Sunni–Shi'i schism. The Sunnis would accept all four of the first caliphs as legitimate, while the Shi'a – whose name comes from the Arabic phrase *shi'at 'Ali*, 'the party of 'Ali' – thought that 'Ali, as the closest surviving blood relative of the Prophet, had been Muhammad's rightful heir from the beginning.[4]

Yet while the Sunnis and the Shi'a would be defined to a large extent by how they interpreted these foundational events, none of the participants in these early disputes saw themselves as Sunni or Shi'i. It was only much later – in the tenth and eleventh centuries – that those names would begin to acquire something like their full range of meaning.

For the majority of Muslims up to the present day, Islam would mean Sunni Islam. This was a form of the faith defined above all by compromise and consensus. The Qur'an had described the community of Allah as *ummatan wasatan*, 'a community of the middle way' (2:143), and, after the tragedy of the Fitna and the agonies of the Mihna, the Sunnis were those who turned moderation into their guiding motto. When they looked back on the momentous events of early Islamic history, they searched for an interpretation that most Muslims could agree on; hence they settled on the view that each of the first four caliphs had been 'rightly guided' (*rashidun*), and that all of the Prophet's companions had been righteous believers.[5] Similarly, when they looked at the contemporary political landscape, the Sunnis opted for moderate pragmatism over radical idealism. When the 'Abbasid caliphs lost effective control of their realm, first to the Shi'i Buyid dynasty in the 940s, then to the Seljuq Turks in 1055 − rulers whose political authority rested on brute force rather than religious criteria − Sunni thinkers would come up with theoretical justifications for the new status quo, prioritizing the harmony of the community over the caliphal ideal.[6]

The Sunnis applied this principle of moderation to all areas of Islamic thought, including the all-important sacred law. A clue to their approach to the Shari'a lay in their very name. They were *ahl al-sunna wa'l-jama'a*, 'the partisans of prophetic custom and community'. There were, they said − building on the work of al-Shafi'i, the 'renewer of the second century' − four valid sources of the law (*usul al-fiqh*). First, and most obviously, there was the Qur'an, which was authoritative insofar as it was the direct and 'uncreated' speech of Allah. Second, there was the Hadith and Sunna, the prophetic 'custom' of the Sunnis' name. The most reliable accounts of these sayings and customs, the Sunnis believed, were the so-called 'six books', carefully selected collections of prophetic sayings, helpfully arranged by subject matter, of which the *Sahihayn* ('Authentic Collections') of Bukhari (810–70) and Muslim ibn al-Hajjaj (822–75) were especially trusted and revered.[7] Third, there was *ijma'*, the consensus of a community that, according to a well-known Hadith, would 'never agree upon error'.[8] This was the Muslim *umma* or *jama'a*, the 'community' of the Sunnis' name. Lastly, there was *qiyas* or analogy, that form of legal reasoning that was reliable precisely because it was grounded in the rulings of the Qur'an and Sunna.[9]

Based on these sources of the law, a legal scholar could work out Allah's view on every act and issue. Five *ahkam* or 'categories' of action were identified (in both Sunni and Shi'i jurisprudence). At either end of the scale were those that were classed as 'mandatory' (*wajib*) and 'forbidden' (*haram*). Mandatory actions, the Sunni scholar Abu Ishaq al-Shirazi (1003–83) explained in *The Illuminating Rays of Legal Theory* (*al-Luma' fi usul al-fiqh*), were those that a Muslim had to perform in order to avoid hell, such as the five daily prayers, fasting during Ramadan, and almsgiving. Forbidden actions, conversely, were those that led straight to hell, among which al-Shirazi included fornication, sodomy, and theft, among other major sins. In between these two extremes came 'the recommended' (*al-mandub*), those acts that would help a believer attain salvation but that weren't mandatory, such as extra prayers, voluntary almsgiving, or using a toothpick to clean one's teeth; 'the permitted' (*al-mubah* or *al-halal*), those acts that merited neither punishment nor reward, like eating good food or wearing comfortable clothes; and 'the reprehensible' (*al-makruh*), those things which it was better to avoid but which wouldn't inevitably lead to damnation, like praying inattentively.[10]

The doctrine of the four sources of the law was a typically Sunni compromise between those (like Ahmad ibn Hanbal and the partisans of Hadith) who wanted to base the law entirely on Qur'an and Hadith, and those (such as Abu Hanifa and the partisans of reasoning) who wanted to give a wider remit to human judgement. This attempt at compromise was largely successful. Out of the early disputes in legal theory emerged four *madhhabs* or schools of legal thought – the Shafi'is, Hanafis, Malikis, and Hanbalis – which would recognize one another as fellow Sunnis.[11]

Each madhhab – whose real founders were the disciples of the pioneering scholars after whom they were named – had its own particular doctrines, methodologies, and institutions. Lengthy books were written on the subject of *khilaf*, the differences between the madhhabs on particular points of law, and 'everyone,' as the North African historian Ibn Khaldun (1332–1406) wrote in his *Introduction to History* (*al-Muqaddima*), 'argued in favour of the correctness of the school to which he adhered'.[12] Thus, to take the seemingly trivial example of whether it was permitted to eat horsemeat (a question on which there was contradictory information in the Hadith), the Shafi'is and Hanbalis said that it was permitted (*mubah*); the Malikis that it was reprehensible (*mandub*) but not punishable; and the Hanafis that it was reprehensible bordering on forbidden (*haram*).[13] Less trivially (because it pertained to the worship of Allah), the Malikis held that believers should let their hands hang by their sides when standing during the ritual prayer; the other three schools that they should hold their right hand over their left.[14] And while the Hanafis, Shafi'is, and Malikis held that a person who intentionally and persistently neglected to pray ought to be imprisoned until they resumed the ritual prayer, the Hanbalis ruled that such a person was an unbeliever who should be killed (though this was a theoretical position that they rarely had an opportunity to implement).[15]

Such differences reflected the different origins and emphases of the four schools: while the Malikis sought to preserve the customary practice (*'amal*) of Medina, the Hanbalis clung to Hadith; while both the Hanafis and Shafi'is gave scope to human reasoning, the former allowed the public good (*istihsan*) to be taken into account while the latter generally stuck to reasoning by analogy (*qiyas*).

From the mid-eleventh century, the madhhabs had their own madrasas or law colleges, funded by private individuals, for training scholars in their particular doctrines and approach. In 1067, Nizam al-Mulk (1018–92), the Seljuq Turks' powerful Iranian vizier, founded the Nizamiyya College in Baghdad for training scholars in Shafi'i jurisprudence. In the same year, a Hanafi benefactor established a Hanafi madrasa adjacent to the shrine of Abu Hanifa in the same city. In this way, a degree of rivalry between the madhhabs was encouraged. Sometimes, a Hanbali would impugn the reliability of a Shafi'i's scholarship – or vice-versa – for partisan motives.[16] Occasionally, particularly when politics intervened, this degenerated into civil conflict, as happened in 1053, when al-Kunduri (1024–64), Nizam al-Mulk's predecessor as Seljuq vizier, and a staunch Hanafi, launched a *mihna* against the Shafi'is of Nishapur in north-eastern Iran.[17]

More often, however, the spirit of compromise and moderation won out. All four madhhabs broadly accepted the doctrine of the four sources of law, and those who refused to compromise – like the Zahiris, who remained unflinching in their commitment to the explicit (*zahir*) meaning of the Qur'an and Hadith and hostile to all reasoning, including analogy

– were excluded from the Sunni mainstream.[18] Differences between the four madhhabs on particular points of law were generally accepted, and even celebrated, the earlier quest for unanimity being effectively abandoned. 'Difference of opinion within my community is a divine mercy,' declared an often-cited Hadith.[19] The founding fathers of the four madhhabs, it was said, had accepted one another as believing Muslims, and so too should their followers.[20] A Sunni Muslim could convert from one madhhab to another without loss of face.[21] 'We follow al-Shafi'i, Malik, Abu Hanifa, and the great Ibn Hanbal,' wrote the later Shafi'i scholar al-Subki (1327–70) in his biographical dictionary of Shafi'i scholars, 'and we shall meet in the garden [of paradise]'.[22] In this respect, the Sunnis were similar to the Jews, who recognized the schools of Iraq and Palestine as equally Jewish, but unlike the Eastern Christian churches, who refused to acknowledge each other's orthodoxy.[23]

It was geography, more than anything else, that would determine which madhhab a Sunni followed. Outside of North Africa and Spain, where almost all were Malikis, and Baghdad, where many ordinary people were Hanbalis, most Sunnis adhered either to the Shafi'i or Hanafi schools. The former, traditionally strong in Iraq and Khorasan, would from the thirteenth century become the leading school in Syria, Egypt, and Yemen, from where it spread across the Indian Ocean to Southeast Asia. The Hanafi school, meanwhile, expanded from Kufa into the rest of Iraq, Syria, Khorasan, Central Asia, and India. It became the preferred madhhab of Turkish Muslims, and, as we shall see, would be made the official school of law of the Ottoman Empire.

★

The founding fathers of the Sunni law schools had had an uneasy relationship with theology. Al-Shafi'i had been on bad terms with the rationalist Mu'tazila, while Ahmad ibn Hanbal, in the words of his biographer Christopher Melchert, 'had a distrust of all *kalam*, even apologetic'.[24] Yet the Sunnis, being the party of compromise, would find a place for revealed theology within their system. Alongside the four schools of law, they acknowledged two schools of theology – the Ash'ari and Maturidi – as legitimate.

The Ash'ari school took its name from Abu'l-Hasan al-Ash'ari (874–936). A one-time student of the eminent Mu'tazili theologian Abu 'Ali al-Jubba'i (d. 915/6), one Friday around the year 913, it was said, al-Ash'ari had ascended the pulpit of the congregational mosque of Basra and dramatically renounced Mu'tazili *kalam*: 'Bear witness to the fact that my religion was not Islam,' he proclaimed, 'and that at this moment I have become a Muslim, and have repented of my Mu'tazili beliefs.'[25] In exchange for Mu'tazilism, al-Ash'ari embraced the doctrine of Ahmad ibn Hanbal, whom he declared 'the virtuous guide and perfect leader'. 'The religion that we profess,' he said, 'is that of clinging to the Book of our Lord and the Sunna of our Prophet.'[26]

From Basra, al-Ash'ari moved to Baghdad, the centre of the caliphate and a stronghold of Sunni Islam. There he attended weekly classes on Shafi'i law at the Mosque of al-Mansur, and began to write in defence of Sunni doctrine and against the views of the 'heretics' and 'partisans of deviation and innovation (*bid'a*)', meaning his erstwhile Mu'tazili colleagues.[27] Significantly, however, he also wrote in defence of *kalam*. Against those followers of Ahmad who shared their master's allergy to revealed theology, al-Ash'ari argued that rational argumentation was not simply useful in refuting heretics, but had in fact been recommended by the Qur'an and Sunna.[28] *Taqlid*, the unthinking emulation of others' opinions, was not good enough; Sunni Islam had to make room for reason.[29]

Though he upheld the rational methods of his former colleagues, the theological positions advocated by al-Ash'ari and his followers were the opposite of those defended by the Mu'tazila. When he stood up in the mosque of Basra to announce his conversion, al-Ash'ari was said to have declared: 'I ... used to proclaim that the Qur'an was created, that Allah will not be seen visually, and that when I do evil things, it is I who do them. Behold, I am repenting, uprooted, committed to refuting the Mu'tazila, casting off their disgraces and shameful errors.'[30] Here were three issues on which the Ash'aris would reject the characteristic Mu'tazili teaching. First, where the Mu'tazila had insisted that the Qur'an was created in time, al-Ash'ari and his supporters would say with Ahmad ibn Hanbal and the ulema that it was 'uncreated'. Yet where Ahmad had asserted this on the basis that there was no Hadith to the contrary, al-Ash'ari, being a theologian, made the rational case for the uncreatedness of the Qur'an. The Qur'an – so one of his arguments went – was Allah's word or speech. Allah created by speaking: as the Qur'an declared, when He wanted to create something He had merely to say 'Be!' and that thing would exist (e.g. 2:117). Now, if Allah's speech were created, then those acts of creation would themselves require creative acts of speech to create them, in turn creating a chain of such acts extending to infinity. Since such an infinite chain was impossible, Allah's speech had to be uncreated, and so too, therefore, did the Qur'an.[31]

Second, on the Day of Judgement, al-Ash'ari insisted, the saved would see Allah with their eyes. This issue was important because it touched not only on the reality of the resurrection but also on the nature of Allah Himself. According to the Mu'tazila, the Qur'an's references to Allah's attributes and body parts were meant to be taken metaphorically: when the Qur'an said that 'faces on that day [the Day of Judgement] will shine, looking at their Lord' (75:22–3), it meant that the believers would see Allah 'with their hearts'. For al-Ash'ari and his followers, this was to fail to take scripture sufficiently seriously. Allah's attributes, he affirmed, were real. If one could not rationally understand the scriptural passages in which they were mentioned, one was obliged not to reinterpret them but simply to accept them *bi-la kayf*, 'without asking how'.[32] When in doubt, reason had to give way to revelation.

Third, al-Ash'ari rejected the Mu'tazili belief in human free will. 'In truth,' he declared, 'there is no agent, except Allah.'[33] This doctrine – which historians of philosophy would call occasionalism – was founded on Qur'anic statements like 'Allah created you and all that you do' (37:96). It also rested on the atomistic view of the universe that al-Ash'ari had inherited from the Mu'tazila. According to that theory, the world was made up of atoms (called in Arabic *juz' la yatajazza'*, 'a part which cannot be made into smaller parts') and 'accidents' (attributes like heat or cold, movement or rest, which resided in bodies or groups of atoms). In the Ash'ari view, the whole assembly of atoms and accidents that made up the world was continuously being constructed and reconstructed by Allah in what the theologians described, drawing on the Qur'an (e.g. 13:5), as a 'renewed creation' (*khalq jadid*). This meant that, for the Ash'aris, there were no laws of nature, only the customary will of Allah. As a famous example given by the later Ash'ari theologian al-Ghazali (1058–1111) had it, when cotton came into contact with fire, it was not the fire but Allah's creation of the accident of burning that caused it to burn.[34] Human actions worked the same way: it was Allah who created them and their effects. Humans only performed them, or, as the Ash'aris put it, they merely 'acquired' (*kasb*) them from Allah – a doctrine consistent with the mindset of a society which saw the hand of God in everything.[35]

All in all, the Ash'ari school of theology adopted what was a characteristically Sunni middle position – between literal adherence to the Qur'an and Hadith on the one hand, and rational thought on the other. It would stand, in the words of a modern Ash'ari scholar, for 'the middle ground between revelation and reason in epistemology, between divine incomparability and comparability [to creation] in theology, and between compulsion and free will in human affairs.'[36] In this way, the Ash'aris succeeded in marrying the sophisticated reasoning of the intellectuals with the scripture-based beliefs of the humble believers.

The result was that most Sunnis would identify as Ash'aris in their theology. This was especially true of Sunnis who adhered to the Shafi'i school. Al-Shafi'i's attempt to reconcile reason and revelation in legal theory resembled al-Ash'ari's in theology, and the schools named after the two great scholars became virtually synonymous. Almost all Shafi'is were Ash'aris and vice versa: the influential Ash'ari theologian al-Juwayni (1028–85), for instance, was also an authority on Shafi'i law, revered by his followers as 'the Imam of the Two Sanctuaries' because he had taught in both Mecca and Medina, and famed for his lengthy

Demonstration of Legal Theory (al-Burhan fi usul al-fiqh), in which he offered rational arguments for the use of Hadith, consensus, and analogy in working out the law.[37] There were also prominent Ash'aris within the Maliki school: al-Baqillani (d. 1013), a Baghdad-based scholar widely regarded as the leading Ash'ari theologian and 'renewer' (*mujaddid*) of the fourth Islamic century, was a Maliki judge,[38] as was the aforementioned North African historian Ibn Khaldun, who would commend Ash'ari theology as 'one of the best speculative disciplines and religious sciences' in his *Introduction to History*, at the same time as he credited the Maliki school of law with preserving the hardy desert attitude and simple piety of Muhammad and his companions.[39]

Adherents of the Hanafi madhhab, by contrast, invariably tended to follow the Maturidi school of theology. An almost exact contemporary of al-Ash'ari, Abu Mansur al-Maturidi (*c.*870–944) was born in the ancient Central Asian city of Samarqand, a wealthy and populous trading centre along the Silk Road that was famous for its papermaking. In al-Maturidi's time, the region was under the control of the Samanids (819–999), an independent Persian dynasty who would play a key role in the introduction of Persian as a literary language into the world of Islam. Al-Maturidi himself was a native Persian speaker who wrote in halting Arabic and seems never to have left his native town. There, in a city noted for its religious diversity, he continued the old tradition of *kalam* as reasoned polemic: his writings contain refutations of Jews, Christians, and the dualist Manichaeans and Zoroastrians, as well as the Mu'tazila, the Shi'a, and other misguided Islamic sects.[40]

Against these various opponents, al-Maturidi argued for doctrines that were essentially close to those of al-Ash'ari. He insisted, for instance, that the believers would see Allah with their eyes in the afterlife – though they would not 'comprehend' Him – and that, when the Qur'an said that Allah sat upon the throne, this had to be accepted as literally true.[41]

That said, both his general approach and his positions on the controversial theological questions tended to be more rationalist than al-Ash'ari's. This was particularly in evidence in his response to the question of how good and evil could be known. The Mu'tazila had proposed that there was an objective set of ethical values that humans could know through their innate reason. Al-Ash'ari, by contrast, had argued that good and evil were just what Allah said they were; if human beings wanted to know what was right or wrong, they had simply to consult the Qur'an and Hadith, which were a record of Allah's will.[42] Al-Maturidi's position cut a path between the two: while he agreed with al-Ash'ari that it was Allah who determined what was good or bad, he also thought that Allah had given humans intellects to enable them to work this out.[43] Similarly, on the thorny issue of free will versus determinism, al-Maturidi opted for a middle position, one that tried to preserve both divine omnipotence and human free choice through subtle linguistic distinctions. Allah 'created' actions, he explained, but humans 'did' them – or, in another formulation, while Allah 'willed' all deeds, this did not 'compel' humans to perform them.[44]

Al-Maturidi's teachings spread across Central Asia, and by the eleventh century most Hanafis in the region had aligned with the school named after him. When, in the mid-eleventh century, the Seljuq Turks broke out of their Central Asian homeland and conquered Iran and Iraq, they therefore took the Maturidi school of theology with them. Previously confined to their own geographical spheres, Ash'aris and Maturidis now rubbed shoulders in the heartlands of Islam. Though relations were initially less than harmonious – a situation aggravated by the Seljuqs' general hostility to Ash'arism and the Shafi'i school of law – mutual toleration was eventually agreed and the differences between the two schools largely glossed over.[45] Compromise, as ever, was the watchword of the Sunnis.

If the jurists of the four madhhabs looked after most Muslims' approach to the law, and the Ash'ari and Maturidi theologians took care of their beliefs, then the Sufis looked after their hearts. This may have seemed unlikely at the beginning of the tenth century, when Baghdad was rocked by what the Catholic scholar Louis Massignon called the 'passion' of al-Hallaj (857–922) (meant in the Christian sense of the 'passion' or redemptive suffering of Christ). A native of southern Iran and former student of al-Junayd, al-Hallaj had travelled through Iran, Central Asia, and India, calling Muslims and non-Muslims alike to the spiritual life. Back in Baghdad, he courted controversy with his *shatahat* or ecstatic 'outpourings'. He announced that Satan, in refusing to bow down before Adam, had been a true monotheist who worshipped only Allah, proposed that the true pilgrimage was to the 'Ka'ba of one's heart', and, most notoriously, proclaimed *ana'l-haqq*, 'I am the Truth' (meaning, 'I am God'). Sober Sufis from the circle of al-Junayd condemned him for divulging the mysteries of Sufism and being too clever for his own good. 'Al-Hallaj and I are of one belief,' said al-Shibli (861–945), another of al-Junayd's students, 'but my madness saved me, while his intelligence destroyed him.'[46] The political authorities, fearful of his popularity, accused him of plotting revolution. In 922 he was sentenced to death, hanged on the scaffold, and beheaded – the ultimate form of execution.[47]

In response to this trauma, the Sufis insisted that their teachings were compatible with Sunni principles. 'The whole science [of Sufism],' wrote al-Sarraj (d. 988), the author of *The Illuminating Rays of Sufism* (*al-Luma' fi'l-tasawwuf*), one of the oldest handbooks of Sufi teachings, 'can be found in the Book of Allah and the sayings of the Messenger of Allah.'[48] This, al-Sarraj stressed, was not just his own view, but the position of the great Sufis of the ninth century: 'Our science,' he quoted al-Junayd as saying, 'is interwoven with the Hadith of the Messenger.'[49] According to al-Qushayri (986–1073), a Sufi, Ash'ari theologian, and Shafi'i legal scholar whose *Epistle on Sufism* (*al-Risala*) would become the most widely read introduction to Sufism, al-Junayd had gone even further: 'Whoever does not memorise the Qur'an and write down Hadith is not to be followed in this matter [i.e. Sufism], for this science of ours is limited by the Book and the Sunna.'[50]

Following the Qur'an and Sunna meant adhering to the Shari'a and orthodox theological beliefs. 'The Sufis,' al-Sarraj wrote, 'agreed with the doctrines of the legal scholars and partisans of Hadith, accepted their sciences, and did not oppose their views or their methods.'[51] Al-Junayd had been a student of al-Shafi'i's leading disciple, and those Sufis who were not themselves experts in the law, it was stressed, would go to the jurists for legal rulings.[52] In theology, the Sufis adopted the Sunni view that the Qur'an was 'uncreated', that the attributes ascribed to Allah in the Qur'an were real, and that it was Allah who created all actions and humans who 'acquired' them.[53] Those who rejected these views were condemned as false Sufis who, as al-Sarraj put it, merely 'looked like them, wore their clothes and took their name',[54] while the idea that Allah became incarnate in man – as the Christians believed of Jesus and al-Hallaj was said to have taught – was rejected as having nothing to do with true Sufism.[55]

In this way, the Sufis sought to carve out a niche for mysticism within Sunni Islam. While legal theory and theology were the sciences of 'outward' (*zahir*) commandments and beliefs, Sufism, they said, was the science of 'inward' (*batin*) practices and ideas; or rather, it was the science that combined the outward and the inward dimensions of Islam.[56] They claimed to have special ways of drawing out the hidden meaning of the Qur'an: when the Qur'an talked about jihad, for instance, the Sufis, citing a prophetic Hadith, said that this meant the 'greater jihad', the holy war against the urge to sin.[57] They undertook special practices like withdrawing from society (*khalwa*) or repeatedly chanting the name of Allah (*dhikr*) in order to induce a heightened state of consciousness. And, aware of the need to present Sufism as a systematic science comparable to theology and law, they spoke of Sufism as a mapped-out 'path' (*tariqa*) punctuated by certain mystical 'stations' (*maqamat*) and 'states' (*ahwal*) such as poverty and patience, fear of Allah and trust in Him, which culminated in mystical proximity to the divine.[58]

Nor did the Sufi authors shy away from addressing the more controversial aspects of the mystic path. Contentious topics like *walaya* ('friendship' with Allah, a concept comparable to the Christian idea of sainthood) and *sama'* (the ritual use of music to induce mystical experiences) were dealt with in such a way as to render Sufi theory and practice acceptable to the scholars of theology and the law. The saints or 'friends of God' (s. *waliy*, pl. *awliya' Allah*), insisted 'Ali Hujwiri (1010–72), author of *The Unveiling of the Veiled* (*Kashf al-mahjub*), the oldest Sufi treatise in Persian, were inferior to the prophets: though they performed miracles, their miracles were different to prophetic miracles, nor were they immune to sin as the prophets were.[59] The Prophet himself, remarked al-Sarraj in his chapter on the *sama'*, had been fond of song, while Sufi masters like al-Junayd had imposed clear restrictions on the use of music to ensure that the Sufis' mystical concerts never got out of hand.[60]

All this helped give Sufism an intellectual and doctrinal respectability, enabling it to take its place alongside the legal doctrines of the four madhhabs and the theology of the Ash'ari and Maturidi schools as a key part of the Sunni compromise. As we shall see, this was a compromise that would remain largely intact up to the present day.

Chapter Five

THE SHI'I
VISION

I f the Sunnis were the party of compromise, the Shi'a were
those who held onto the early vision of a living guide. 'You are
a forewarner (*mundhir*), and to every people there is a guide (*hadin*)'
(13:7), Allah had said to Muhammad. With the 'forewarner'
gone, the Shi'a believed, it was the turn of the 'guide' to lead
the Muslim community in its religious and political affairs.[1]

They called this guide their Imam. This was the same title
that the mainstream tradition gave to the caliph, but the Shi'a
gave it a special meaning. The Imams, the Shi'a believed, were
to be found among the *ahl al-bayt* or 'People of the Household',
a Qur'anic term (33:33) used to denote the Prophet's family. In
the Shi'i view, the special status of the *ahl al-bayt* had been clearly
established by the Qur'an and Hadith. 'I am leaving you with
two weighty things,' the Prophet had told his followers just before
his death, 'the Book of Allah and the People of the Household.
As long as you cling to these two, you will not go astray.'[2]

The first Imam had been 'Ali. According to the Shi'a, the
Prophet had explicitly designated his cousin and son-in-law
as his heir and legatee (*wasiy*). 'Whoever's master I am,' they

quoted Muhammad as having said, 'their master is 'Ali also.'[3] In the majority Shi'i view, the Imamate had subsequently been passed down through the descendants of 'Ali and his wife Fatima, each of whom had received the designation (*nass*) and religious knowledge (*'ilm*) of his predecessor. This knowledge came from the divine realm – for the Imams were believed to have been spoken to by the angels – and was infallible and all-encompassing.[4] The Imams were said to possess knowledge of the unseen world, of the past, present, and future, of all human and animal languages, and of the inner meaning of all the sacred scriptures.[5] 'I contain the knowledge of the Qur'an,' the sixth Imam Ja'far al-Sadiq (*c*.700–65) was quoted as saying.[6] Some even thought that the Imams had in their possession a secret and more complete version of the Qur'an than the one used by the Sunnis, whom they accused of deleting references to 'Ali and the Imams from the sacred text.[7]

History, however, had been unkind to the People of the Household. First Abu Bakr had seized the caliphate from 'Ali. Then 'Ali had had to bear the wrongful caliphates of 'Umar and 'Uthman, only acquiescing in their rule to preserve the unity of the community. When he finally became leader, 'Ali had met with disobedience and rebellion, culminating in his murder in 661 at the hands of the extremist Kharijites (whom we've already met as proponents of the view that the grave sinner was an unbeliever), who had seceded from 'Ali's camp when he agreed to submit his claim to the caliphate to an arbitration committee. In his stead came the iniquitous Umayyads, who, in words attributed to 'Ali's younger son Husayn (626–80), 'practised obedience to Satan and forsook obedience to God'.[8] Most tragically of all, in 680, on the tenth day (*'ashura'*) of the Islamic month of Muharram,

Husayn and a band of seventy-two of his supporters had been brutally cut down at Karbala on the orders of the Umayyad caliph Yazid (r. 680–83) – an event that would forever after be mourned and reimagined by the Shi'a on the holy day of Ashura. Subsequent rebellions in support of the sons of 'Ali had also come to nothing, as the Umayyads and then the 'Abbasids strengthened their grip on the caliphate. Though the latter had raised Shi'i hopes by rebelling in the name of 'the chosen one' (al-rida) from the family of Muhammad – a vaguely pro-Shi'i formula – they were descendants neither of 'Ali nor Muhammad, and after their rise to power they kept the Shi'i Imams under close surveillance and even, so the Shi'a alleged, had them killed.

In the face of these tragedies, the Imams had opted to withdraw from the political fray. This attitude crystallized under the aforementioned sixth Imam Ja'far al-Sadiq, who won a broad following among the Shi'a of Kufa, particularly among those who refused to support the unsuccessful rebellion in 740 of Husayn's grandson Zayd ibn 'Ali (694/5–740). (The latter's followers, who became known as the Zaydis, would continue to insist that the Imam ought to seek political power, if necessary by armed struggle.[9]) Soon, however, the Shi'a were hit by another crisis, this time from within. Ja'far al-Sadiq had apparently designated his second son Isma'il (721–55) as his successor, only for Isma'il to predecease him. When Ja'far himself died in 765, his followers were split over who should succeed him. On one side – the majority – were those who thought that the Imamate should pass to another of his sons, Musa al-Kazim (745–99). On the other side were those who believed that the rightful Imam was in fact Isma'il's son Muhammad (740–813), since, as an infallible Imam, Ja'far's designation of Isma'il could not have been a mistake.[10] These two positions would form, respectively, the basis of the two major Shi'i groups: the Imamis or Twelvers and the Isma'ilis.

Just over a century after this schism came another major turning point. In 874, the eleventh Imam of the Imami Shi'a died, apparently without leaving an heir. Soon it was argued that there had in fact been a son, who had gone into hiding or 'occultation' (*ghayba*) in order to escape 'Abbasid persecution. In the ensuing decades, so the Imami Shi'a came to believe, this twelfth Imam remained in contact with the Shi'i community through an 'ambassador' (*safir*). In 941, however, the fourth ambassador declared on his deathbed that after him there would be no further contact with the Imam, initiating the period that came to be known as the 'greater occultation'.[11] The twelfth Imam, it was said, had not died; rather he was one of those individuals who had been endowed with an extraordinarily long life, like the prophet Noah (who according to Genesis 9:29 had lived to be 950).[12] He was, moreover, declared the *final* Imam. In support of this idea, the Imamis – or Twelvers as they now came to be called – found evidence in the Qur'an, Hadith, and even the Bible: the twelve sons of Ishmael mentioned in Genesis 25:12–16, for instance, were said to be the twelve Imams.[13] Most importantly, the Twelvers believed that the twelfth Imam would return at the End of Time as the Mahdi or Divine Guide, a messianic figure tasked with ridding the world of evil and restoring justice, wisdom, and true Islam. This, in fact, was declared to be the reason for his occultation, for it was only because he was free of all loyalty to the worldly authorities that the Imam would be able to lead an uprising against the forces of oppression.[14]

The doctrine of the occultation had a number of important implications for Twelver Shi'i thought. First, it further encouraged an attitude of political quietism. The task of the Shi'a was not to bring down the unrighteous rule of the Sunni caliph, but instead to wait for the Mahdi, the messianic saviour, to accomplish this task at the appropriate point in history. Emphasising the Qur'anic virtue of patient endurance (*sabr*), the Twelvers quoted a statement attributed to the fifth Imam Muhammad al-Baqir (*c.*676/7–733), the father of Ja'far al-Sadiq: 'Be content with performing your religious obligations, and bear your enemies with fortitude, and cling to your awaited Imam.'[15] To this end, like the Sufis, they transformed the concept of jihad from holy war into spiritual or intellectual struggle,[16] and developed the principle of *taqiyya*, dissimulation for self-preservation, or, as the eleventh-century Shi'i theologian al-Shaykh al-Mufid (948–1022) defined it in his *Correction of Beliefs* (*Tashih al-i'tiqadat*), 'the concealing of truth, covering up of belief about it, and confounding of opponents' in order to avoid persecution.[17]

Just as important, the disappearance of the Imam meant that the Twelvers could no longer seek the infallible guidance of a living and divinely inspired guide on questions of law and theology. As a consequence, they were forced to develop their own traditions of legal and theological thought, similar to those of the Sunnis. In this regard, the greater occultation came at a convenient moment. In the 940s the central Islamic lands were conquered by the Shi'i Buyids from northern Iran, who, though they kept the 'Abbasids in place, were only too happy to provide protection and support to Shi'i scholars.

In the Buyid capital Rayy – today a southern suburb of Tehran – and Qom in central Iran, Shi'i scholars worked out a new approach to questions of law and theology. The stance they adopted was close to that of the Sunni ulema. The religious law, these scholars argued, was founded on the Qur'an and Hadith of the Prophet. 'The discussion of legal matters,' one early Twelver scholar was quoted as saying, 'is based on the Book and the Sunna, for as Allah has said: "Should you disagree about something, refer it to God and the Messenger" (4:59).'[18] But there was also another, equally important, source of the law, and that was the sayings or 'reports' (akhbar) of the Imams. Much effort went into collecting these akhbar, and the sayings of Muhammad that the Imams had passed on, as source material for Shi'i legal doctrine. Like the six books of the Sunnis, four collections of such sayings – compiled over the course of the tenth and eleventh centuries, and together amounting to some 38,000 reports – would be accepted as canonical in Twelver Shi'i thought.[19]

This was essentially a continuation of Shi'i practice in the period when the Imams were still physically present. While a Shi'i Muslim could no longer consult the living guide on questions of theology or law, he or she could do the next best thing by consulting the record of the Imams' pronouncements. For many Shi'a, these inspired sayings were a sufficient guide to life. Rational argument, according to this view, was superfluous and misleading. As the Imam Ja'far al-Sadiq was quoted as saying, 'The partisans of theology will perish, while the Muslims will be saved.'[20]

Yet, there were others, in ever-greater numbers, who recognized that because the sayings of the Imams were necessarily limited in number and scope, supplementation would be needed. In support of their approach, they cited Qur'anic verses like 16:125 – 'Debate with them in the most courteous manner' – and the precedent set by those of the Imams' disciples who had engaged in *kalam*.[21] Swayed by this view, Twelver ulema, like their Sunni counterparts, came to accept that the inerrant guidance of revelation and the inspired words of the Prophet and Imams could be filled out, where appropriate, by human reasoning.

This process started in Baghdad, where a group of Shi'i scholars fell under the influence of Mu'tazili theology. It came to fruition in the work of the aforementioned al-Shaykh al-Mufid and his students, al-Sharif al-Murtada (967–1044) and Shaykh al-Ta'ifa al-Tusi (995–1067). These scholars were hugely influential and widely revered. Their homes in al-Karkh, the Shi'i quarter of Baghdad on the left bank of the Tigris, became the intellectual centres of the Shi'i community: students would come there to study Hadith and theology, and petitions would be sent in from Iraq and Iran, Syria and Egypt, seeking their guidance on particular questions of law. Al-Murtada, who was born into Shi'i nobility, also held the office of *naqib*, political representative of the Twelver community to the Buyid sultan and 'Abbasid caliph. He was also fabulously wealthy: when he died, the library he left to al-Tusi was said to contain some 80,000 books.[22]

In theology, these Shi'i scholars adopted the key doctrines of the Mu'tazila. Thus al-Mufid argued that Allah was utterly 'one' and totally just, that human actions had not been created by Allah but were freely willed, and that the Qur'an had been 'produced in time' (the preferred formulation of the Baghdad school of the Mu'tazila).[23] His student al-Murtada, who had also studied under 'Abd al-Jabbar (935–1035), the leading Mu'tazili theologian of the day, likewise emphasized the justice of Allah and insisted that the Qur'an was not eternal.[24] Of course, they remained Shi'a first and Mu'tazila second: against the Mu'tazila, both al-Mufid and al-Murtada insisted on the Shi'i view of the Imamate as the exclusive inheritance of the descendants of 'Ali and Fatima through the line of Husayn.[25] Nevertheless, in immersing themselves in Mu'tazili thought, they helped make Mu'tazilism the theological school of the Twelver Shi'a, just as Ash'arism and Maturidism were the theological schools of the Sunnis. The result, as the scholar of Shi'ism Mohammad Ali Amir-Moezzi has put it, was that 'the rationalist tendency became the majority and dominant view' within Twelver Shi'ism.[26]

In their approach to the law, too, the three Twelver scholars opened the door to a more rationalist approach. While privileging the Qur'an, Hadith, and sayings of the Imams as sources of law, al-Mufid also proposed that reason was one of the 'roads' leading to knowledge of the revealed sources, while his student al-Murtada allowed some scope for *ijtihad* – a term, close in meaning to *ra'y*, which denoted the legal scholar's use of his or her independent reasoning to work out the law from the fundamental sources.[27] They also developed a specifically Shi'i theory of consensus (*ijma'*) as a source of law, further entrenching the authority of scholars like themselves whose role it was to set that consensus.[28]

In this way, the Twelvers moved from an insistence on the Imam as the sole authoritative guide towards a position that was not so far from that of the Sunnis. In the absence of the Imam, the Shi'i ulema had become the effective arbiters of truth. Like the Sunnis, they embraced *kalam*, the rational defence of religious dogma; indeed, in adopting the theology of the Mu'tazila, they could be said to be more rationalist in their theology than the Sunnis. Like the Sunnis, too, they developed a legal theory that was grounded in revelation, yet which also allowed for some rational interpretation of the revealed sources. In their positive legal rulings, meanwhile, they tended to differ from the Sunni madhhabs on relatively minor issues, like whether rings should be worn on the right or left hand (the Shi'a said the right; the Sunnis, the left), whether anal intercourse was allowed (al-Murtada said yes; Malik and most Sunni authorities, no), or whether it was permissible to eat rabbit (the Shi'a said no; the Sunnis, yes).[29] They also developed their own school of legal thought – later known as the Ja'fari school after the sixth Imam Ja'far al-Sadiq – on the model of the four Sunni madhhabs.[30]

Yet while the Twelvers may have moved closer to the Sunni position, a crucial and insurmountable difference remained. Aside from the Qur'an itself, the Sunnis relied upon the Sunna of the Prophet, as interpreted by their religious scholars. The Twelvers, by contrast, still sought the guidance of their Imams, recorded for posterity in the four canonical collections. While the Imams' authority had been delegated to the religious scholars who interpreted those sayings, this was only a temporary loan, for the twelfth and final Imam remained alive and in hiding, liable to return at any moment as the Mahdi, the perfect guide to the realization of a perfect world.

At its roots, Shi'ism was an idealistic and activist movement, dedicated to the installation of the rightful Imam as ruler. While the Twelvers had moderated this initial idealism, opting for political quietism and deferring their expectations until the coming of the Mahdi, the Isma'ili branch of Shi'ism retained the early vision.

Though the split between the Twelvers and Isma'ilis went back to the dispute over who should succeed Ja'far al-Sadiq as Imam in the mid-eighth century, the Isma'ilis only really emerged onto the historical scene a century later, about the time that the last Imam of the Twelvers was said to have gone into occultation. The first Isma'ili missionaries or *du'at* (s. *da'i*) appeared in the countryside around Kufa, and soon could be found across the Middle East, North Africa, and India, calling on people to pledge allegiance to the true Imam. This was an underground, revolutionary movement, headquartered at Salamiyya in western Syria, whose goal was nothing less than the overthrow of the 'Abbasid caliphate. As such, it appealed in the first instance to the less privileged – to the peasants and Bedouin of the Kufan countryside and Bahrain, the mountain tribes of Yemen, and the Berber mountain dwellers of the Maghreb – as well as to educated Shi'a who disagreed with the quietist policies of the Twelvers.

Alongside revolution, the earliest Isma'ili missionaries preached a radical and complex religious doctrine. There had, they said, been seven great prophets: Adam, Noah, Abraham, Moses, Jesus, Muhammad, and Muhammad ibn Isma'il (the son of Ja'far al-Sadiq's son and successor Isma'il). These 'speaker' (*natiq*) prophets, as the Isma'ilis called them, had taught the outer (*zahir*) dimension of divine revelation, that is, legal rulings and commandments that changed according to historical circumstances. Yet each speaker prophet, the missionaries taught, also had a 'silent' (*samit*) companion, or 'foundation' (*asas*), who knew the immutable inner (*batin*) dimension of revelation: Moses, for instance, had Aaron, Jesus had Peter, and Muhammad had 'Ali. These silent companions had in turn inaugurated a parallel cycle of Imams – seven for each prophetic cycle – who likewise knew the inner truth of scripture. As if that wasn't complicated enough, the Isma'ili missionaries also taught that Muhammad ibn Isma'il was both the seventh and final prophet *and* the last Imam of the present era, and that he therefore knew both dimensions of religion, the outer and the inner. He was believed to be still alive and in hiding – some said in Byzantium – and to be on the verge of returning as the Mahdi. When he did, the early Isma'ilis believed, he would reveal the secret meaning of the scriptures to all people and establish perfect justice on earth.[31]

Further adding to the complexity, around 899 the leadership at Salamiyya announced a dramatic change of course. Muhammad ibn Isma'il, it was now said, was not about to return. Instead, the latest in the line of his descendants, who had until that point been living in *satr* or 'concealment', would now reveal himself as the Imam and take his rightful place at the head of the Muslim community. This announcement had the adverse effect of provoking the 'Abbasid authorities' interest in the Isma'ilis, and, fearing for his life, the newly declared Imam fled Salamiyya, first for Ramla in Palestine, then Egypt, and finally to North Africa, where the Isma'ili missionaries had found success among the Kutama Berbers. For four years he lay low in Sijilmassa, a remote Moroccan town on the edge of the Sahara, while the North African missionary 'Abd Allah al-Shi'i (d. 911) and his Berber troops swept through the province of Ifriqiya – at that time under the control of the Sunni Aghlabid dynasty – in modern Tunisia. When Qayrawan, the Aghlabid capital, fell in

909, the Imam finally emerged from hiding. He was proclaimed the first Imam and caliph of the Fatimid dynasty – so named to highlight the Imams' descent from 'Ali and Fatima – and took the messianic title al-Mahdi (the Divine Guide). The age of concealment, so the Isma'ilis believed, was over, and the age of righteousness had begun.

The goal of the Isma'ili mission, however, had been the total overthrow of the 'Abbasid caliphate. For that, provincial Ifriqiya would not do as a centre of power. In 969, the Fatimid army conquered Egypt. There, next to the old Arab garrison town of Fustat, they founded *al-Qahira*, 'the Victorious', or, in a nod to the Fatimids' fondness for astrology, 'the City of Mars'. This new city, known to us as Cairo, would from 973 be the capital of the Fatimid caliphate, an empire that at its peak would stretch from North Africa to the holy cities of Mecca and Medina, and whose influence could be felt in places as diverse as Sicily and Sind (in modern Pakistan). For the first time in their history, the Shi'a had a worthy alternative to the Sunni caliphate.

Egypt and North Africa were majority Sunni, and the Fatimids did not force their subjects to convert to Isma'ili Shi'ism. They did, however, continue to direct missionary activity throughout their territories and the wider Muslim world. One of the great offices of the Fatimid state was the position of chief missionary or *da'i al-du'at*. He directed a highly organized Isma'ili missionary network: the Muslim world was divided into twelve 'islands', into each of which the Fatimids sent their missionaries with tactics specific to the inhabitants of that region.[32] The chief missionary also hosted the *majalis al-hikma*, 'wisdom sessions' held every Thursday in the Fatimid caliphal palace, in which he would lecture initiates on the secret teachings of the Isma'ili faith. Lectures on more general Isma'ili topics, open to the wider public, were also given after the communal Friday prayer in the great congregational mosques of Cairo.[33] Non-Muslims as well as Sunnis were targeted for conversion. Ibn Killis (930–91), the first Fatimid vizier, who was himself a convert from Judaism, would host interreligious debates in the caliph's palace, while Fatimid missionaries interpreted the sacred texts of other faiths in accordance with Isma'ili beliefs, identifying the messianic king whose coming was foretold in the Hebrew Bible – and whom the Christians identified as Jesus – with the Fatimid Imam and caliph.[34]

To support this missionary work, the Fatimids, sustained by Egypt's thriving agricultural sector and their extensive network of maritime trade, were generous patrons of educational institutions. Fatimid Cairo was famous for its well-stocked libraries: the palace library was said, fantastically, to contain some 1.6 million books. The most famous college in the Fatimid capital was al-Azhar. Founded just after the conquest as a congregational mosque, its name, meaning 'the Resplendent', came from one of the titles of Fatima. In 988, the vizier Ibn Killis, who reputedly spent the princely sum of 1,000 dinars a month on supporting Isma'ili scholars, established a residential college in the precinct of the mosque, which, in a cruel twist of fate, would later become the most important centre of Sunni education in the Muslim world.[35]

The main subject taught at al-Azhar in Fatimid times, and one of the topics of the 'wisdom sessions', was Isma'ili law. This intellectual tradition was in effect the creation of al-Qadi al-Nu'man (c.903–74), the chief da'i and judge of the Fatimid state under the caliph al-Mu'izz (r. 953–75), the conqueror of Cairo. The basis of the Isma'ili legal tradition was the doctrine of *walaya*, the spiritual authority of the Imam. (The word was the same as the Sufis used for divine 'friendship' or sainthood.) *Walaya*, al-Nu'man explained in *The Pillars of Islam* (*Da'a'im al-Islam*), his textbook of Isma'ili law, was the first and greatest pillar of the faith. When Allah instructed Muslims to 'obey Allah, and obey the Messenger, and those in authority among you' (4:59), he said, this meant that they were bound, respectively, by the Qur'an ('Allah'), the Hadith of the Prophet ('the Messenger'), and the opinions of the Shi'i Imams ('those in authority').[36]

This was basically the same as the Twelver view. The crucial difference, however, was that the Imam of the Isma'ilis – the Fatimid caliph – was alive and present in the world. In addition to referring to the sayings of past Imams, al-Qadi al-Nu'man and his fellow Isma'ilis were able to consult their Imam-caliph on those questions to which the Qur'an and Hadith provided no ready answer.[37] So when, for instance, al-Nu'man considered the legal problem of when to begin and end the Ramadan fast, the answer he gave was that Isma'ilis could simply follow the lead of the Imam, 'fasting when he fasted, and breaking the fast when he broke it', rather than going by the sighting of the new moon like the Twelvers and the Sunnis.[38]

This, in essence, was an argument against legal theorizing. If the law was what the living Imam said it was, there was no need for jurisprudential techniques like consensus or analogy. Anyone who wanted proof of the inadequacy of juristic reasoning, al-Nu'man suggested, needed only to look at the severe disagreements that bedevilled Sunni law.[39] For this reason, in fact, Isma'ili thinkers after al-Qadi al-Nu'man would show relatively little interest in legal theory, and *The Pillars of Islam* would remain the principal book of Isma'ili law up to the present day.

The period from roughly 900 to 1100 witnessed the crystallization of Sunni and Shi'i Islam, and the definitive split between the two forms of the faith. Mutual hostility was the dominant note of the relationship. The Isma'ilis came in for the severest criticism from the Sunni majority. 'Externally they feign the Shi'i faith,' wrote the Ash'ari theologian and Maliki judge al-Baqillani, the 'renewer' of the fourth century, 'internally they hide pure unbelief.'[40] Yet nor did the Twelvers escape Sunni censure. In the late 1020s, the 'Abbasid caliph al-Qadir (r. 991–1031), seeking to reassert the caliph's religious authority, issued a series of decrees condemning the Mu'tazili-Twelver doctrine of the 'created Qur'an' as a mark of unbelief, and commanding reverence for those companions of the Prophet whom the Shi'a despised.[41] Twelver attempts to have the 'Ja'fari' madhhab recognized as a fifth school of legal thought were likewise rejected by the Sunnis.[42] The Shi'a, in their turn, were contemptuous of Sunnism. In the view of the Twelver thinker al-Sharif al-Murtada, though the Sunnis were not exactly unbelievers, they were also not believers in the true sense.[43]

Sectarianism at the theological level sometimes spilled over into physical violence. This was especially true in Baghdad, where Sunni Hanbalis lived side by side with Twelver Shi'a. Shi'i festivals like Ashura, the commemoration of the martyrdom of Husayn, were often flashpoints for anti-Shi'i rioting. During one such episode, the home of the eminent Twelver scholar Shaykh al-Ta'ifa al-Tusi was burnt down, forcing him to flee to the Shi'i shrine city of Najaf about a hundred miles to the south.

Politics, as well as theology, played a part in all this. If the period from the early tenth to the early eleventh century, when the Buyids took control of Iraq and Iran and the Fatimids conquered North Africa and Egypt, could be called the 'Shi'i Century', the period after that was the age of the 'Sunni Revival'. Around the same time that the caliph al-Qadir was proclaiming his Sunni creed in Baghdad, the Turkish warlord Mahmud of Ghazna (r. 998–1030), an aggressive persecutor of non-Sunnis, was taking the Indian city of Multan from the Isma'ilis and conquering Rayy from the Buyids. Then, in 1055, the Seljuq Turks took Baghdad, putting an end to Buyid rule and declaring themselves the 'right hand' of the 'Abbasid caliph. Soon after, their vizier Nizam al-Mulk, another who loathed the Shi'a, began his programme of madrasa-building for the spread of the Sunni faith.[44]

While the Fatimids held out in Egypt for a time, their empire was beset by economic and military crises, and in 1171 they were finally overthrown by the Kurdish Sunni vizier Salah al-Din al-Ayyubi (1138–93) – the legendary Saladin of the Crusader chronicles – who, declaring himself 'the reviver of the empire of the Commander of the Faithful [a title of the Sunni caliph]', brought Egypt back under the dominion of the 'Abbasid caliphate, introduced the first Sunni madrasas into Egypt, and – so Isma'ili tradition has it – shut the famous Fatimid libraries and destroyed many of the great works of Isma'ili thought.[45]

Sunnism presented itself as the Islam of the majority – indeed, the majoritarian instinct was built into its teachings – and the Sunni Revival helped ensure that it would indeed be so.

Yet Shi'ism, in its Twelver and Isma'ili forms, would survive as an important part of Islamic intellectual culture. The Sunnis, though dominant, would never have a monopoly on Islamic thought.

Chapter Six

RATIONALISTS
AND RADICALS

In developing their systems of legal theory and theology, both the
Sunnis and Twelver Shiʿa sought to modify and control what they
saw as a potentially dangerous tendency: an excessive indulgence
of human reasoning. They labelled this tendency *zandaqa*, a term
originally denoting the dualist doctrine of the Manichaeans, but
which came to be used for all kinds of heresy and freethinking.[1]

One whose thought was labelled *zandaqa* was Ibn al-Rawandi
(c.850–910). A theologian with links to the Muʿtazila of
Baghdad, he denied the reality of prophecy, ridiculed the rites
of pilgrimage and prayer, and praised human reason as the
only way to truth.[2] Another was the physician and philosopher
Muhammad ibn Zakariyya al-Razi (c.854–925). A medic
whose books on smallpox and kidney stones would be read in
Latin translation in medieval Europe, he proclaimed his Imam
to be Plato's teacher Socrates, dismissed the miracles of the
prophets as 'fraudulent tricks' (*makhariq*) and their teachings as
mutually contradictory, and proposed pleasure and pain as the
proper basis of ethical judgements.[3] Then there was the blind
Syrian poet Abu'l-ʿAlaʾ al-Maʿarri (973–1058). An advocate of

veganism, he mocked those who preferred Greek philosophy, Twelver Shi'ism, or Ash'ari or Mu'tazili theology to common sense and critical thought.[4] 'Be a servant of God,' he advised his readers, 'but not a servant of His servants: the law makes slaves, independent thinking frees.'[5]

In doubting prophecy and revelation, these thinkers made no attempt to render their views acceptable to their coreligionists. As such, they met with unremitting hostility from the majority, their names becoming watchwords for the irreligion and immorality that resulted from too much independent thinking and reading of ancient books.[6] Yet there was also a larger tradition of philosophers, writing in Arabic and sometimes in Persian, who sought to reconcile philosophy with religion, and so to make it acceptable to those who believed in divine revelation. This tradition, as we have seen, had begun with al-Kindi, the Philosopher of the Arabs, and was continued by the man revered as 'the Second Teacher' (al-mu'allim al-thani) after Aristotle: Abu Nasr al-Farabi (c.870–950).

Of Khorasanian or Central Asian origin, al-Farabi seems to have begun his philosophical career in Baghdad, where he studied logic with a Syriac Christian cleric, and probably encountered the philosophy of al-Kindi and the rationalist theology of the Mu'tazila. Towards the end of his life he spent time in Egypt and Syria, where he associated with the Shi'i ruler of Aleppo Sayf al-Dawla (r. 945–67). A prolific author on music as well as philosophy, many legends, like the claim that he knew over seventy languages, would be attached to him.[7]

As a philosopher, al-Farabi believed that natural reason was a trustworthy guide to the true nature of things, and that a human being's happiness consisted in the perfection of his or her rational capacities. For him, as an Aristotelian, this meant the use of logic. This he defined as 'the laws on which rational thought is based, and by which man is led towards the path of truth', celebrating logic as a kind of universal language that allowed anyone with the requisite intellectual capacity to obtain certain knowledge.[8]

From al-Farabi's Aristotelian perspective, the pinnacle of logic was *burhan* or rational demonstration. To prove something demonstratively meant to argue from inarguable premises to certain conclusions. This meant reasoning through the use of syllogisms, logical proofs such as 'Socrates is a man; all men are mortal; therefore, Socrates is mortal.' Demonstrative logic showed not only that something was true ('Socrates is mortal'), but also why it was so ('because he is a man'). For al-Farabi, this was the only kind of reasoning that gave certain knowledge. As such, it was the method of the philosophers; indeed, it *was* philosophy in the strict sense.

If the demonstrative reasoning of the philosophers provided the surest path to the truth, then where did that leave religion? In al-Farabi's view, religions like Islam dealt in other, lesser yet still useful forms of argumentation. Where the philosophers employed demonstration, the theologians used dialectic (*jadal*), the form of reasoning employed in polemical debates. Though it could provide only what al-Farabi termed 'strong supposition', it remained valuable insofar as it could be used to defend religious beliefs against the arguments of heretics and unbelievers. As for the prophets, they made use of what Aristotle had called 'poetics' (*shi'r*). This form of argumentation, al-Farabi proposed, drawing on an idea advanced by the philosopher-physician Galen in the second century AD, conveyed not so much true and certain knowledge as symbols of the truth.[9] The prophet's aim was not to demonstrate how things really were through rational argument, but to move the imaginations of his audience in the hope of eliciting a positive reaction from them. The Qur'an's vividly 'poetic' depictions of the pleasures awaiting those admitted to paradise – and of the torments in store for those condemned to hell – then, were to be understood as parables designed to encourage ordinary Muslims to live a virtuous life.[10]

Unlike the freethinkers, therefore, al-Farabi did not reject religion outright. On the contrary, he found a place for it within a hierarchy of paths to the truth. For a society to function properly, he insisted, both philosophy and religion were needed – philosophy to uncover the truth, and religion to convey that truth to ordinary people and defend it from the arguments of its enemies. Adapting Plato's famous notion of the philosopher-king to his Islamic context, in *The Opinions of the Inhabitants of the Virtuous City (Ara' ahl al-madina al-fadila)*, his major political work, he identified the ideal ruler of the community as the 'philosopher-prophet', the individual who had both perfected his rational intellect *and* developed the capacity to explain these truths to the masses in a poetic way. While religion was clearly subordinate to philosophy, the virtuous community still needed scripture and prophecy.[11]

Al-Farabi's vision was essentially idealistic and elitist. His view of the role of religion was built on a hierarchical conception of society which, as S.D. Goitein has indicated, was common in an age when most believed that their lot had been ordained by God.[12] Al-Farabi, however, gave this idea a metaphysical basis. The hierarchy in the ideal state, he proposed, mirrored a hierarchy in the cosmos. Adopting the emanation theory of the

Neoplatonists, al-Farabi mapped out a metaphysical scheme in which existence flowed out from God – or what he called 'the First Being' (*al-mawjud al-awwal*) – down through ten secondary causes or cosmic 'intellects', ending with the so-called 'active intellect' (*al-'aql al-fa''al*), which governed the sublunar world. Through logical reasoning, al-Farabi held, the human mind could make contact with this active intellect and so attain rational illumination. Such would be the case for the philosopher-prophet who ruled the virtuous community.[13]

As an intellectual elitist, al-Farabi's target readership was not the ordinary believer but his fellow philosophers. Among the adherents of *falsafa*, he had many admirers. 'As for works on logic,' the Jewish philosopher Moses Maimonides (1138–1204) would declare, 'one should only study the writings of Abu'l-Nasr al-Farabi.'[14] Al-Farabi's greatest devotee, however, and the one Islamic philosopher who would outstrip him in terms of influence, was Abu 'Ali ibn Sina (*c.*970–1037), or, as he was known in Latin Europe, Avicenna.

Ibn Sina grew up in Bukhara, the capital of the Samanid dynasty, those rulers of Central Asia who patronized the revival of Persian as a language of literature; indeed, Ibn Sina himself was the first philosopher to write in his native Persian as well as Arabic. This was an intellectually fertile atmosphere, conducive to the development of the philosophical spirit. The Samanid royal library, Ibn Sina recalled in his autobiography, contained 'chests of books piled one on top of the other', including the philosophical works of the ancient Greeks.[15] Making the most of the opportunity to consult these books, the young Ibn Sina progressed swiftly through the Aristotelian curriculum. While still in his teens, he mastered the logical, physical, and mathematical sciences, as well as medicine, which he found was 'not one of the difficult sciences'.[16]

That left only metaphysics, the study of existence itself. Yet here the young prodigy was initially stumped. Despite reading Aristotle's *Metaphysics* forty times and committing it to memory, he struggled to decipher its meaning. Help, however, was at hand. Among the works of al-Farabi was a treatise on *The Aims of Metaphysics*, in which the Islamic philosopher had explained how Aristotelian metaphysics was distinct from theology: while the latter dealt specifically with God, al-Farabi explained, the subject matter of metaphysics was broader, treating universal properties like existence and unity.[17] The clarification seems to have proved helpful to the budding philosopher. After buying a copy of al-Farabi's treatise at the market in Bukhara, Ibn Sina found the mysteries of Aristotelian metaphysics suddenly revealed. He was only eighteen, and he had, as he put it, 'finished all of the sciences'.[18]

In 999 the Samanids were overthrown and Ibn Sina, who had entered their service as a physician and administrator, was forced to flee Bukhara. Henceforth he lived a peripatetic existence, moving between the rival courts of Iran in search of patronage and protection. He would spend roughly the last two decades of his life at the Buyid courts of Rayy, Hamadan, and Isfahan, working as a doctor and government official. What free time he had he devoted to philosophy. According to one of his pupils, in Hamadan students would gather every night at his house to read from his writings – and, the disciple added, to drink wine and listen to music.[19] In Isfahan, the same student recalled, the Buyid sultan 'designated Friday nights for learned discussions in his presence, which all of the different classes of learned men attended, the Master [Ibn Sina] among them, and he was not outclassed in any of the sciences.'[20]

Like his fellow philosophers, Ibn Sina believed in the ability of human reason to work out the truth on its own. His understanding of human beings and their capabilities was based on a tripartite division of the soul that went back to Plato. Everyone, Ibn Sina held, possessed a vegetative soul (the spirit of life, which they shared with plants and animals), a sensible soul (the ability, shared with animals, to perceive things through the senses), and a rational soul (the ability to work things out through reason). In keeping with the Aristotelian dictum that man was essentially a rational animal, Ibn Sina explained that it was the rational soul that made humans special, and that the purpose of human existence, therefore, was to perfect this rational soul through the philosophical life.[21]

Those who did so would be masters of logical reasoning, able to construct demonstrative arguments almost at will. They would achieve this, Ibn Sina said, through their *hads*, the intuitive ability to guess correctly the middle term common to both premises of a syllogism.[22] Asked why it was that Socrates was mortal, the *hads*-inspired philosopher would instantly be able to say that it was because he was a man. This exercise of logic, Ibn Sina thought, was an inspired, almost mystical capability. Closely following al-Farabi, Ibn Sina proposed that rationally perfect individuals were able to know middle terms because their intellects had made 'contact' (*ittisal*) with the active intellect, the cosmic mind that governed the sublunar world and contained the universal forms of all things.[23]

This capability, Ibn Sina held, again following al-Farabi, was characteristic of the prophets.[24] Like the Second Teacher, and

97

in contrast to those freethinkers who had dismissed the prophets as impostors, Ibn Sina saw the prophets as master philosophers, distinguished from the rest of mankind by the strength of their intellects and their knowledge of the highest metaphysical truths. Knowing that those exalted truths would be incomprehensible to most people, however, they had also been blessed, he thought, with exceptional imaginations, which enabled them to convey basic religious truths to the masses in a symbolic or poetic way.[25]

This was an extension of al-Farabi's theory of the hierarchy of truths. Though essentially in agreement with his predecessor, Ibn Sina was perhaps more insistent in his commitment to Islam.[26] To those who accused him of heresy, or drew attention to his wine-drinking or what the historian Ibn Khallikan later called his 'extreme addiction to sexual pleasure',[27] he retorted in Persian verse:

It is not so easy and trifling to call me an unbeliever;
No faith is better founded than my faith.
I am singular in my age; and if I am an unbeliever –
In that case, there is no single Muslim anywhere![28]

Certainly, Ibn Sina directed much of his intellectual energy to theological questions. His most celebrated achievement, set out in his major philosophical compendia *The Cure* (*al-Shifa'*) and *The Salvation* (*al-Najah*), as well as in the more allusive *Pointers and Reminders* (*al-Isharat wa'l-tanbihat*), was his proof for the existence of God. This was a metaphysical proof, hinging upon ideas about the nature of existence. It began with a simple proposition: there is no doubt that there is existence. Then Ibn Sina introduced a crucial distinction, the 'big idea' that had first come to him when he had mastered metaphysics at eighteen: everything that exists, he said, must either be 'necessary' (*wajib*) or 'possible' (*mumkin*).[29] A necessary being he defined as one whose non-existence was unimaginable, while a possible being was one that might conceivably not exist.[30] If you could prove the existence of an intrinsically necessary being, Ibn Sina suggested, then you would prove the existence of God, for one of Allah's most beautiful names, after all, was 'the Self-Sustaining' (*al-qayyum*) (e.g. 2:255).

Ibn Sina next turned his attention to the category of possible beings. In order to acquire actual existence, he reasoned, a possible existent must have a cause. Like all other beings, this cause itself had to possess either necessary or possible existence. If the latter, then it too would require a cause, and this could be extended until one was faced with a chain of beings, each of which was the cause of the one following them in the chain. This, said Ibn Sina, was the universe. Now, since this chain was made up of possible beings, it could not itself be intrinsically necessary. And since the chain of beings could not go on forever, there must be a necessary being that existed outside of the chain: a 'first cause' of the universe. And this was God – or, as Ibn Sina referred to Him, *wajib al-wujud bi-dhatihi*, 'the Intrinsically Necessary Being'.[31]

This was a momentous argument, whose impact would be felt far and wide. Christian and Jewish theologians and philosophers – from the founders of the Franciscan order in thirteenth-century Paris to the radical Jewish philosopher Baruch Spinoza (1632–77) in seventeenth-century Holland – came under its sway.[32] So too did Muslim thinkers. In the centuries following Ibn Sina's death, 'the Necessary Being' (*wajib al-wujud*) would become one of the most common names for Allah.[33] More fundamentally (as we shall see later), under Ibn Sina's influence Muslim theologians would begin to move away from the apologetic defence of scriptural truths towards a more systematically philosophical investigation of basic questions like the source of true knowledge, the existence and nature of God, and the origin of the world.[34]

Nevertheless, as influential as his language and methods were, Ibn Sina's philosophy would never be adopted wholesale into Sunni Islam. Some aspects of *falsafa* were just too radical to be accepted as fully Islamic. This ambivalence is best represented by the thought of Abu Hamid al-Ghazali (1058–1111). Born in the Khorasanian city of Tus, as a young man al-Ghazali studied Shafi'i law and Ash'ari theology with al-Juwayni, the aforementioned 'Imam of the Two Sanctuaries'. A rationalizing legal theorist and theologian who argued that sound reasoning led inevitably to reliable knowledge, al-Juwayni was one of the first theologians to study the works of Ibn Sina in depth and to talk about Allah as the Necessary Being.[35] When he died in 1085, al-Ghazali attached himself to the court of the Seljuq vizier Nizam al-Mulk, patron of the great network of Nizamiyya madrasas. Six years later, he was appointed to the chair of Shafi'i law at the Nizamiyya in Baghdad, the most prestigious academic job in the Sunni world.

Once in post, al-Ghazali further familiarized himself with the writings of al-Farabi and Ibn Sina, and wrote a summary of their views, based on one of Ibn Sina's Persian treatises, which he titled *The Aims of the Philosophers* (*Maqasid al-falasifa*). Though this would be highly regarded in medieval Europe as an exposition of Aristotelian philosophy, al-Ghazali presented it as essentially a preparatory work for his main exercise: to demonstrate, as the title of his famous book had it, *The Incoherence of the Philosophers* (*Tahafut al-falasifa*).

In that book, al-Ghazali turned the philosophers' logical argumentation against them. Accusing them of 'blind emulation' (*taqlid*) of clever-sounding names like Socrates, Plato, and Aristotle, he identified twenty teachings that the philosophers had failed to prove by their own standards of rational demonstration. Three of these he singled out for special criticism: the Aristotelian view that the world had always existed; their idea that Allah knew particulars only 'in a universal way' (meaning that He was oblivious to the details of what went on in the world); and their belief in the resurrection and immortality of the soul but not the body. As al-Ghazali saw it, these three philosophical doctrines were not only unproven; they were positively irreligious, being irreconcilable with the Qur'an and Sunna. Unlike the other seventeen doctrines attacked in the *Incoherence*, which al-Ghazali deemed merely heretical, they constituted what he called 'self-evident unbelief'. Anyone who held them, he ruled, was an apostate who, by the laws of the Shari'a, deserved death.[36]

The Latin translation of the *Incoherence* was given the title *Destructio philosophorum*, 'The Destruction of the Philosophers', and for a long time it was thought that al-Ghazali – as the historian of Arabic philosophy Salomon Munk put it in the mid-nineteenth century – had 'delivered a blow to philosophy from which it would never recover in the Orient'.[37] It is true that *falsafa* would never become a fully accepted part of Islam. The fourteenth-century North African historian and Maliki jurist Ibn Khaldun probably reflected wider Sunni opinion when he declared that the 'harm that [philosophy] can do to religion is great' and that the philosophers' teachings on metaphysical topics like the nature of God or the origin of the world were 'wrong in all respects'.[38]

At the same time, under the influence of rationalizing Ash'ari theologians like the 'renewer' of the fourth century al-Baqillani and al-Ghazali's teacher al-Juwayni, the language, books, and methods of the philosophers were gradually integrated into Islamic theology. In the words of the same Ibn Khaldun, after al-Juwayni 'the science of logic spread in Islam' and *kalam* and *falsafa* 'in a way came to be one and the same discipline'.[39] Al-Ghazali himself was a key contributor to this trend. Though he condemned the philosophers as unbelievers, he was hardly anti-philosophical in his approach. *The Incoherence of the Philosophers* was a philosophical critique of philosophy, designed to show up the logical errors of the philosophers when they argued for doctrines that contradicted the Qur'an and Sunna. Far from bringing philosophical thought in Islam to an end, then, the book actually further encouraged the integration of the philosophers' methods into *kalam*, helping to create a tradition of philosophical theology comparable to the scholastic tradition in medieval Europe.

If the Sunnis looked upon philosophy with some ambivalence, the Isma'ili Shi'a embraced it wholeheartedly. This began with Isma'ili missionaries in Iran in the mid-tenth century. Working independently of the Fatimids of Cairo, whose claim to the Imamate they rejected, these missionaries turned to Neoplatonism in an attempt to give Isma'ili doctrine a philosophical basis. The first to do so was the tragic missionary Abu'l-Hasan al-Nasafi (d. 943), who managed to convert the Samanid ruler and his entourage to Isma'ilism, before falling from favour and being brutally slaughtered along with his followers.[40] While his philosophical writings have not survived, the extant works of his successor, Abu Ya'qub al-Sijistani (d. *c*.971), bear all the hallmarks of Neoplatonic thought. He interpreted *tawhid* (the doctrine of God's unity) to mean that Allah, like the One of the Neoplatonists, was utterly transcendent and totally indescribable, explained that the world had come into existence through a three-stage process of emanation from this unknowable deity, and asserted that the life of the intellect was the surest path to paradise, which would, he said, be an intellectual, rather than physical, experience.[41]

Around the same time, in the Iraqi city of Basra, another group of Isma'ilis who rejected the authority of the Fatimids were also turning to philosophical speculation. This was the secret intellectual society known as the Brethren of Purity (*Ikhwan al-Safa'*), authors of a collection of fifty-two philosophical epistles (*rasa'il*) inspired by Neoplatonic emanation theory and Neo-Pythagoreanism (the interpretation of reality according to mathematical principles). 'The relation of the Creator to existent beings,' the Brethren wrote in their first epistle (on mathematics), 'is like the relation of the number one to the other numbers.'[42] The world's existence emanated from the divine being, they said, just as light emanated from the sun.[43] Contrary to Fatimid doctrine, they also taught the underlying unity of all revealed religions, and placed little emphasis on the doctrine of the Imamate, arguing that a 'brethren' of enlightened individuals was just as sure a guide to salvation as an Imam.[44]

Though neither the early philosopher-missionaries in Iran nor the Brethren of Purity were affiliated to the Fatimids, however, their philosophical outlook was soon absorbed into mainstream Isma'ili thought. By the tenth century, the Fatimids' leading missionaries had adopted the Neoplatonic perspective. In *The Comfort of the Intellect (Rahat al-'aql)*, Hamid al-Din al-Kirmani (996–1021), the leading Fatimid missionary in Iraq, developed an account of the emanation process that closely resembled that of al-Farabi, albeit with an Isma'ili twist. Like al-Farabi, al-Kirmani proposed that God's existence flowed into the world of nature through a series of ten secondary causes or 'intellects'; unlike the philosopher, he identified these intellects with the speaker-prophets, silent-companions, Imams, and chief missionaries of the Isma'ilis.[45] After him, the Persian poet and travel writer Nasir-i Khusraw (1008–72/8), the head of the Fatimid mission in Khorasan, would likewise attempt to demonstrate the essential harmony of Isma'ili Shi'ism and Neoplatonic philosophy in a book pointedly titled *The Harmonizing of the Two Forms of Wisdom (Jami' al-hikmatayn)*.[46]

The philosophical Isma'ilism taught by these missionaries, like the *falsafa* of al-Farabi or Ibn Sina, was designed to appeal to an educated elite, and often succeeded in converting philosophically minded thinkers to Isma'ilism. But there were also other, more radical kinds of Isma'ilism, which had a potentially broader appeal. In 899, as we have seen, the Isma'ili leadership had announced the reappearance of the Imam, a change in doctrine that precipitated the rise of the Fatimid state. Some Isma'ilis, however, refused to go along with the change, clinging to the old doctrine of the imminent return of Muhammad ibn Isma'il as the Mahdi. They became known as the Qaramita, after their leader Hamdan Qarmat, whose name was said to mean either 'short-legged' or 'red-eyed' in Aramaic.[47] Winning over the Bedouin of Arabia and Iraq with the promise – so their opponents alleged – to waive the obligatory prayers, the Ramadan fast, and the prohibition of wine, they succeeded in establishing a small rebel state at Bahrain in the Persian Gulf.[48] In 930, they stole the black stone from the Ka'ba in Mecca – an act thought to symbolize their belief that, on his return, the Mahdi would annul the religious law of Muhammad.

While the Fatimids repudiated this scandalous doctrine, encouraged the Qaramita to return the black stone (which they did in 951 after the 'Abbasids paid a large ransom), and eventually succeeded in bringing many of the dissidents back into the fold, other radical movements would soon spring up.[49] One such was the movement that convulsed Cairo during the reign of the Fatimid caliph al-Hakim (r. 996–1021). Al-Hakim was a charismatic yet eccentric figure, who was said to ride out into Cairo on a donkey, sometimes at night, to speak and pray with his subjects. At various points in his reign he cancelled all Isma'ili missionary activity and the sessions of wisdom, ordered the destruction of churches and synagogues across the empire (including the Church of the Holy Sepulchre in Jerusalem), and even banned the consumption of certain vegetables.[50] Around 1017, a group of renegade Isma'ili missionaries, perhaps encouraged by the caliph, began to teach that he was Allah Himself.

Those who accepted this claim called themselves *al-muwahhidun*, 'the true monotheists'. Outsiders called them the Druze, after al-Darazi (d. 1018), one of those renegade missionaries. They developed a highly secretive doctrine, encapsulated in a new scripture called *The Epistles of Wisdom* (*Rasa'il al-hikma*), and saturated in Neoplatonic metaphysics.

Al-Hakim, they believed, was the divine 'One' of Neoplatonic emanation theory; Hamza (*c*.985–1021), the first and only Imam of the Druze faith, and one of the authors of the *Epistles*, was an embodiment of the cosmic intellect; and human souls were reincarnated after death – a process which the Druze called *taqammus* or 'putting on a new shirt'.[51] Breaking definitively from the Isma'ilis, they survive up till the present day, mainly in the mountains of Syria and Lebanon, a one-million-strong religious community on the fringe of Islam.[52]

Though a threat to Isma'ili unity, the Druze posed little threat to the wider Muslim community. The same could not be said of the Nizari Isma'ilis. The origins of the Nizaris lay in 1094, when the Isma'ili community was split over the succession to the eighth Fatimid caliph al-Mustansir (r. 1036–94). On one side stood those who supported the accession of al-Mustansir's son al-Musta'li (r. 1094–1101). They were henceforth known as the Musta'lis, and, after the fall of the Fatimid caliphate, would establish an important centre in Yemen, where they developed a philosophical doctrine that combined the ideas of the Brethren of Purity with the emanation scheme of al-Kirmani. (In modern times, they are found mostly in India, where they are known as the Bohras, from the Gujarati word for 'traders'.[53]) On the other side stood the Nizaris, so called because they supported the claim of al-Mustansir's elder son Nizar.

The stronghold of the Nizari movement was Iran, and its leading figure was the Iranian missionary Hasan-i Sabbah (*c*.1050–1124). Born into a Twelver Shi'i family in Qom, Hasan had converted to Isma'ili Shi'ism while a student in Rayy, the prominent site of Isma'ili missionary activity just to the south of Tehran. After visiting Cairo to learn the essentials of Isma'ili doctrine, he returned to Iran with the goal of overthrowing the Seljuq Turks and realizing the original Isma'ili vision of establishing the Imamate across the entire Muslim world. In 1090, disguising himself as a tutor, Hasan infiltrated and seized one of the castles of Alamut, a remote valley in the Alborz mountain range in northern Iran. There he established a strict religious society in which the Shari'a was harshly implemented: Hasan even had two of his sons executed on charges of murder and drunkenness. He also built up an impressive library, made the castle a near impregnable military base, and encouraged the establishment of other Nizari strongholds in eastern Iran and Syria. His military strategy was founded on targeted assassination. The Nizaris' opponents, believing that the fearless killers must have been drugged, took to calling them *hashishiyyin*, 'hashish addicts' or, as the Crusader chroniclers nicknamed them, 'Assassins'.[54]

For the Sunnis of Iran and the surrounding region, the Nizari threat was terrifyingly real. At its root was a religious ideology, a radical interpretation of Isma'ili Shi'ism. Though Nizar had probably been killed in his attempt to seize the Fatimid caliphate, the Nizaris believed that he was still alive and in hiding and that, in his absence, his authority had devolved to Hasan-i Sabbah, his *hujja* or 'proof'. This gave Hasan the authority to reformulate Isma'ili doctrine, and this he did with his so-called 'new preaching' (*da'wa jadida*).

At the heart of this new preaching was the concept of *ta'lim*, the 'authoritative instruction' of the Imam. A trained logician, Hasan explained his doctrine in four propositions simultaneously designed to demonstrate the truth of the Isma'ili view and nullify the positions of his opponents. First, against the philosophers,

Hasan argued that the human intellect was unable to know the Creator without the authoritative instruction of a teacher. Second, against the Sunnis, he declared that what was needed was a single truthful and reliable teacher, not multiple religious scholars as in Sunnism. Third, he proposed, this time against the Twelver Shi'a, that the authority of this teacher must be convincingly proven *before* the instruction begins, for otherwise why should anyone submit to the teacher's instruction? Finally, he attempted to show that the one true teacher was none other than the Isma'ili Imam.[55] For the Nizaris, knowledge of God could only be obtained through the authoritative instruction of the rightful Imam. Though similar to the mainstream Isma'ili doctrine of *walaya* (the spiritual authority of the Imam), there was a difference of emphasis here. Such was the Imam's authority, Hasan taught, that each Imam was entirely free to overturn the rulings of his predecessor.[56]

The task of responding to Hasan's ideas fell to al-Ghazali, author of *The Incoherence of the Philosophers*. In *The Scandals of the Esotericists (Fada'ih al-batiniyya)*, a treatise dedicated to the 'Abbasid caliph al-Mustazhir (r. 1094–1118), al-Ghazali attacked the Nizari movement on three principal grounds. First, he condemned their use of deception in winning new converts. Next, he argued that their symbolic interpretation of scripture – for example, their assertion that the mysterious 'pillar of cloud' that had guided the Israelites during the Exodus from Egypt (Exodus 13:21–2) was a symbol of the Isma'ili Imam – was an anarchic exercise, allowing them to make scripture say whatever they wanted it to mean.[57] Finally, he pointed out that Hasan's argument for the inadequacy of reason and the necessity of an infallible Imam was itself a rational argument, meaning that his key doctrine of *ta'lim* was built on a contradiction.[58] And though it was true, al-Ghazali acknowledged, that an infallible source of knowledge was needed to supplement reason, that infallible source was not the Isma'ili Imam, but the Prophet Muhammad, who had left mankind the Qur'an and Hadith as their guides to the truth.[59] As for the true Imam of the age, this was none other than the 'Abbasid caliph.

Al-Ghazali's book was no mere academic exercise. In his mind, the errors of the Nizaris had political implications, and so warranted an assertive response. There were, al-Ghazali said, two kinds of Shi'a: those who simply believed that 'Ali had been the rightful successor to Muhammad and that the imamate should belong to his descendants, and those who rejected the fundamentals of the Muslim faith and thought nothing of shedding Muslim blood or stealing Muslim property. Members of the first group, he declared, were in error, but could still be considered Muslims. The latter group, on the other hand, which evidently included the Nizaris, were to be declared unbelievers and killed.[60]

Despite al-Ghazali's best efforts, however, the Isma'ili threat remained. In 1138, the new 'Abbasid caliph al-Rashid (r. 1135–6) was assassinated, prompting great festivities at Alamut. Three decades later the most radical implications of Hasan's 'new preaching' were worked out. On the seventeenth day of Ramadan, 1164, Hasan II (r. 1162–6), the fourth Nizari ruler at Alamut, announced a series of radical claims: that he was the true caliph (understood by his followers to mean the true Imam); that the Shari'a had been abolished; and that the day of resurrection had come, and the Isma'ili faithful admitted into a paradise of perfect knowledge. Soon afterwards, his son, Muhammad II (r. 1166–1210), went even further, openly claiming to be not only the Imam, but a manifestation of Allah Himself.[61]

These extraordinary claims, like the claims of the Druze about al-Hakim, were probably self-defeating, at least if the goal was to spread Isma'ilism across the Muslim world. In abolishing the Shari'a and shutting out non-Isma'ilis from a 'resurrection' that had already taken place, the Nizaris had in effect given up on converting the masses to their version of the faith. Though they soon announced the re-establishment of the sacred law, never again would Nizari Isma'ilism offer a serious alternative to Sunni Islam.

Nevertheless, the Nizaris lived on, blending into the Iranian religious landscape as a Sufi brotherhood (which, as we'll see, were becoming increasingly popular in this period), and continuing to proselytize, achieving considerable success in India among the Hindu merchant caste of Gujarat. Known as Khojas, from the Persian word for 'spiritual master' (khwaja), this Indian Isma'ili community would be led in modern times by the Aga Khans. Heirs to the doctrine of ta'lim, they would use their untrammelled religious authority to guide their followers to an easy and harmonious relationship with secular modernity.[62]

Chapter Seven

SUFISM
ASCENDANT

Al-Ghazali, as we've seen, was the most influential Sunni thinker of his day. Professor at the Nizamiyya of Baghdad since 1091, refuter of the philosophers and the Isma'ilis, he was unquestionably at the height of his career. Yet in 1095, he gave it all up. The reason, he later explained, was an intellectual 'sickness', a loss of faith in the foundations of his knowledge. Realizing that his career up to that point had been little more than a quest for fame and fortune, and fearing the judgement of the life to come, al-Ghazali turned away from the world. Abandoning his post and possessions on the pretext of going on the pilgrimage to Mecca, he headed to Damascus on spiritual retreat.[1]

There al-Ghazali occupied himself, as he later wrote, with 'cleansing my soul, rectifying my morals, and purifying my heart for the remembrance of Allah', and began work on a new book, *The Revival of the Religious Sciences* (*Ihya' 'ulum al-din*), which he taught to the students who gathered around him at the Umayyad Mosque.[2] When he wasn't teaching, he would shut himself away in a cell located high up in the mosque's western minaret.[3] Six months later, uneasy again at his growing renown among the Damascenes, he left for Jerusalem, where he would go every day to the Dome of the Rock to sit in seclusion. From there he finally set out on the pilgrimage to Mecca, stopping on the way at Hebron, where he made a vow at the tomb of Abraham never again to consort with worldly rulers. After a short spell back in Baghdad, in 1097 al-Ghazali returned to his native Khorasan, building himself a private madrasa and a Sufi lodge in his hometown of Tus. There he taught and wrote until 1106, when he took up his teacher al-Juwayni's old post as professor at the Nizamiyya madrasa in Nishapur.[4]

Back in Nishapur, with only a few years left to live, al-Ghazali sat down to write his autobiography, *The Deliverer from Error* (*al-Munqidh min al-dalal*). Though partly an attempt to justify his return to mundane affairs, he presented it as a record of his lifelong effort to find the surest path to true and certain knowledge. 'Thirsting for knowledge of the true nature of things,' he wrote, 'had been my custom since the beginning of my life.' Specifically, he had tried and tested the methods of four different groups of 'seekers' (*tullab*) – the theologians, the Isma'ilis, the philosophers, and the Sufis – and, in his moment of spiritual crisis, had come to see that Sufism was the most reliable.[5] 'I knew for certain,' he wrote, 'that the Sufis, more than anyone, were travelling on the path to God, that their way was the best way, that their path was the truest path, and that their morals were the purest morals.' While others relied on fallible human reasoning or blind obedience (*taqlid*) to authority, the mystics, like the Prophet himself, were in direct contact with Allah. 'All that they do and do not do, both outwardly and inwardly, is drawn from the lamp of prophecy.'[6]

Al-Ghazali, however, did not abandon his old attachment to theology and the law. Rather, in *The Revival of the Religious*

Sciences, the book he had begun during his Damascene retreat, he sought to re-establish theology and law on a new foundation of Sufi piety. A massive work in forty volumes divided into four 'quarters', the *Revival* was devoted to the recovery of what al-Ghazali called the 'science of the path to the hereafter'.[7] It was, as al-Ghazali's biographer Eric Ormsby has put it, a 'manual for salvation', covering everything from the hidden significance of the pillars of Islam, through the importance of table manners and sexual propriety, to the reprehensibility of pride and the virtue of reflecting upon death.[8]

Al-Ghazali's treatment of each subject was suffused with his Sufi perspective. In his discussion of the secrets of ritual purity (*al-tahara*), for example, he explained that this important legal requirement consisted of four levels: first, what he described as 'purifying one's outward appearance of innovations and ugly and wasteful things'; second, 'purifying one's limbs of crimes and sins'; third, 'purifying one's heart of reprehensible morals and loathsome, vile things'; and fourth, at the deepest, most mystical level, 'purifying one's innermost self of everything but Allah'.[9] Through hierarchical schemes like this, al-Ghazali was able to set out a comprehensive vision of Islam that accounted, in true Sufi fashion, for both the outward (*zahir*) and inward (*batin*) dimensions of the faith. In his mind, Sufism and the Shari'a were as one.

The *Revival* quickly came to be regarded as one of the great works of Islamic thought, and helped to further integrate Sufism into mainstream Sunnism. Al-Ghazali himself was revered as the 'Proof of Islam' and the *mujaddid* or 'renewer' of the fifth Islamic century, just as al-Shafi'i had been for the second century and al-Ash'ari and al-Baqillani for the third and fourth.[10] 'Al-Ghazali has been acclaimed as the greatest Muslim after Muhammad,' observed the orientalist William Montgomery Watt, 'and is certainly one of the greatest.'[11]

Like all great thinkers, however, al-Ghazali was not universally loved by his contemporaries. His ideas would prove especially controversial in the Muslim west – the Maghreb (western North Africa) and al-Andalus (Muslim Spain) – which at that time was under the control of the Berber Almoravids (1040–1147). Nominally Muslim since the ninth century, in the eleventh century these Berbers – whose name, from the Arabic *al-murabitun*, means 'border-warriors' – had been converted to a strict and militant form of Maliki Islam, that form of the faith which, in the view of the Maliki scholar Ibn Khaldun, was most consistent with the mindset of the desert. Soon afterwards they had founded an empire, centred on the new city of Marrakech, which stretched, in the words of Ibn Khallikan, 'from the gates of Tlemcen [in western Algeria] to the shore of the Surrounding Ocean [the Atlantic]'.[12] They had subsequently come to the Iberian Peninsula on the invitation of the Muslims of Spain, who hoped that the rugged Berbers would beat back the Christian advance from the north, and proceeded to add al-Andalus to their domains.

Al-Ghazali, it was claimed, had been impressed by what he'd heard of Yusuf ibn Tashfin (r. 1061–1106), the founder of the Almoravid Empire, and even contemplated making the trip west to meet him. The feeling, however, was not mutual. Devoted to their law books, the Maliki ulema whose support gave the Almoravids their religious legitimacy believed, as the Tunisian historian Mohamed Talbi has written, that 'there existed only one single unique truth, that which had been taught by Malik and his school'.[13] They therefore saw in al-Ghazali's work a dangerous claim to an alternative, mystically inspired source of religious authority. In 1109, armed with a fatwa from the chief Maliki judge of Cordoba, the highest religious authority in the land, Yusuf's son and successor 'Ali (r. 1106–43) had copies of *The Revival of the Religious Sciences* cast to the flames in the courtyard of the city's Great Mosque.[14]

Such drastic action, of course, only goes to show the influence of al-Ghazali's ideas, for, as S.D. Goitein has observed, 'No one, but fools, takes the trouble to burn irrelevant books.'[15] The Sufi thinker's fortunes in North Africa, moreover, were about to change. In 1120, a man appeared at Marrakech, preaching a new doctrine of religious reform. This was Ibn Tumart (1092–1130). A Berber of the Masmuda tribal confederation, Ibn Tumart had been to Baghdad, where he'd studied at the Nizamiyya madrasa and supposedly met al-Ghazali, who was said to have tasked him with taking revenge on the Almoravids.[16] Though the story is legend, Ibn Tumart certainly returned to North Africa with a clear sense that his countrymen were practising a false version of Islam. Inspired by both the literalist approach of the Zahiri madhhab (still alive in the Muslim west despite being largely defunct in the central lands) and al-Ghazali's condemnation of unthinking emulation of authority (*taqlid*), he charged the Almoravids and their subjects with neglecting the Qur'an and Sunna in favour of the hairsplitting legal arguments of the Maliki jurists. The result, as Ibn Tumart saw it, was moral decay. Adopting a literal interpretation of the Qur'anic principle of 'commanding good and forbidding evil', he went round Marrakech and other cities of the Maghreb smashing musical instruments and pouring out wine jugs, with the aim, he said, of 'reviving the Sunna and destroying innovations (*bid'a*)'.[17]

In place of the Maliki scholars, Ibn Tumart, sounding much like the Shi'a, proposed that the best guide to the truth was an infallible Imam.[18] Inventing a genealogy for himself that went back to 'Ali, he claimed to be both the Imam and the Mahdi, the messianic saviour who would fill the earth with justice.[19] He gave those who accepted his claims the sobriquet of Almohads (*al-muwahhidun*), the 'true monotheists' (the same name that the Druze gave to themselves), and led them in a jihad against the 'unbelieving' Almoravids. When he died in 1130, the jihad was continued under his successor, 'Abd al-Mu'min (r. 1130–63). In 1147, Marrakech fell, as did Cordoba the following year. By 1172, the whole of al-Andalus was under the sway of the Almohads, whose leaders took the title Commander of the Faithful (*amir al-mu'minin*), a historic title of the caliph.[20]

The Almohads were infamous for their brutality. The Hanbali religious scholar Ibn Taymiyya (1263–1328), himself no shrinking violet, would lament the fact that Ibn Tumart had 'made licit the blood of thousands upon thousands of people in Maliki North Africa who were adherents of the Book [the Qur'an] and the Sunna.'[21] Just as the works of al-Ghazali had been cast to the flames under the Almoravids, so too did the Almohads now organize public bookburnings of Maliki texts.[22] And they adopted an equally harsh policy towards non-Muslims, abolishing the protected status that Jews and Christians enjoyed in Islamic law, and forcing their Jewish subjects – including the great Maimonides – to choose between conversion, exile, and death.[23]

Brutality and intolerance, however, did not preclude an interest in philosophy. Ibn Tumart himself had used his education in philosophical Ash'arism to compose a proof for the existence of God in terms reminiscent of Ibn Sina, and his successors kept up this interest in the rational sciences.[24] The Almohad caliph Abu Ya'qub Yusuf (r. 1163–84), the North African historian al-Marrakushi (1185–*c*.1228) observed, 'was constantly collecting books from all over al-Andalus and the Maghreb and searching for scholars, especially those learned in rational speculation'.[25]

One of those scholars was Ibn Tufayl (*c*.1110–85). A native of Guadix, near Granada, like most Muslim philosophers Ibn Tufayl was a polymath and a politician, serving Abu Ya'qub as his court physician and chief minister. His only surviving book is an allegorical tale, designed, he said, to explain the esoteric parts of Ibn Sina's philosophy. Titled *Hayy ibn Yaqzan* – literally, 'Alive, Son of the Awake' – it tells the story of the eponymous Hayy, who grew up alone on a desert island. (Translated into English at the beginning of the eighteenth century, it is thought to be one of the sources of inspiration for Daniel Defoe's *Robinson Crusoe*.)

Devoid of human contact, Hayy is forced to learn everything by himself. Raised by a doe, from the age of seven he begins to fend for himself. When his deer 'mother' dies, he tries to revive her, and in the process discovers the difference between the body and the soul. Desiring to find out more about the life process, he studies fire, and dissects the bodies of the deer and other dead animals to learn about their organs. Having taught himself physics and biology in this way, around the age of twenty-one Hayy moves onto metaphysics, discovering the existence of the Platonic 'forms' and, ultimately, of God Himself. Progressing further still, he next considers rational proofs for metaphysical truths. He ponders whether the world is eternal or created in time, and develops a kind of intelligent design argument for the existence of God. Soon, like the mystics, he comes to love God. Realizing that he has a rational soul, that this is in fact his true self, and that it is divine, he seeks to cultivate it through ascetic mortification of the body.

Finally, as he approaches his forties, Hayy attains his supreme goal.[26] This, Ibn Tufayl wrote, was 'a state so wonderful the tongue cannot describe or explain it.'[27] It was what the Sufis called the 'passing away' (fana') of the self in the presence of Allah, and the philosophers the intellect's 'contact' (ittisal) with the cosmic mind. It consisted in the realization that God was the one true existent, and in Hayy perfectly resembling God Himself.[28] This final stage, the stage of 'rational mysticism', was the summit of Ibn Sina's philosophy. It was a stage, Ibn Tufayl said, known to al-Ghazali too, though the great theologian and mystic, conscious of the sorry fate of al-Hallaj, had wisely concealed this secret from the uninitiated.[29]

Hayy's story symbolized the innate powers of the unassisted human intellect. This didn't mean, however, that religion was superfluous. Ibn Tufayl's story ends not with Hayy's mystical experience, but with a meditation on the relationship between reason and revelation. Near to the island, Ibn Tufayl explains, was another island, 'in which had settled the followers of a certain true religion, based on the teachings of a certain ancient prophet'.[30] One of the inhabitants of this second island, a pious ascetic called Absal, has come to Hayy's island in search of solitude. The two meet, Absal teaches Hayy about religion, and eventually they both return to Absal's island. After trying, unsuccessfully, to teach people the truths that he has discovered for himself, Hayy now sees 'that most men are no better than unreasoning animals, and realize[s] that all wisdom and guidance, all that could possibly help them, was contained already in the words of the prophets and the religious traditions.'[31] While philosophy was appropriate and useful for an enlightened few, from Ibn Tufayl's elitist philosophical perspective most people still needed religion, which made philosophical truths accessible to them in symbolic form.

Like al-Farabi and Ibn Sina, therefore, Ibn Tufayl, as the historian al-Marrakushi put it, was 'eager to reconcile philosophy and religion'.[32] Perhaps the most successful exponent of this reconciliation, however, was his friend and contemporary, the physician, legal scholar, and philosopher Ibn Rushd (1126–98) – or, as he would be known in the Latin world, Averroes. Born into an eminent Cordoban family of scholars, Ibn Rushd had travelled to Marrakech, where Ibn Tufayl introduced him to the court of the Almohad caliph Abu Ya'qub. There the caliph asked him to explain the philosophers' views on whether the world was eternal (as Aristotle had claimed) or created (as the Qur'an and the Islamic theologians taught). Afraid to engage in so controversial a question, Ibn Rushd kept silent, only for the caliph to proceed to discuss the opinions of Plato, Aristotle, and other philosophers, putting his mind at rest. On another occasion, when the caliph, complaining of 'Aristotle's obscurity of expression, or the obscurity of expression of his translators', asked that someone who understood Aristotle's philosophy summarize his works and explain his aims, Ibn Tufayl suggested Ibn Rushd as the man for the task.[33]

Ibn Rushd would go on to write Arabic paraphrases and commentaries on almost all the major works of Aristotle, earning him the nickname 'the Commentator' in the Latin world.[34] Yet he was also, like his father and grandfather before him, a major religious scholar of the Maliki madhhab, and, from 1182, the holder of the chief judgeship of Cordoba. He was, therefore, a passionate believer in the inherent compatibility of religion and philosophy. 'Truth,' he famously declared in a treatise devoted to the topic, 'cannot be opposed to truth.'[35] This meant following the principle first outlined by al-Farabi: the Qur'an had to be interpreted in accordance with truths established through demonstrative reasoning. For Ibn Rushd, therefore, philosophy was not simply acceptable; rather, it was *necessary* if the Qur'an was to be understood correctly. When the Qur'an announced that it contained 'some verses that are clear … and others that are unclear … whose hidden meanings are known only by Allah and those firmly established in knowledge' (3:7), it was the philosophers who were 'those firmly established in knowledge', and so it was they who were the surest guides to the truth.[36]

As the story of his first encounter with the caliph Abu Ya'qub indicates, Ibn Rushd was aware of the controversial nature of philosophy. He had good reason to be wary, for Abu Ya'qub's successor, Abu Yusuf (r. 1184–99), courting the support of the Maliki ulema for his campaigns against the Christians in the north, would for a time ban philosophy, banish Ibn Rushd, and condemn his works to be burned. The most famous critique of *falsafa*, of course, was al-Ghazali's *The Incoherence of the Philosophers*. Since the Almohads had rehabilitated al-Ghazali's reputation, this was a critique that needed to be dealt with, and this Ibn Rushd proceeded to do in *The Incoherence of the Incoherence* (*Tahafut al-tahafut*). In defending Aristotelian philosophy, Ibn

Rushd tried to show that al-Ghazali's critique did not apply to Aristotle himself, only to his Muslim interpreters. Ibn Sina, he alleged, had taken his famous distinction between necessary and possible existence from the Mu'tazila, while al-Ghazali was right that it was contradictory to claim, as Ibn Sina had appeared to do, that the world's existence was both contingent on God and eternal. Much better, Ibn Rushd said, to agree with Aristotle that God caused the movement of a world whose existence was eternal.[37] For the Commentator, as for the participants in the translation movement, true philosophy was the philosophy of Aristotle, the First Teacher.

Ibn Rushd's return to Aristotle, however, would have relatively little impact on subsequent Islamic thought. Though widely read by Christians and Jews in Latin and Hebrew translation, his works were rarely studied in their original Arabic, *falsafa* being associated much more with the ideas of Ibn Sina than the thought of the Andalusian Aristotelian. Of the Muslim thinkers of al-Andalus, it was Ibn Rushd's younger contemporary, the Sufi Ibn 'Arabi (1165–1240), who would have the greatest influence on later Islam.

The two thinkers had met when Ibn 'Arabi was an adolescent, and Ibn Rushd already an eminent jurist and philosopher. According to Ibn 'Arabi's own account, Ibn Rushd had heard of the young man from Murcia's exceptional mystical gifts and asked him to come to see him. As soon as Ibn 'Arabi arrived, Ibn Rushd rose from his seat, showering him with affection and praise. Ibn Rushd embraced him, and exclaimed, 'Yes!' To which the youth responded, 'Yes!' At this, Ibn Rushd's joy increased, but on noticing this, Ibn 'Arabi then said, 'No!' At this point Ibn Rushd shrunk back, the colour draining from his face. Then Ibn Rushd asked the key question: 'What have you discovered through mystical unveiling and divine effusion? Is it the same as what rational enquiry provides us?' Ibn 'Arabi delivered his judgement: 'Yes and no! Between "yes" and "no" spirits fly out from their substance and necks from their bodies.' At this, Ibn 'Arabi wrote, Ibn Rushd turned yellow and began to tremble.[38]

Ibn 'Arabi's enigmatic account of his meeting with the great philosopher was intended not so much as an accurate historical report as a comment on the relationship between mystical experience and rational thought. 'Yes and no,' said Ibn 'Arabi. Yes, on the one hand, mystical insight and rational enquiry could lead to similar results; but no, on the other hand, there *was* a difference. And the difference was this: despite his wide learning, his many years of working through Aristotle, Ibn Rushd knew less than an adolescent who had 'unveiled' the truth through Sufi practice.

The superiority of mystical insight was a principle that Ibn 'Arabi had learnt and tested through his own experience – not just as a young man in al-Andalus, but throughout a nomadic life that took him to Fez and Tunis, Cairo and Jerusalem, Mecca and Baghdad, Konya in Seljuq Anatolia, Aleppo, and, from around 1230 until the end of his life, Damascus.[39] His two greatest works were *The Gemstones of Wisdom* (*Fusus al-hikam*), a meditation on the metaphysical truths associated with each of the Qur'anic prophets, and *The Meccan Revelations* (*al-Futuhat al-Makkiyya*), an encyclopaedic treatment, like al-Ghazali's *Revival*, of every conceivable topic in Islamic theology and law from a Sufi perspective. Both, he claimed, were the product of his own mystical experience: the former had been given to him by the Prophet Muhammad in a vision that he'd had in Damascus; the latter while he was circling the Ka'ba in Mecca.[40]

These mystical experiences, however, produced thoughts that were profoundly intellectual. Like the philosophers, Ibn 'Arabi was interested in metaphysical questions concerning the nature of existence. Central to his Sufi metaphysics was the concept of 'manifestation' (*tajalli*). This was close to the Neoplatonic concept of emanation, which Ibn 'Arabi may have picked up from the *Epistles* of the Isma'ili Brethren of Purity, which were widely circulated in the Maghreb.[41] The world that we see around us, Ibn 'Arabi thought, was a reflection or manifestation of Allah, who had created the universe in order to see His own most beautiful names and attributes reflected in it. This idea struck many of Ibn 'Arabi's critics as tantamount to pantheism, and his later followers would indeed talk of *wahdat al-wujud* or 'the unity of existence'.[42] Yet Ibn 'Arabi's own idea of Allah's manifestation in creation was more nuanced than that label would allow. Though existence was essentially one, there was a difference, he said, between the 'absolute' existence of the divine and the 'limited' existence of creation. Allah, as he cryptically put it, was both 'identical and not identical' (*huwa la-huwa*) to His creation, both transcendent and immanent.[43]

Moreover, in Ibn 'Arabi's view, not all created things reflected Allah to the same degree. The ideal embodiment of the divine attributes, Ibn 'Arabi taught, was man, for as a famous Hadith (echoing Genesis 1:26–7) had declared, 'Allah created Adam in His image.' If Allah had created the world as a mirror for His names and attributes, then He had created man as the 'polishing' of that mirror.[44] Those who perfectly reflected the divine attributes were, in Ibn 'Arabi's terminology, 'the perfect humans' (s. *al-insan al-kamil*). Adam had been one such perfect man, and so too were the other prophets and the great Sufis of old. Yet the most perfect of all was the Prophet Muhammad. Though the Qur'an insisted that the Prophet was 'a human being like you' (41:6), Ibn 'Arabi and his followers made him into a superhuman figure, the cosmic light from which the world was created and from which the other prophets and saints drew their inspiration.[45]

For Ibn 'Arabi and the Sufis, then, the goal of Sufism was to 'adorn oneself in the traits of Allah', just as the Hadith advised and the Prophet himself had done.[46] Those who were successful in doing so were the saints or 'friends of Allah' (*awliya*') – a status which Ibn 'Arabi, who had studied with female teachers in al-Andalus, believed that women as well as men could obtain.[47] Though the concept of sainthood was a longstanding one in Islam by this time, Ibn 'Arabi gave it new significance. While the friends of Allah did not receive a scripture, he suggested, they nonetheless possessed a kind of 'general prophecy' (*nubuwwa 'amma*) insofar as they maintained the connection between Allah and His creation in an age where scriptural prophets were no more.[48] As the recipient of revelatory mystical experiences, Ibn 'Arabi classed himself among the saints; indeed, he went so far as to declare himself 'the seal of Muhammadan sainthood', which was to say, the greatest of Allah's friends.[49]

These ideas constituted a daring challenge to the long-standing Sunni position, which interpreted the Qur'an's declaration that Muhammad was 'the seal of prophets' (33:40) to mean that there would be no prophet, of any kind, after him. No less shocking to his contemporaries were the things Ibn 'Arabi said about other religions. According to a Hadith, on the Day of Judgement the severest punishment would be handed out to the creators of graven images, *shirk* or polytheism being the one unforgiveable sin. For Ibn 'Arabi, however, since all things were a manifestation of Allah, idol-worshippers too could be said to worship a form of the one true God.[50] Correspondingly, all humans would experience Allah's mercy in the life-to-come: the chastisement (*'adhab*) promised to the unbelievers, he wrote, exploiting the associations of the Arabic language, would ultimately turn sweet (*'adhib*).[51]

All this did not mean, however, that Ibn 'Arabi had lost his attachment to Islam. Though he denounced the jurists as 'scholars of superficialities' (*'ulama' al-rusum*), his *Meccan Revelations* was full of reflections on Islamic law; indeed, in legal matters he advocated the strictly literalist approach of the Zahiri school and took an uncompromising stance on issues such as the use of music in Sufi ritual and the imposition of the *dhimmi* restrictions on Christians and Jews.[52] Ibn 'Arabi's *Gemstones of Wisdom*, similarly, was effectively a commentary on the prophet-stories of the Qur'an, and his works were so saturated with quotations from the Qur'an and Hadith that when his critics called for his books to be burned, one of his later followers could retort that to do so would be to burn the very word of Allah.[53] Daring and original though they were, Ibn 'Arabi's ideas were unquestionably Islamic.

Ibn 'Arabi's writings were notoriously impenetrable, and it fell to his disciples to explain them in a way that Muslims educated in theology, philosophy, and Sufism could understand.

This effort was led by the circle that congregated around his son-in-law and designated successor Sadr al-Din al-Qunawi (1207–74) in Seljuq Konya. Yet though he helped to make Ibn 'Arabi famous throughout the Muslim world, al-Qunawi was not the most celebrated resident of that Anatolian city in this era. That accolade belonged to his friend, the Persian Sufi and poet Jalal al-Din Rumi (1207–73). Rumi was born in Vakhsh, in Central Asia. His father, Baha' al-Din Walad (1151-1231), was a mystically inclined scholar and preacher who claimed that the Prophet himself had given him the title 'Sultan of the Religious Scholars'. Around 1216, the family headed west, ending up in Anatolia – or, as it was known in Islamic languages, Rum ('Rome' or Byzantium), from where Rumi derived his name. In Konya Baha' al-Din found employment as a madrasa professor, and when he died, Rumi, who'd been in the meantime to Syria to study Hanafi law, inherited his position.

As a madrasa teacher, the young Rumi taught the law and, as one of his hagiographers put it, 'wound his turban in the manner of the religious scholars'.[54] Yet all this changed in 1244 with the arrival in Konya of Shams al-Din Tabrizi (d. *c.*1247). There was by this time a well-established tradition of Sufis engaging in deliberately shocking behaviour to attract condemnation and keep their pride in check – the so-called *malamatiyya* or 'way of blame'.[55] Taking inspiration from this tradition, Shams set out to scandalize Konyan society, asking Rumi to bring him wine, consorting with beautiful young boys, and wondering aloud whether the Sufi Abu Yazid Bistami had reached a higher spiritual station than the Prophet Muhammad.[56] The effect on Rumi was transformational. Under Shams's influence, he abandoned his teaching of the law and embraced a new vocation as a poet of mystical love. As his son would later write: 'Through love, a fatwa-writing Shaykh turned poet.'[57]

But Shams was more than just a spiritual guide. Rumi saw in him a physical embodiment of the divine, a living exemplar of the Sufi 'perfect man'. God, Rumi said, was the Sun – *shams* in Arabic – and Shams was the light of God:

You are that light which told Moses:
'I am God, I am God, I am God I am' [cf. Exodus 3:14][58]

And just as the mystic sought union with God, so did Rumi imagine himself to have been mystically united with his beloved teacher: 'It is your voice,' he said to Shams, 'that mouths all my words.'[59] Indeed, he often signed his poems with Shams's name.[60]

Shams had changed Rumi's life, but within a year or two he had vanished, driven out or even murdered by Rumi's jealous disciples. Yet his convention-defying Sufism would leave an indelible mark on Rumi's poetry, and through that on Islamic thought in the entire Persian cultural sphere from the Balkans to Bengal.[61]

Perhaps the most widely read work of that Persian tradition is Rumi's *Masnavi-yi Ma'navi* or *Spiritual Couplets*. The *masnavi*, a long teaching poem in internally rhyming couplets, had already been put at the service of Sufism by the Persian poets Sana'i (d. 1131) and 'Attar (*c.* 1145–1221). The latter's *Conference of the Birds* (*Mantiq al-tayr*) tells the story of the quest of a group of birds to find a mythical bird called the Simurgh – a metaphor for the mystics' quest for the divine. Encountering numerous perils on their journey, one by one the birds fall away until there are only thirty who reach the goal. The moral of the story is revealed in a pun: the Persian for 'thirty birds' is *si murgh*. Just as the birds *were* the Simurgh, so God was to be found within the heart of the believer.[62]

Taking inspiration from 'Attar, Rumi composed a twenty-five-thousand-verse *masnavi* whose aim was to teach 'boys' (*pesaran*) – meaning Sufi novices – how to become spiritual 'men' (*mardan*). The subject of these poetic lessons, Rumi explained, was 'the roots of the roots of the roots of religion'.[63] Rumi believed that the inner aspect of things was more real than their exterior aspect – that the 'kernel' was superior to the 'shell'. The path to mystical enlightenment therefore required aspiring Sufis to cultivate their spiritual nature and combat their *nafs* or lower self, a Qur'anic term denoting that part of humans' psychological makeup that attracted them to the evils of this world. 'Whoever cleanses their soul of sensual desires,' Rumi proclaimed, 'will at once be in the holy presence and the court of the Pure One.'[64]

The human soul's relationship with Allah, Rumi thought, was characterized above all by *'ishq*, a word which the philosophers had defined as 'an excess of love'.[65] In their passionate love of God, he said, the Sufis were like the legendary Majnun, a figure in Arab and Persian folklore who had driven himself mad (*majnun*) with desire for his beloved Layla.[66] Such love could not be taught, only experienced. 'Someone asked, "What is love?" I said, "When you are like us, you will know."'[67] It also turned conventional religious values upside down. Even the prophet Moses's message of pure monotheism was rendered meaningless by the power of *'ishq*:

Kindle a fire of love (*'ishq*) in your soul;
   Burn up thought and expression completely!
O Moses! Some know [religious] customs;
   Others are burnt in their mind and soul.[68]

Yet while Rumi said things that challenged conventional sensibilities, like Ibn 'Arabi and the other Sufis his overall framework remained thoroughly Islamic. The Qur'an was his guiding light: he called the *Masnavi* the 'unveiler of the Qur'an', and cited more than 2,000 Qur'anic verses over the course of the poem. The Shari'a likewise remained important to him, and from Shams he'd learnt the necessity of following the Prophet's example in all things.[69] 'Strive that no fine point of our Prophet's Sunna remains unobserved or neglected,' Rumi instructed his disciples.[70] Following a widespread Sufi tradition, Rumi called on his followers to see the 'inner reality' (*haqiqa*) of the law (*shari'a*), explaining that they could only do so by following the path (*tariqa*) of the Sufis. The law, he said, was like studying medicine; the path like taking the right medicine and eating well; and the attainment of the inner reality like enjoying true health.[71] The *Masnavi* was a textbook in how to become spiritually healthy.

In the years following his death, Rumi's work attained near sacred status. He became known throughout the Muslim world by the Persian title *Mawlana*, 'Our Master', while the *Masnavi*, which helped make Persian the pre-eminent language of Islamic mystical poetry, was revered as 'the Qur'an in Persian'. Outside the formal setting of the madrasa, few works would be so widely read as a key to understanding the Qur'an and the teachings of the Prophet.[72]

★

The careers of Ibn 'Arabi and Rumi coincided with the diffusion of Sufism into almost all areas of Islamic intellectual and ritual life. Crucial to this process was the emergence of the Sufi *tariqas*, mystical orders or brotherhoods, comparable to Christian mendicant orders like the Franciscans or Dominicans, which taught a distinctive path (*tariqa*) to Allah.[73] Like the legal madhhabs, these were named after a great saintly figure – the Mevlevi tariqa, for instance, was named after 'Mawlana' Jalal al-Din Rumi – but were actually founded by the disciples of the 'founder'. They had special initiations – those entering the Mevlevi order had first to work in the kitchen of one of the order's lodges for 1,001 days – and rituals, like the famous whirling dance of the Mevlevi dervishes.[74]

Though controversial in some circles, these Sufi orders and rituals appealed to Muslims of all social and religious backgrounds. 'The people of the world,' declared a Mevlevi source, 'high and low, powerful and weak, jurist and man of poverty, religious scholar and the unlettered, Muslim and infidel, all adherents of the religious communities, leaders of Islamic denominations and rulers turned towards Mawlana and they all became reciters of poetry and men of music and merriment.'[75] And while the Mevlevis were particularly popular in Anatolia, elsewhere in the Muslim world other tariqas – like the Shadhilis in Egypt and North Africa, the Suhrawardis in Iraq, the Naqshbandis in Central Asia, and the Chishtis in India – would prove equally appealing to the lowly and powerful alike.[76] Once marginal and suspect, then accepted and respected, by the thirteenth century Sufism was in the ascendant throughout the world of Islam.

Chapter Eight

REASON, REVELATION, AND INSPIRATION

I f Sufi mysticism was becoming mainstream, then so, too, was
philosophical theology. As with Sufism, a key figure in this
development was al-Ghazali. As we've seen, his logical critique of
the philosophers played an important role in the development and
diffusion of the more philosophical Ash'arism of his teacher al-
Juwayni. After al-Ghazali, the next great philosophical theologian
was Fakhr al-Din al-Razi (1150–1210).[1] Born in Rayy, al-Razi
had studied Ash'ari theology in Nishapur – reportedly learning
one of al-Juwayni's theological treatises by heart – and philosophy
at Maragha in north-western Iran.[2] Like many scholars of the
time, he was constantly on the move, travelling from city to city
in search of patronage and protection from the various ruling
dynasties of the Muslim world. Wherever he went, three hundred
students reportedly came in tow. Eventually he settled in Herat in
modern Afghanistan, where he was given his own madrasa and
honoured as the 'master of Islam' (shaykh al-islam).[3]

Much like al-Ghazali, al-Razi had an ambivalent relationship
with falsafa. A critical commentator on the works of Ibn Sina as
well as a prolific author of original works of Ash'ari theology,

Shafi'i legal theory, and Qur'anic exegesis, al-Razi identified several fallacies in the theories of the philosophers.[4] In his commentary on Ibn Sina's *Pointers and Reminders*, for instance, he criticized the great philosopher's proofs for the existence and unity of God, his doctrine of emanation, and his view (also criticized by al-Ghazali in the *Incoherence*) that Allah only knew things 'in a universal way'.[5]

Yet, again like al-Ghazali, al-Razi also saw much that was useful and good in philosophy. Conceding that Ibn Sina's book contained, as he put it, 'important points and remarkable insights', he studied and absorbed the philosophers' logical methods, adopted their tripartite view of the soul, and came to think that the highest form of human happiness lay in attaining intellectual perfection.[6] Nor was al-Razi afraid to deviate from earlier Ash'ari views, dismissing the classical Ash'ari doctrine of *kasb* – the deterministic notion that humans 'acquired' their acts from Allah – as 'a name indicating nothing', and criticizing al-Ghazali's arguments against the philosophers and Isma'ilis where he found them wanting.[7] He even spoke highly of the freethinking poet al-Ma'arri and engaged with the ideas of the heretical philosopher Muhammad ibn Zakariyya al-Razi (their shared name indicates that both hailed from the Iranian city of Rayy), hinting at a more radical rationalism hidden beneath the surface of his writings.[8]

Just as important as his engagement with philosophical ideas, al-Razi also wrote his works in the way that philosophers did, adopting what the historian Ibn Khallikan called a 'systematical arrangement of topics' in his theological treatises.[9] A typical al-Razi treatise proceeded step by step through the key topics of philosophical theology, beginning with a section on epistemology and logic, then moving onto questions relating to the nature of existence, then to matters connected to God and the divine realm, and finally to issues arising from revelation, such as the nature of prophecy and the afterlife.[10]

This way of presenting theological material set a model for others to emulate. In the wake of the Mongol conquests of Iran and Iraq in the mid-thirteenth century, a Mongol dynasty known as the Ilkhanids (1256–1335) had established themselves in north-western Iran. In the early fourteenth century, the chief judge of the Ilkhanid state, 'Adud al-Din al-Iji (c.1300–55), composed *The Stations of Theology* (*al-Mawaqif fi 'ilm al-kalam*), a systematic textbook of Ash'ari theology, divided like al-Razi's treatises into separate sections, and advocating, as al-Razi had done, a philosophical approach to *kalam*. This and similar textbooks – and the many commentaries written to explain them – would soon be incorporated into the Sunni madrasa curriculum, ensuring that almost all educated Sunnis were exposed to philosophical theology, and that philosophical thinking would continue to thrive under the guise of *kalam*.[11]

The Shi'a, too, continued to cultivate the philosophical sciences. The greatest philosopher of the age – 'the most learned and wisest man in the world', in the words of the Ilkhanid vizier Rashid al-Din (c.1247–1318) – was the Shi'i scholar Nasir al-Din al-Tusi (1201–74).[12] Born a Twelver, al-Tusi embraced Isma'ili Shi'ism early in life, and came to prominence as an astrologer and theologian at the Nizari Isma'ili courts in eastern Iran and Alamut. When the Mongols swept through Iran and destroyed the Isma'ili strongholds in the 1250s, al-Tusi reverted to Twelver

Shi'ism and put himself at the service of the conquerors, who built him a fabulous astronomical observatory – with a library of 40,000 books – at Maragha by way of thanks.[13]

Amid his shifts of political and sectarian allegiance, a consistent thread ran through al-Tusi's intellectual outlook, and that was his commitment to philosophy.[14] Among his major works were an influential treatise on Aristotelian ethics and a commentary on Ibn Sina's *Pointers and Reminders* in which he attempted both to explain Ibn Sina's philosophical ideas and to refute the criticisms made by al-Razi, defending, among other things, the validity of Ibn Sina's famous proof for the existence of God.[15] Al-Razi's commentary on the *Pointers*, al-Tusi sniped, was a *jarh*, not a *sharh* – a 'defamation' rather than an 'explanation'.[16] Where al-Razi had taken from Ibn Sina a spirit of critical enquiry, al-Tusi saw the philosopher's teachings as truth itself.[17]

Al-Tusi's rationalism would leave a heavy imprint on Twelver Shi'i thought. His student al-'Allama al-Hilli (1250–1325), the most influential Shi'i theologian and legal theorist of the age, was the author of the earliest commentary on Ibn Sina's philosophical encyclopedia *The Healing*. In his view, as the historian of Islamic philosophy Robert Wisnovsky has put it, Twelver Shi'ism was the 'natural home of Avicennian [Ibn Sina-inspired] metaphysics', and al-Tusi, not al-Razi, the best interpreter of Ibn Sina.[18] He also deepened the Twelver commitment to Mu'tazili *kalam*, arguing, against the Ash'arism of al-Razi, that there was an objective set of ethical norms knowable to unaided human reason; that Allah was as much subject to these ethical standards as anyone else; and for the existence of human free will – all classic Mu'tazili views.[19]

Al-Hilli's rationalist outlook also figured in his approach to the law. Building on the work of the Twelver scholars of Buyid times, he accepted *ijtihad* – the independent reasoning of the scholar – as a valid source of law, and declared it the duty of the ordinary Shi'a to follow the rationally derived opinions of their scholars. This doctrine, which came to be known as Usulism because it was based on the jurist's rational analysis of the fundamental sources (*usul*), would dominate Shi'i legal thinking until the seventeenth century.[20]

Though both Sufism and philosophical theology had become widely accepted by the thirteenth century, this remained a contentious age. Besides his Shi'i opponents, al-Razi had many critics, both in his own day and later. He was attacked by Rumi's master Shams-i Tabrizi as 'the apostate of the age',[21] criticized by both Ibn 'Arabi and Rumi for his excessive reliance on reason,[22] and wrote a whole book detailing his debates with his contemporaries in Central Asia and India.[23] The philosophical theologians in their turn took exception to Sufism. Al-Iji, the aforementioned author of *The Stations of Theology*, declared that Ibn 'Arabi had been a delusional hashish-eater, an accusation echoed by his follower Sa'd al-Din al-Taftazani (1322–92) – the most influential exponent of philosophical theology in Central Asia – who produced an extended rationalist critique of the Sufi doctrine of the unity of existence.[24] For his part, the historian and Maliki jurist Ibn Khaldun attacked *both* the philosophical theologians and the philosophical Sufis for illegitimately mixing religion and philosophy, going so far as to issue a fatwa ordering that the books of Ibn 'Arabi and his ilk be destroyed by fire or water.[25]

The most vociferous critic of these recent trends, however, was Taqi al-Din ibn Taymiyya. Born into a family of Hanbali scholars in Harran, an ancient centre of pagan astrology in northern Mesopotamia, Ibn Taymiyya was raised in the Hanbali quarter of Damascus, to which his family had fled from the Mongol advance. Damascus was at that time under the rule of the Mamluks, slave-soldiers who had beaten back the Mongols at the Battle of 'Ayn Jalut (1260) and established an independent kingdom in Egypt and Syria, deriving their Islamic legitimacy from the 'Abbasid caliphs whom they had brought to Cairo after the Mongols destroyed Baghdad. At the age of twenty-one Ibn Taymiyya succeeded his father as director of the Sukkariyya madrasa, a Hanbali institution located just outside the walls of old Damascus, and soon afterwards began to teach the interpretation of the Qur'an at the Umayyad Mosque.[26]

As a Hanbali, Ibn Taymiyya's guiding principle was absolute reliance on the revealed word of Allah and the inspired sayings of His Prophet, and for him, this meant being faithful to the literal meaning of the scriptural texts. A Muslim, he declared, should profess 'belief in Allah as He has described Himself in His Book and as His Messenger has described Him, without any distortion, alteration, reasoning or representation'.[27] When the Qur'an or Hadith were unclear, the believer should resort to the unerring interpretation of Muhammad's collectively righteous companions and their immediate successors, who constituted the special class of Muslims known to the Sunnis as *al-salaf al-salih*, 'the pious predecessors'. As a Hadith often quoted by Ibn Taymiyya put it, 'The best generation is my [Muhammad's] generation, then the generation following them, and then the generation following them.'[28] Islam, then, was nothing more than the Qur'an, Hadith or Sunna, and the practices and interpretations of the *salaf* – a view Ibn Taymiyya called *madhhab al-salaf* or 'the doctrine of the predecessors'. Anything not found in these unimpeachable sources was *bid'a*, reprehensible deviation from original Islam.

As a literalist and reactionary, Ibn Taymiyya was scathing of what he called *ta'wilat falsafiyya*, 'philosophical interpretations' of the Qur'an. The notion that the Qur'an was made up of poetic symbols open to allegorical interpretation (*ta'wil*), he thought, was pure heresy, an 'alteration' (*tabdil*) of the meaning of scripture serving only to justify misguided beliefs.[29] The rationalist Qur'an commentary of Fakhr al-Din al-Razi, he said, 'contained everything other than Qur'an commentary'.[30] Philosophically minded Ash'aris like him, Ibn Taymiyya wrote, were 'innovators who prefer the pseudo-philosophical approach of recent ages, and such like, to the approach of the *salaf*',[31] while the Shi'i philosophical theologian Ibn al-Mutahhar al-Hilli – whose Shi'ism only compounded his error – was not 'the Son of the Purified' (the meaning of his name), but 'the Son of the Polluted'.[32]

If the philosophical theologians were bad, the philosophical Sufis were even worse. Ibn 'Arabi's teachings, Ibn Taymiyya declared in a fatwa, 'were contrary to the Shari'a and to reason, besides being contrary to Allah's prophets and saints'.[33] In particular, they undermined one of the most important teachings of the Qur'an, namely, the radical distinction between Allah and His creation.[34] In speaking of creation as a manifestation of Allah, Ibn Taymiyya alleged, Ibn 'Arabi and his followers had collapsed that crucial distinction.[35] Their position, he said, was unadulterated monism, an illegitimate extension of Neoplatonic metaphysics that was socially harmful as well as theologically mistaken.[36] If all things were a manifestation of Allah, there would be no difference between the lawful and the prohibited, the good and the bad, and the Shari'a would therefore be rendered null and void; indeed, he said, the Sufi position could be summed up by the scandalous phrase, 'Everything is licit (*halal*)!'[37]

With the spread of heretical Sufi ideas, Ibn Taymiyya thought, Muslims in Damascus, Cairo, and other historic centres of Islam had fallen into deviant ways of living. Popular piety had been sullied by 'innovations' not seen in the early days of Islam: if the *salaf* had not prayed at the tombs of the prophets, celebrated the Prophet Muhammad's birthday (an obvious imitation of the Christian festival of Christmas) or engaged in mystical chanting or walking on fire, Ibn Taymiyya reasoned, why should any Muslim do so now?[38] The illegitimate practice of visiting Muslim saints' shrines, he noted, had become widespread under the Shi'i Fatimids, Buyids, and Qaramita, while those who venerated the purported severed head of Husayn in Cairo had been duped by Isma'ili propaganda.[39]

These views would get Ibn Taymiyya into serious difficulties. He was sent to prison on no fewer than six occasions, each time on the basis of a controversial religious stance that he refused to recant. He was accused of teaching that Allah had a body (an idea that smacked of the Christian doctrine of the Incarnation), of violating the consensus of the ulema, and of throwing the minds of the common people into confusion. On one occasion, the Mamluk sultan signed a decree threatening anyone who adopted his views on the divine attributes with death. On another, a group of five hundred Sufis staged a protest at the Cairo citadel, demanding he be sent back to prison. The North African traveller Ibn Battuta (1304–68/9), who passed through Damascus in 1326 and heard one of Ibn Taymiyya's Friday sermons, was of the opinion that he had 'some kink in his brain'.[40] In the same year, a council of Damascene judges ordered his incarceration on the basis of his mistaken teachings on the veneration of saints.[41]

Today, Ibn Taymiyya is commonly regarded as one of the most influential Muslim thinkers of pre-modern times. As we shall see, his doctrine of the *salaf* would inspire the Salafi movement in the late nineteenth and early twentieth centuries, while his fatwas permitting jihad against the unbelieving Mongols would be used as justification for the terrorism of Islamic Jihad – the group that assassinated Egyptian president Anwar Sadat in 1981 – and al-Qaeda.[42] Nevertheless, though he did have his devoted students and admirers, his influence on his own age was relatively slight. Only in the seventeenth century, as Muslim thinkers sought ways out of what they saw as the decline of Islam, would Muslims return to his writings in any great number.[43] Despite his reactionary temperament, he was also a more nuanced and sophisticated thinker than both his modern acolytes and detractors would allow. The Qur'an and Sunna, he wrote, were 'full of rational proofs', for there was no conflict between 'pure reason' and 'authenticated revelation'.[44] Unlike the radical Kharijites in the early days of Islam, he did not think that Muslims who sinned were unbelievers.[45] Like Ibn Sina, al-Ghazali, and Ibn 'Arabi, he believed that this was the best of all possible worlds.[46] And even those condemned to hell, he and his leading student Ibn al-Qayyim al-Jawziyya (1292–1350) taught, would ultimately be embraced by Allah's mercy – a view, again, which was close to that of his opponent Ibn 'Arabi.[47] Like most medieval thinkers, Ibn Taymiyya does not fit easily into modern stereotypes.

*

Despite the force of Ibn Taymiyya's polemics, the manuals of theology would continue to be taught and the works of Ibn 'Arabi would continue to be studied, copied, and commented upon, into the early modern and modern periods. Among the Sunnis, the philosophical theologian al-Razi would come to be widely seen as the 'renewer' (*mujaddid*) of the sixth century, just as al-Ghazali had been for the fifth.[48] Al-Razi's philosophical exegesis of the Qur'an would become one of the most widely read commentaries on the holy text, and his rationalist approach would leave its imprint on everything from Maturidi theology in Central Asia to Maliki jurisprudence in al-Andalus.[49] Among the Shi'a, similarly, the philosophical writings of al-Tusi and al-Hilli would serve as a guide to how to approach questions of theology and law. In both theological traditions, Sunni and Shi'i, *tahqiq* or philosophical truth-seeking would remain an ideal, and intellectual attainment would be regarded as the height of human perfection.[50]

Sufism, too, would prove practically inescapable. In a Muslim world torn apart politically, it was the glue that united Muslims of different schools and social classes, an 'institutionalized mass religion', as Marshall Hodgson has put it, capable of complementing the Shari'a as a guide to the spiritual life.[51] Even Sufism's critics were caught in its web: Ibn Taymiyya had good things to say about the sober Sufism of early mystics like Junayd, and Ibn Khaldun was appointed the director of the most illustrious Sufi lodge in Cairo.[52] Ideas like the miraculous powers of the friends of Allah or the superhuman status of the Prophet Muhammad, meanwhile, became the common currency of popular preachers, prayer-writers, and poets.[53]

The framework for all of this, however, remained the Shari'a, as interpreted by the scholars of the madhhabs: 'The one who studies Sufism but not the law,' went a popular saying attributed to the early legal scholar Malik, 'is a heretic; and the one who studies the law but not Sufism is a sinner; yet the one who combines the two will reach the truth.'[54] Reason, revelation, and mystical inspiration would all be integral to Islamic thought.

Chapter Nine

THE AGE
OF EMPIRE

Politically divided and economically weakened by the Mongol invasions in the thirteenth century, the Muslim world had nonetheless managed to retain its cultural unity and strength through the ideas and institutions of Islam. A medieval traveller like Ibn Battuta could wander from Morocco to India, confident that wherever he went he would find like-minded legal scholars and theologians in their madrasas and Sufis in their lodges.[1] In the work of a polymath like al-Suyuti (1445–1505), a prolific author from Mamluk Cairo who claimed to be the 'renewer' of the ninth century, the disciplines of Hadith study and legal theory, Sufism and Qur'anic exegesis, could be said to have reached their peak of refinement.[2]

Yet culture was only one half of the Islamic ideal. From the beginning, the truth of Islam had been linked to political success. Muhammad's taking of Mecca, the rapid success of the Arab conquests, the magnificence of Umayyad Damascus and 'Abbasid Baghdad – all were proof of Islam's claim to be the final and complete religion. From this perspective, the perfect society was one in which intellectual and spiritual attainment were married to worldly glory, where powerful rulers patronized and protected scholars and mystics and saw to it that the Shariʿa was implemented and the true faith propagated and preserved. This ideal had survived the Mongol devastation and the brutal destruction of the ʿAbbasid caliphate in Baghdad in 1258. Under the great Muslim empires of the early modern world, it would come close to being attained once again.

The conquest of Constantinople had been a Muslim dream from the very first days of Islam. Since Umayyad times, many attempts had been made to conquer the ancient Byzantine capital, the city revered as the 'New Rome' and a symbol of the good fortune of the Christian faith. In 1453, the city finally fell to the Ottoman Turks, giving the rulers of what once had been a small principality in north-western Anatolia a capital worthy of their ambitions to be a global power, and making their ruler Mehmed II (r. 1444-6, 1451–81), in the words of the Turkish historian Halil Inaclik, 'the most celebrated sultan in the Muslim world'.[3] Nor was that the summit of Ottoman achievement. Under Selim I (r. 1512–20), the Safavids of Iran were defeated at the Battle of Chaldiran, and Syria, Egypt, and the Hijaz taken from the Mamluks. Under Suleyman I (r. 1520-66) – known in Europe as 'the Magnificent' and in the Ottoman world as 'the Lawgiver' (*qanuni*) – the empire entered what many saw as its golden age, its navy controlling the Mediterranean, and its army advancing up to the gates of Vienna in the west and taking the Safavid capital Tabriz, and Baghdad, in the east.

The Ottomans presented these victories, and their empire, in religious terms. From the beginning, they styled themselves as *ghazis*, holy warriors on the frontier with Byzantium, tasked, as an early Ottoman epic poem had it, with 'sweeping the world clean' of polytheism.[4] 'Sultan Mehmed conquered Constantinople with the help of God,' declared the endowment deed of the Conqueror's (Fatih) Mosque in Istanbul (the Turkish form of the Greek name). 'It was an abode of idols ... He converted its churches of beautiful decoration into Islamic colleges and mosques.'[5] Most famously, Mehmed converted the Hagia Sophia – the greatest church of the Eastern Christian world – into the Aya Sofya Mosque, a place of Islamic worship believed to offer a foretaste of paradise, where a prayer, the Ottoman court poet Yusuf Nabi (1642/3–1712) declared, was worth a hundred prayers.[6] The Suleymaniye Mosque, designed by the master architect Sinan (1490–1588) in the sixteenth century, was likewise seen as a symbol of paradise, and the light streaming in through its many windows said to be the light of Allah.[7] Thanks in large measure to these monuments, Istanbul was punningly known as *Islambol*, 'abounding in Islam', and after the conquest of the holy cities of Mecca and Medina, the Ottomans felt entitled to style themselves as 'Guardian of the Two Sanctuaries' (*khadim al-haramayn*) and to claim the functions of the great caliphs of old.[8]

If the Ottoman sultan-caliphs were responsible for protecting Islam, the ulema were responsible for articulating it. Integrated into the state system in a way never seen before, the scholars were given ranks in the imperial bureaucracy, with corresponding titles, pay grades, and special clothing. There was a fixed hierarchy of madrasas, and any scholar who aspired to prominence hoped for an appointment to a professorship at one of the great colleges – the eight madrasas founded by Mehmed II in the vicinity of the Conqueror's Mosque, or, from the sixteenth century, the six madrasas in the precinct of the Suleymaniye. From there he might hope to obtain one of the great judgeships in Istanbul or the former capitals Bursa and Edirne, or, better still, the post of military judge in Anatolia or the Balkans.[9]

At the summit of the scholarly hierarchy was the Mufti of Istanbul or Shaykh al-Islam. The holder of this title, as one seventeenth-century Ottoman writer put it, was 'possessed of absolute power in matters of religion'.[10] Western observers often compared him to the Pope.[11] The Mufti was tasked with giving legal opinions – his office would issue as many as 1,000 fatwas a day – on everything from a woman's right to kill a rapist in self-defence to the permissibility of accepting eggs from one's Christian neighbours at Easter, and was often called upon to advise the sultan on religious and political matters.[12] Sometimes he would challenge an imperial edict when he thought it violated the Shari'a. When Selim I once ordered the mass execution of a hundred and fifty treasury officials on an apparently spurious charge, the Mufti protested, leading the Sultan to pardon the accused – a measure of the Mufti's moral standing.[13] Yet, as state appointees, the Mufti and his fellow scholars could more often be relied upon to give religious legitimacy to the sultan's decrees. When Selim II (r. 1566–74) invaded Venetian-controlled Cyprus despite the existence of a peace treaty with the maritime republic, the Mufti Ebu Su'ud (1490–1574) justified the invasion on the grounds that 'peace treaties with infidels are valid only so long as they benefit the Muslim community'.[14]

Like other Turkish Muslims, the Ottomans followed the Hanafi madhhab, which, in another break with precedent, they made the official legal doctrine of their empire. This meant that members of the scholarly hierarchy had to be Hanafis; that Hanafi law was taught in the official madrasas; that state-salaried judges had to rule according to Hanafi law; and that Hanafi courts – open to adherents of all schools and religions – could be found across the Ottoman domains.[15] Hanafis in Anatolia and the Balkans were barred from converting to another of the four Sunni madhhabs, while scholars who followed those other schools would often convert to Hanafism in order to advance their careers.[16] For those areas where the Shari'a was felt to be impractical or inadequate, meanwhile, the Ottomans introduced a code of secular customary law called *qanun*, which Muftis like Ebu Su'ud explained in terms taken from Hanafi legal theory, thereby aiming to show its essential compatibility with the sacred law.[17]

Aside from the law, Ottoman intellectuals also cultivated philosophical theology. As Turks and Hanafis, they adhered to the Maturidi school of theology, yet they were also receptive to Ash'ari *kalam* and sought to minimize the differences between the two schools. The Mufti of Istanbul Ibn Kemal Pasha (1468/9-1534) described al-Ash'ari as 'the Imam and leader of the Sunnis', ahead of al-Maturidi, and Ottoman scholars would pore over the works of the Ash'ari theologian Fakhr al-Din al-Razi and the later handbooks of Ash'ari theology, composing innumerable commentaries to explain them and adopting their rationalist perspective.[18] In an updated version of al-Ghazali's *The Incoherence of the Philosophers* commissioned by Mehmed II himself, for instance, the Ottoman theologian Khojazade (d. 1488) rejected al-Ghazali's objections to the philosophers' proof for the existence of God and explained prophetic miracles by appealing to Ibn Sina's understanding of prophecy.[19] The

Mufti Ibn Kemal Pasha – who was known as 'the Ottoman Ibn Sina' and 'the First Teacher' (the title usually applied to Aristotle) – likewise took exception to al-Ghazali's decision to label the philosophers as unbelievers, and denied that Allah's foreknowledge of events necessitated the rejection of human freedom to act.[20] In his essay collection *The Balance of Truth* (*Mizan al-haqq*), meanwhile, the seventeenth-century Ottoman bibliographer Katib Çelebi explained that reason and revelation were twins, and logical argument 'a staircase and a ladder to the heights of certainty'.[21]

If philosophical thought was alive and well under the Ottomans, so too was Sufism. Sufis of the more popular kind had been a prominent feature of the Anatolian environment in which the Ottoman state had emerged.[22] This folk mysticism would survive among the Janissaries – the sultan's elite infantry – who embraced Bektashism, a syncretic form of Islam which combined a Shi'i-like reverence for 'Ali and a Christian-like belief in a Trinity of Allah, Muhammad, and 'Ali.[23] While the Ottoman scholarly establishment rejected these heretical beliefs, they would embrace the mainstream Sufism of the tariqas; indeed, by the eighteenth century, most official ulema – and sometimes the sultan himself – were affiliated to one or more of the Sufi orders.[24]

The underlying view of reality espoused by these Sufi tariqas was inspired by the ideas of Ibn 'Arabi, who became a kind of Ottoman patron saint. Both the first professor of the first Ottoman madrasa and the first Ottoman Shaykh al-Islam were important commentators on the Andalusian Sufi's work, and, after the conquest of Damascus in 1516, Selim I had Ibn 'Arabi's tomb renovated and ordered his chief scholars to issue a fatwa declaring Ibn 'Arabi 'a perfect religious scholar and virtuous guide to the right path'.[25]

Thinkers across the empire subsequently embraced Ibn 'Arabi's ideas. For the seventeenth-century Bosnian Sufi Abdullah al-Bosnawi (1584–1644), author of commentaries on Ibn 'Arabi's *Gemstones of Wisdom* in Ottoman Turkish and Arabic, Ibn 'Arabi was Muhammad's 'most perfect heir' and 'the reviver of the truth and of religion', and his *Gemstones* a guide for those 'who desired to reach the Muhammadan level and so attain Muhammadan sainthood'.[26] The Hanafi Mufti of Damascus 'Abd al-Ghani al-Nabulusi (1641–1731), the first Arab author of a commentary on the *Gemstones*, likewise described Ibn 'Arabi's books as 'the pillar of my belief'.[27] Considering the origin of the world, Ottoman intellectuals cited a Hadith beloved by Ibn 'Arabi and his followers – that Allah was a hidden treasure who wanted to be known, and so created the world in order to be known.[28] Even the caliphate was presented in Sufi terms: the Ottoman sultan-caliph, it was said, was the 'perfect man' and mystical pole (*qutb*) of the cosmos, without whom the whole world would cease to exist.[29]

If the Ottomans stood for the Sunni version of the Islamic ideal, the Safavids of Iran represented its Shi'i alternative. Named after Safi al-Din (1252/3–1334), a Sufi shaykh of Ardabil in north-western Iran, the Safavids began life as a Sufi order committed to Sunnism and the Shafi'i school of law. In the middle of the fifteenth century, however, they transformed themselves into a militant Shi'i movement. Drawing on the fervent support of the Turkish tribesmen of Azerbaijan and eastern Anatolia – known as Qizilbash ('redheads') because of their distinctive red turbans – the Safavids cast themselves as *ghazis* fighting the Christians of Georgia and the Greeks of Trebizond.[30] Exploiting the popularity of millenarian Shi'ism and antinomian Sufism among the peasants and artisans of the region, they presented their mission in messianic terms. In poetry written in the Turkish vernacular, the Safavid leader Isma'il (1487–1524) announced himself as the perfect man of the Sufis, the Twelfth Imam and Mahdi of the Twelver Shi'a, a reincarnation of 'Ali, and even Allah Himself, demanding that his Qizilbash followers bow down before him like the good Muslim before Allah.[31]

Emboldened by the millenarian spirit, in 1501 the Safavids took Tabriz, the former capital of the Ilkhanid Mongol state, paving the way for the conquest of the rest of Iran. At the same time, they also embraced a more orthodox form of Twelver Shi'ism, which they imposed on the conquered country as the official state religion. Isma'il restored the Friday congregational prayer – a public ceremony which Twelvers had traditionally considered illegitimate in the absence of the rightful Imam – and ordered that every mosque include in its call to prayer the Shi'i addition to the declaration of faith: 'I bear witness that 'Ali is the Friend of God.'[32]

Prior to the Safavid conquest, most Iranians were Sunnis who followed the Shafi'i madhhab, while the great centres of Twelver scholarship were in Iraq and Lebanon. The Safavids organized a mass importation of Shi'i scholars from these regions, tasking them with defining and regulating Shi'ism for a public largely ignorant of that tradition. Above all, this meant clarifying Shi'i law. Under Isma'il's son and successor Shah Tahmasp (r. 1524–76) and Shah 'Abbas I (r. 1588–1629), the émigré scholars set to work translating into Persian the major Shiʿi legal texts – like the four canonical collections of the sayings of the Imams – and writing standardized codes of Twelver doctrine and practice. The most popular such code was *The Compendium of ʿAbbas* (*Jamiʿ-yi ʿAbbasi*) by Shaykh Bahaʾi (1547–1621), Shaykh al-Islam (chief religious authority or mufti) of Shah ʿAbbas's new capital, Isfahan. He introduced it as an answer to the Shah's request for 'a book that taught the essential principles of religion' – a category that included the five pillars of Islam, jihad, and the visitation of the tombs of Muhammad, ʿAli, and 'the other holy, infallible Imams' – as well as a collection of rulings on more mundane matters like eating and drinking, what clothes to wear, and hunting.[33] Other legal works commissioned by the Shah dealt at length with a single issue, like Shaykh Bahaʾi's treatise justifying the Shiʿi prohibition on consuming meat slaughtered by the People of the Book.[34]

As important as such texts were, however, Iranian hearts and minds were won over to the Shiʿi cause not by the law, but the story of Karbala – the tragic tale of the brutal slaughter of Husayn and his followers by the Umayyad caliph Yazid. The most famous account of the tragedy, *The Garden of the Martyrs* (*Rawdat al-shuhada'*), written by Husayn Vaʿiz Kashifi (*c.*1436/7–1504/5) at the very moment the Safavids came to power, made the story a paradigm of the eternal battle between the tyrannical oppressor and the righteous oppressed. During the reign of Shah ʿAbbas, works like this began to be recited in public on Ashura, the anniversary of Karbala, with the aim of enabling the audience to relive the suffering of Husayn and his companions for themselves. 'By praising you,' wrote Kashifi, addressing Husayn, 'we cure our hearts. / With your beloved name, we purify our hearts.'[35] The Italian traveller Pietro Della Valle (1586–1652), who was in Isfahan for Ashura in 1602–3, described how the recital of the tale of Karbala was met by 'the moans and groans of the hearers', especially the women, who would 'beat their breast and make piteous gestures', crying out, 'Ah Husayn! King Husayn!'[36]

If the story of Yazid and Husayn stood for an eternal tale of good versus evil, then as far as the Safavids were concerned the Sunni Ottomans were the modern incarnation of Yazid. From the beginning, Safavid Shi'ism was viciously anti-Sunni. After the conquest of Iran, the Safavids forced the erstwhile Sunni populace to publicly curse the memory of their 'rightly guided' caliphs Abu Bakr, 'Umar, and 'Uthman, who had robbed 'Ali of his birthright.[37] During the Ashura commemorations, an effigy of 'Umar would be publicly burned.[38] When the Safavids captured Baghdad in 1508, their troops desecrated the tomb of Abu Hanifa, the founding father of the Ottomans' official madhhab. When they took the Afghan city of Herat two years later, they burnt the tomb of Jami (1414–92), a noted Sufi poet of the staunchly Sunni Naqshbandi order, which, like other Sunni tariqas, the Safavids drove out of Iran.[39]

This hostility was mutual. To the Ottoman travel writer Evliya Çelebi (1611–c.1684), the Safavids and their subjects were 'evil-living' (bad-ma'ash). 'In Iran,' Evliya reported a convert from Shi'ism saying, 'they don't pray in a congregation, and they don't follow the precepts of the Qur'an at all, let alone recite it properly.'[40] Jihad against the Safavid heretics, the Mufti of Istanbul Ibn Kemal Pasha declared, was 'the greatest form of ghaza', a legal obligation on every believing Muslim.[41] Death in this holy war, his successor Ebu Su'ud agreed, was a 'great martyrdom'.[42] In this way, sectarian allegiance became intertwined with loyalty – or opposition – to the state, thus planting the seeds of the culture of sectarianism that would often plague the modern Middle East.[43]

Nevertheless, Islamic thought under the Safavids was not confined to assertive expressions of Shi'ism. Philosophy and mysticism also flourished in Shah 'Abbas's Iran.[44] Aside from his legal works, the jurist Shaykh Baha'i, who was said to have travelled to Egypt, Jerusalem, and Syria dressed as a Sufi dervish, also wrote a treatise defending the Sufi doctrine of the unity of existence.[45] Mir Damad (d. 1631), his successor as Shaykh al-Islam, meanwhile, was an out-and-out philosopher. He developed a complex synthesis of the Aristotelian philosophy of Ibn Sina and the so-called 'philosophy of illumination' (*hikmat al-ishraq*) of Suhrawardi (1154–91), an Iranian Neoplatonist who had taught that existent beings were lights issuing from God, the Light of Lights.[46] With his theory of 'perpetual creation' (*huduth dahri*), Mir Damad also tried to resolve the long-standing conflict between the theological position that Allah had created the world out of nothing and the philosophical view that the world was eternal.[47]

Though Mir Damad was revered in some circles as the 'Third Teacher' after Aristotle and al-Farabi, it was his student Mulla Sadra (*c.*1571/2–1640) who was the most celebrated philosopher of Safavid Iran. A student of Shaykh Baha'i as well as Mir Damad, Mulla Sadra thought that the path to true knowledge lay in both the intuitive perception of the Sufis and the rational enquiry of the philosophers: in creating what he called his 'transcendent philosophy' (*al-hikma al-muta'aliyya*), he drew variously from the *falsafa* of Ibn Sina, the Sufism of Ibn 'Arabi, and the 'illuminationism' of Suhrawardi.[48] His key philosophical insight was what he called 'the primacy of existence' (*asalat al-wujud*), the idea that existence (*that* something was) came before 'essence' (*what* something was).[49] Like Ibn 'Arabi, he held that pure existence was identical with God. Yet he also thought that this divine existence appeared in various 'modes' (*anha*). Just as some forms of light were closer to the pure light of the sun than others, he said, so the existence of some things was closer to the original existence of God.[50] This hierarchy wasn't fixed, however; since all things 'desired' a more intense form of existence, everything was constantly moving, an idea Sadra explained with reference to Qur'an 27:88: 'When you see the mountains, you think they are stable but they are [in fact] fleeting just like clouds'.[51]

In Mulla Sadra's philosophy, those who came closest to the purest kind of existence were what Ibn 'Arabi had called the perfect men. As the Safavid thinker explained in his major work, *The Transcendent Philosophy of the Four Journeys of the Intellect* (*al-Hikma al-muta'aliyya fi'l-asfar al-'aqliyya al-arba'a*), these perfect men had undergone four journeys: the journey from creation to God; the journey within God accompanied by God; the journey from God back to creation accompanied by God; and the journey within creation accompanied by God.[52] In this way, they served as a link between Allah and His creation. For Mulla Sadra, as a Shi'i, they were identical to the Imams, and the task of interpreting their words and inheriting their role now fell on those who knew the transcendent philosophy.[53]

Such a claim was a threat to the interpretative authority of the Shi'i legal scholars, and Mulla Sadra received his fair share of opposition, particularly after returning from Isfahan to his native Shiraz. At the beginning of *The Four Journeys*, he complained of his persecution by 'a group who were strangers to understanding, whose eyes were blind to the lights of philosophy and its mysteries ... who viewed delving into divine matters and reflecting upon scriptural verses as innovation (*bid'a*) ... and who, through their hostility, stood in the way of knowledge and gnosis.'[54] After his death, his students met with similar difficulties, and were often forced to pass on his teachings orally to avoid suspicion.[55]

As we've seen, however, a strong current of rationalist thought had long run through Twelver Shi'ism, and Sadra's philosophy could not be suppressed. By the nineteenth century, Hadi Sabzavari (1797–1878), widely regarded as the leading Iranian philosopher of modern times, was able to teach a six-year course on Mulla Sadra's thought to as many as 1,000 students. In the twentieth century, Ayatollah Khomeini (1902–89) himself would begin his career as a proponent of the transcendent philosophy.[56]

The third and final great Muslim dynasty of the period, the Mughals of India, held by birth the strongest claim to universal empire. The founder of the Mughal Empire, Babur (1483–1530), was descended on his mother's side from Genghis Khan and on his father's from the equally ferocious Timur (the Tamerlane of European literature), who had torn through Central Asia, India, and the Middle East in the late fourteenth and early fifteenth centuries, laying the foundation for the Timurid Empire in Central Asia. Babur saw himself as heir to this empire. Yet when the Uzbeks swept across the region in the early sixteenth century, he was forced to turn his attention to India.

The Muslim presence in Hindustan, as the Indian subcontinent was known to Persian and Turkish speakers, went right back to the Arab conquest of Sind in the early eighth century. From the eleventh century, Perso-Islamic culture had flourished in the region, first under the Ghaznavids (the heirs of the Turkish warlord Mahmud of Ghazna), and then, from the beginning of the thirteenth century, under the Delhi Sultanate (1211–1556). Yet, by Babur's time, the region was in disarray: the Delhi Sultanate had never really recovered from Timur's sacking of their capital in 1398, and when Babur and his followers arrived in Hindustan, they found no fewer than seven dynasties – five Muslim and two Hindu – competing for control of the region.[57] Into this chaos stepped Babur and the Mughals. With his decisive victory over the Delhi Sultan at the Battle of Panipat in 1526, Babur launched an empire which, at its height in the late 1600s, would control most of the subcontinent and rule over up to a hundred and fifty million people.[58]

Prior to the Mughal conquest, the Islamic culture of India had been defined to a great extent by Sufi mysticism. In the Punjabi city of Lahore, for instance, the practice of Islam revolved around veneration of the tomb of 'Ali Hujwiri, the author of the oldest Persian treatise on Sufism, who was revered locally as Data Ganj-Bakhsh, a Sanskrit-Persian hybrid meaning 'Bestower of Treasures'. From the thirteenth century, Sufi orders like the Suhrawardis and especially the Chistis began to spread throughout Hindustan: Mu'in al-Din Chishti (1141/2–1236), the Iranian mystic after whom the Chishti order was named, was believed to have won over countless Hindus to Islam through his sermons on the love of Allah and His Prophet, while, under the Delhi Sultanate, the order was associated with the revered saint of Delhi Nizam al-Din Awliya (1243/4–1325) and his disciple, the poet Amir Khusraw (1253–1325), widely celebrated as the greatest representative of Indo-Persian literature.[59]

This inclination to mysticism was continued under the Mughals. Babur himself had links to Sufism. The Persian poet Jami, a Sufi of the Naqshbandi order, was one of his heroes, and after his victory at Panipat he made a point of paying his respects at the tombs of the saints of Delhi, including the great Nizam al-Din Awliya.[60] His grandson Akbar (r. 1556–1605), who through his military victories and centralizing reforms did more than anyone to turn the Mughal state into a major empire, was likewise drawn to mystical Islam, naming his first son after a Chishti shaykh, making an annual pilgrimage on foot to the city of Ajmer to seek blessings at the shrine of Mu'in al-Din Chishti, and issuing a decree instructing government bureaucrats to devote their free time to reading the *Masnavi* of Rumi and the *Revival* of al-Ghazali.[61] Such views reflected more general trends in Indo-Islamic piety and literature. Through poetry in Persian and the Indian vernaculars, the ideas of Ibn 'Arabi were diffused through all levels of society: poets conveyed the notion of the unity of existence through the oft-repeated Persian phrase *hama ust*, 'All is He (meaning, God)', while some Indian Sufis, such as the Chishti mystic Muhibb Allah Allahabadi (1587–1648), took to studying Ibn 'Arabi's works in the Arabic originals and writing commentaries on them like their Ottoman counterparts.[62]

Alongside Sufism, the other major intellectual traditions of medieval Islam were also prominent in Indo-Islamic thought. As in all parts of the Muslim world, *fiqh*, the study of the law, was the bread and butter of Islamic scholarship on the subcontinent. Being of Turkish origin, the Mughals, like the

Ottomans, were Sunnis of the Hanafi school: Babur himself had written a versified treatise in Turkish on Hanafi law, and the *Guide* (*al-Hidaya*) of the Hanafi jurist al-Marghinani (d. 1197), whom the Mughals celebrated as a fellow native of Central Asia, was widely used as a textbook of Hanafi law (as it still would be under British rule).[63]

Other, more philosophical, traditions were brought to India by the steady stream of Iranian intellectuals who were drawn to the Mughal realm by tales of its proverbial riches. Some brought the philosophical *kalam* of the later Ash'ari manuals or ethical works inspired by Nasir al-Din al-Tusi's widely read treatise on Aristotelian ethics (another work that the emperor Akbar recommended to his officials).[64] Others, like the Iranian Mir Fendereski (1562/3–1640), the author of a major work of Platonic political philosophy in the tradition of al-Farabi, brought philosophy in the stricter sense, paving the way for the creation in the eighteenth century of the *Dars-i Nizami*, an influential philosophical curriculum that drew heavily on the rationalist traditions of Iran, including the work of the philosophers Mulla Sadra and Mir Damad.[65]

In this way, Mughal India became part of the mainstream Islamic intellectual culture. At the same time, there was also what might be thought of as a distinctly Indian tendency towards eclecticism in Mughal thought. This tendency was driven by the emperors and reached its apex under the aforementioned Akbar. A unique character, who is said to have been a chronic depressive and a dyslexic, in 1574 Akbar moved his capital from Agra to Fatehpur Sikri, a newly built city dominated by a large congregational mosque and the tomb of the Sufi shaykh after whom he'd named his son.[66] There he established an *'ibadatkhane* or house of worship, where, from 1579, he hosted interreligious debates involving Sunnis and Shi'a, Brahmin Hindus, Jains, Zoroastrians, Jesuits, and Jews, at which controversial issues like the unity of God, the eternity of the world, and the nature of the resurrection were freely discussed.[67] In the same year, he abolished the *jizya*, the poll tax paid by non-Muslims in return for the protection of their Muslim rulers, and had a council of scholars declare that, as the 'just Imam' of the age, he had the ultimate authority to decide questions of religious doctrine and law.[68]

All this paved the way for Akbar's policy of *sulh-i kull* or 'peace to all', which called not merely for the toleration of other faiths, but for a syncretistic borrowing of all that was good in them.[69] Inspired by the approach of the second Islamic millennium in 1592, Akbar began to worship the sun, and, like the Imam of the Nizari Isma'ilis and the Safavid Shah Isma'il, to present himself as a semi-divine figure. In the eyes of his chief vizier and annalist Abu'l-Fazl (1551–1602), he was the perfect man of the Sufis, the philosopher-king of the philosophers, and an embodiment of Suhrawardi's divine light.[70] Like Shah Isma'il's Qizilbash followers, his subjects were instructed to prostrate themselves before him. Islam, it seemed, had given way to what would be known as *din-i ilahi*, a universal 'divine religion', centred on the Mughal Emperor as the living god.[71]

Unsurprisingly, this caused a rupture with the ulema. An Islamic judge in the city of Jaunpur issued a fatwa declaring that Akbar had abandoned Islam and that all good Muslims should rise up in revolt, while the scholar and courtier al-Bada'uni (1540–c. 1615) complained in his secret chronicle of Akbar's reign of how the emperor had been swayed by 'bastards' who 'reviled and ridiculed' Islam with their supposedly rational proofs.[72] The pressure generated by such opinions eventually told. Though the cult of sacred kingship and religious syncretism continued under Akbar's son Jahangir (r. 1605–27), the latter's son Shah Jahan (r. 1628–58) moved the Mughals back in the direction of orthodox Islam.[73] He forbade his subjects from prostrating themselves before him, attempted to enforce the Shariʿa rule prohibiting the building of new temples and churches or the repair of old ones, and resumed Mughal patronage of the pilgrimage caravan to Mecca.[74] He also commissioned architectural projects that testified, like the mosques of Ottoman Istanbul, to the glory of Islam, the most famous of which was the Taj Mahal, a memorial for his beloved wife Mumtaz Mahal intended – according to one recent interpretation – as a 'vast allegory of the Day of Judgement'.[75]

These two competing visions of Mughal religion – what the scholar of Indian Islam Annemarie Schimmel called the 'India-oriented' eclecticism of Akbar and the 'Mecca-oriented' Sunnism of the ulema and Shah Jahan – came to a head in the civil war fought between Shah Jahan's sons Awrangzeb (r. 1658-1707) and Dara Shikoh (1615–59).[76] Dara, a Sufi mystic of the Qadiri order, who'd commissioned a commentary on Ibn ʿArabi's *Gemstones of Wisdom* from the aforementioned Muhibb Allah Allahabadi, went even further than Akbar in his religious universalism. The differences between Islam and Hinduism, he proclaimed, were merely verbal, and the roots of monotheism were to be found in the corpus of Hindu scriptures known as the Upanishads, which he had translated into Persian as *Sirr-i Akbar* (*The Greatest Secret*).[77] In the twentieth century, Jawaharlal Nehru, the first Prime Minister of India, would celebrate Dara as a hero who'd striven for 'a common nationality and synthesis of the various elements of the country'.[78] In the eyes of many of his contemporaries, however, he was an apostate, and after defeating him in the civil war, Awrangzeb had his brother executed on that charge.[79]

Like Babur, Awrangzeb adhered to the sober Sufism of the Naqshbandi order. As the Venetian doctor and traveller Niccolao Manucci (1638–1717) observed, he cultivated the image of a 'holy mendicant', and passed his time discussing religious matters with Naqshbandi shaykhs and reading the works of al-Ghazali.[80] It was probably al-Ghazali's emphasis on the harmony between Sufism and the Shari'a that appealed to Awrangzeb, for the emperor was deeply committed to the religious law. Unlike most of his Mughal predecessors, he never touched wine, and forbade his courtiers from doing so. He also discouraged all but Islamic building projects and the celebration of un-Islamic festivals like the Persian New Year (Nowruz), levied a tax on pilgrims to Hindu holy sites, and reinstituted the jizya poll tax on the Mughals' non-Muslim subjects.[81]

Underlying all this was a wish to see the Shari'a enforced throughout India. To that end, Awrangzeb supervised the compilation of a comprehensive code of Hanafi law, known as The Fatwas of the World Conqueror (al-Fatawa al-'Alamgiriyya) after his imperial title of 'Alamgir. Drawing on earlier Hanafi codes such as the Guide of al-Marghinani, it attempted, like the analogous law codes produced in the Ottoman Empire and Safavid Iran, to cover every topic on which a fatwa might be needed.[82] Opening with the declaration that knowledge of the law was what separated the saved from the damned, it proceeded to outline the Hanafi rulings on everything from what to do if you missed a mandatory prayer (you had to make it up, whatever your reason for missing it), to the permissibility of using medical cures (they were permissible, as long as you recognized that the ultimate healer was Allah).[83] It would quickly be accepted as the definitive statement of Hanafi law in India and elsewhere, including the Ottoman Empire, where it was known simply as *The Indian Fatwas (al-Fatawa al-Hindiyya)*.[84]

In modern times, Awrangzeb would often be portrayed as a religious zealot – Nehru called him 'an austere puritan, a bigot' – who abandoned the tolerant policies of Akbar and suppressed the ecumenical vision of Dara Shikoh, and so paved the way for the horrors of Partition in 1947.[85] That, however, is the judgement of a later and different age. Awrangzeb's Islamizing policies can perhaps better be understood against the backdrop of the old Islamic vision – shared by the three great empires of early modern times, Ottoman, Safavid, and Mughal – of a stable society, led by a pious and powerful ruler, and governed according to the principles of the Shari'a.

Chapter Ten

DECLINE
AND REVIVAL

When the early modern Islamic empires were at their height
in the fifteenth and sixteenth centuries, Muslims could
be confident in the strength and vitality of their institutions and
intellectual traditions. The Shari'a, codified in books like *The
Fatwas of the World Conqueror* and *The Compendium of 'Abbas*, was
widely understood and generally implemented. Centuries-old
texts, taught in the madrasas and Sufi lodges and explained by
innumerable commentaries and glosses, provided convincing
explanations of the nature of Allah, the cosmos, and man. The
great imperial mosques in the major cities not only provided places
where Muslims could come together to worship Allah, but also
stood as highly visible symbols of the worldly triumph of Islam.
Beyond the borders of the empires, the Islamic faith was being
carried – mostly by Sufi missionaries and Muslim merchants – to
new peoples in China and Southeast Asia, West and East Africa.[1]

Yet some Muslims had begun to see signs of impending
decay. For the Ottoman Empire, the phase of successful military
expansion had come to an end with Suleyman. Near perpetual
war with the Safavids in the east and frustrated attempts at

further expansion in the west had drained the state coffers and led to both rising indiscipline in the army and the breakdown of order in the provinces. By the early seventeenth century, Ottoman intellectuals could be heard contrasting the present condition of the empire with the golden age of Suleyman. In his *Principles for the Wise Ordering of the World* (*Usul al-hikam fi nizam al-'alam*), the Bosnian scholar Hasan Kafi (1544–1616) identified what he called 'a defect in the ordering of the world, and a slip in the arrangement of the affairs of men, particularly in the abode of Islam'.[2] A little while later, the bibliographer Katib Çelebi worried that Muslims were failing to engage with the secular learning being cultivated in Europe: 'Natural science and religious science,' he wrote in *The Balance of Truth*, 'are, as it were, two wings', and 'two wings are necessary for flying; with one, no progress is possible.'[3] In his *Book of Travels* (*Siyahatname*), Evliya Çelebi likewise lamented the fact that the Christians of *kafiristan* ('the land of the unbelievers') had taken better care of their churches, books, and monasteries than the Muslims had of their sacred places and treasures – a symptom, he felt, of the Ottomans' failure to live up to the ideals of justice established in the reign of 'the Lawgiver' Suleyman.[4]

These were largely secular critiques of the Ottoman *status quo*. Other, more actively Islamic thinkers saw the decline as a symptom of a deeper spiritual malaise, the only way out of which was the revival of 'true' Islam. The first major Ottoman thinker in this revivalist tradition was the madrasa teacher and Hanafi scholar Mehmed Birgivi (1522–73). Objecting to the Mufti of Istanbul Ebu Su'ud's attempt to show that the *qanun* – the Ottoman system of secular law – was basically in harmony with the Shari'a, he attacked the Ottomans' quasi-feudal system of land tenure and the common practice of funding charitable endowments with cash as unacceptable innovations (*bid'a*).[5] The existence of the *qanun*, Birgivi argued, was an affront to Allah. The Qur'an and Sunna were sufficient guides for all theological and legal problems. As he wrote at the beginning of his major work, *The Muhammadan Way* (*al-Tariqa al-Muhammadiyya*), 'Salvation is only attained by following the Seal of Prophets, our master and the master of all people, past and present, in our beliefs, speech, morals, and actions.'[6] It was the personal duty of every individual believer to ensure that the message of Muhammad was implemented, 'commanding good and forbidding evil' as the Qur'an had demanded.[7]

Birgivi's campaign was continued by a group of militant Islamic revivalists known as the Qadizadelis, after Mehmed Qadizadeh (1582–1635), a student of Birgivi's son and preacher at the Aya Sofya Mosque in Istanbul. They sought the eradication of such impious innovations as coffee drinking and smoking – both associated with the Sufis, who were known to use stimulants to keep themselves awake for their nocturnal devotions – and the use of knives, forks, and spoons.[8] Their campaigning bore some fruit. In 1633, Murad IV (r. 1623–40) closed the coffee houses and banned smoking in an attempt, so the aforementioned Katib Çelebi ironically recalled, 'to shut the gate of iniquity'.[9] Not everyone was convinced, however. Katib Çelebi was of the view that those who held 'the absurd notion that all mankind ought to share one creed and one code of behaviour' were 'gibbering fools', and that the Qadizadelis' campaign against popular customs demonstrated only their arrogance and 'stone-like stupidity'.[10] Most Ottomans probably agreed. The bans on smoking and coffee drinking were soon lifted, and in 1656 the

Qadizadelis were outlawed and their leaders exiled to the lonely island of Cyprus.[11]

Nevertheless, outside the empire's Anatolian heartlands, the Islamic revivalist movement continued to gather momentum. In the holy city of Medina, a group of ulema led by the Kurdish scholar Ibrahim al-Kurani (1615–90) turned back to the writings of Ibn Taymiyya. Though a Sufi in the tradition of Ibn 'Arabi, al-Kurani agreed with the controversial Hanbali jurist on issues like the dangers of philosophical theology and the need to cling to the literal meaning of the Qur'an and the way of the *salaf*.[12] Under his influence, the revivalist doctrine spread through the holy city. One of the many who imbibed it was Muhammad ibn 'Abd al-Wahhab (1703–92), a Hanbali from the central Arabian region of Najd on the edge of the Ottoman domains, who came to Medina to study with al-Kurani's disciples and departed with one all-encompassing conviction: that true monotheism meant worshipping Allah to the exclusion of all else. Anyone who venerated anything other than Allah – even the Prophet's tomb – was a polytheist bound for hell.[13]

Everywhere he looked, Ibn 'Abd al-Wahhab saw signs of polytheism. Most blatant was the idolatry of the semi-Islamized Bedouin of his native region, who believed in the spiritual power of trees, stones, and graves, and his first act upon proclaiming his message of monotheism in his hometown of 'Unayna was to cut down a tree held sacred by the local people. Yet Ibn 'Abd al-Wahhab had also travelled to Mecca, Medina, and Basra – and perhaps to Baghdad, Syria, and Iran too – and his definition of polytheism also applied to how Islam was practised in the wider Muslim world. The Qur'an, he noted, had condemned the Jews and Christians for 'taking their rabbis and monks as lords besides

Allah' (9:31), yet Sufi ascetics were revered like Christian monks, and the ulema were esteemed like Jewish rabbis.[14] The 'evilest of the innovators', according to Ibn 'Abd al-Wahhab, were the Shi'a.[15] The 'extremists' among them worshipped 'Ali – just as the Christians worshipped Jesus – and all of them blasphemously believed in the sinlessness of the Twelve Imams and the spiritual power of their tombs.[16]

All of these so-called Muslims, Ibn 'Abd al-Wahhab thought, needed to be called back to Allah. If they refused, they were to be declared unbelievers and fought with the sword.[17] To put this into action, in 1745 he forged a pact with Muhammad ibn Sa'ud (1710–65), the chief of the oasis town of Dir'iyya. According to the terms of the pact, Ibn 'Abd al-Wahhab would recognize the political authority of Ibn Sa'ud, while Ibn Sa'ud would see to it that Ibn 'Abd al-Wahhab's interpretation of Islam was implemented across the region, if necessary by force.[18]

It was an agreement that would change the political and religious map of the Muslim world. By Ibn 'Abd al-Wahhab's death in 1792, the Saudi-Wahhabi movement controlled most of central Arabia. By the end of the century, it had further expanded along the Persian Gulf. In 1801 a Saudi-Wahhabi force sacked the Shi'i shrine city of Karbala in Iraq, razing the 'polytheist' shrine to Husayn. In 1803–4, Mecca and Medina came under Saudi hegemony, and the name of the Ottoman caliph was removed from the Friday sermon. Unsurprisingly, this met with a hostile response from the Ottoman ulema. Like the Almohads of medieval North Africa, Ibn 'Abd al-Wahhab's followers called themselves al-muwahhidun, 'the true monotheists'. Their Ottoman opponents, by contrast, called them Kharijites – after the extremists of early Islamic history who said that sin made someone an unbeliever – and accused Ibn 'Abd al-Wahhab of having founded a new and illegitimate madhhab called Wahhabism.[19] Like his hero Ibn Taymiyya, Ibn 'Abd al-Wahhab's pious activism was unwelcome to many.

Still, there were many who shared his desire to revive Islam. In Mughal India the revivalist mentality was especially strong. The roots of this tendency lay in the time of Akbar. Inspired by the Hadith that said that Allah would send a *mujaddid* – a 'renewer' of the faith – at the beginning of every century, the Sufi Ahmad Sirhindi (1564–1624) had claimed to be the *mujaddid* of the entire second Islamic millennium. A severe critic of the religious syncretism of Akbar, Sirhindi also sought to reform the Sufi tradition, criticizing the dominant monistic interpretation of the Sufi metaphysics of Ibn 'Arabi. The latter, he argued, had suggested not that Allah and creation were one, only that the mystics, in their state of mystical rapture, experienced a temporary vision of unity – what he called *wahdat al-shuhud* ('the unity of vision') as opposed to *wahdat al-wujud* ('the unity of existence'). A member of the ardently Sunni Naqshbandi Sufi order, Sirhindi was also virulently opposed to Shi'ism and non-Muslim faiths. 'The humiliation of infidels,' he declared, 'is for the Muslim life itself.'[20]

Sirhindi's views, like Ibn 'Abd al-Wahhab's later, were controversial. The emperor Jahanagir dismissed him as a charlatan and his work as 'a miscellany of drivel' that 'would lead to infidelity and apostasy'.[21] His interpretation of Ibn 'Arabi was attacked in India and in faraway Mecca.[22] Yet many supported his revivalist project, and his views spawned a new and influential branch of the Naqshbandi order, the Naqshbandi-Mujaddidi tariqa, so named on account of Sirhindi's claim to be the *mujaddid* of the second millennium. Counting the Mughal emperor Awrangzeb among its adherents, by the eighteenth century it would be the dominant form of Naqshbandi Sufism, and one of the most influential Sufi orders in India, Central Asia, and the Ottoman lands.[23]

The most important adherent of this rejuvenated Naqshbandi order, and the man who would do the most to spread Islamic revivalism in the subcontinent, was Shah Wali Allah of Delhi (1703–62). Born in the last years of the reign of Awrangzeb, as a young man Wali Allah had gone to Mecca and Medina, where he'd studied Hadith in the same circles as Ibn 'Abd al-Wahhab, and experienced mystical visions in which, so he recalled in *The Spiritual Effusions of the Two Sanctuaries* (*Fuyud al-Haramayn*), he'd been charged with putting right 'the discomposed state of affairs of the *umma*'.[24]

Back in India, Wali Allah saw signs of this decay all around him. Politically, the Mughal Empire seemed to be heading for inevitable collapse. Hindus, Afghans, and Sikhs competed for Mughal territory, and in 1739 Nader Shah (r. 1736–47), the new ruler of Iran, sacked Delhi and carried off the Peacock Throne and the Koh-i-Noor, the priceless symbols of Mughal power. Though the Mughals survived, their control over their empire was tenuous, and Wali Allah would live through the reigns of no fewer than eleven emperors.[25] This he saw as a symptom of moral and intellectual decline. Government officials, he observed, thought nothing of drinking wine in public, and tolerated the existence of brothels, taverns, and gambling dens.[26] 'I am in an age of ignorance, prejudice, and following the passions,' he explained in his major work, *Allah's Conclusive Argument* (*Hujjat Allah al-baligha*), 'in which every person has a high opinion of his ruinous opinions.'[27] Indian Muslims were in the grip of factionalism, identifying more with their legal madhhab or Sufi order than with the community at large. 'There is no prospect of agreement or compromise,' Wali Allah protested. 'Some are Hanafis, others Shafi'is, and everybody ... censures the others'.[28]

The remedy, as Ibn Taymiyya and more recent revivalists had taught, was a return to the Qur'an and Sunna. Like the Protestant Reformers in Christian Europe, Shah Wali Allah advocated direct engagement with the text of scripture. Breaking with the near unanimous view that the Qur'an, being in the language of God, was untranslatable, he translated the Islamic holy book into Persian – for the benefit, he said, of 'the sons of craftsmen and soldiers', who, being able to read Allah's word for themselves, would be protected against the arguments of heretics, unbelieving philosophers, and Hindus.[29] Applying the same principle, his son would later translate the holy book into Urdu, an Indo-Islamic language heavily influenced by Persian and in increasingly wide use since the sixteenth century. Alongside the Qur'an, Shah Wali Allah also advocated going back to the Hadith. 'No nobler task can one set oneself,' he wrote in *The Spiritual Effusions of the Two Sanctuaries*, 'than to try to become a scholar of Hadith.'[30] Inspired by his time in Medina, the overall message of *Allah's Conclusive Argument* was that if the study of Hadith could be revived, then so too could Islam.[31]

For Shah Wali Allah, however, the return to the Qur'an and Sunna meant something more than just studying the texts. It also involved recapturing the spirit of the prophetic message, and this entailed retaining, reforming, and reconciling the best of the Islamic intellectual heritage. Key to that heritage was Sufism. Like Ibn Taymiyya and Ibn 'Abd al-Wahhab, Wali Allah was opposed to the more popular kinds of mysticism. The worship of 'Allah's friends', he wrote, was 'a sin graver than murder or adultery; indeed, it is equivalent to unbelief (*kufr*)'.[32] Yet Wali Allah was also a Naqshbandi Sufi, who accepted Sirhindi's claim to be the 'renewer' of Islam, and presented his Naqshbandi predecessor as the 'pedestal' (*irhas*) on which he was now standing.[33] Like Sirhindi, part of Wali Allah's revivalist project involved reformulating the teachings of Ibn 'Arabi to show how they – and Sufism more generally – were consistent with the Shari'a and the fundamental scriptural sources.[34]

Fiqh, or the study of the law, was another noble part of the Islamic heritage, and it too needed renewal.[35] To counter the factionalist attachment to the legal schools, Wali Allah emphasized that each of the Sunni madhhabs had something beneficial to offer: the Malikis had the best approach to Hadith; the Shafi'is were the best at independent reasoning; Hanbalis like Ibn Taymiyya were the most attached to the Qur'an and Sunna; and the Hanafis were best at interpreting the law in keeping with the demands of the age.[36] This being the case, Wali Allah attempted to create a new legal method that utilized what was best in each of the schools of law. Like other reformers, he stressed the importance of *ijtihad* – the jurist's rational derivation of the law from the fundamental sources – and condemned *taqlid* – the blind emulation of others' opinions. 'The time has come,' he wrote in *Allah's Conclusive Argument*, 'when every order of the Shari'a and every teaching of Islam should be presented before the world in a rational way.'[37]

Though it could not save the Mughal Empire, Wali Allah's attempt at reviving the faith would leave a deep imprint on modern Islam. His combination of the back-to-the-Qur'an revivalism of the Wahhabis and the reformed Sufism of Sirhindi would win adherents across the wider Muslim world, including in regions as far removed from his own context as West and North Africa. There, over the course of the late eighteenth and early nineteenth centuries, several revivalist movements arose that combined a Sufi piety centred on mystical communion with the Prophet (the so-called *tariqa muhammadiyya* or 'Muhammadan way') with a strict commitment to the Shari'a and militant jihad. These movements, the most notable of which were the Tijani tariqa in West Africa and the Idrisi order and its subsidiaries in Libya, the Sudan, and East Africa, would go on to play a major role in the political and spiritual life of African Muslims.[38] No longer simply a response to Ottoman or Mughal decline, by the turn of the nineteenth century Islamic revivalism had spread across the Sunni world.

Among the Shi'a, too, there were those who sought to revive the original spirit of the faith. Since al-'Allama al-Hilli in the fourteenth century, the dominant approach in Shi'i legal theory had been Usulism – the legal scholars' rational interpretation (*ijtihad*) of the sources (*usul*) of the law.[39] In the early seventeenth century, however, the Shi'i jurist Muhammad Amin al-Astarabadi (d. 1623/4 or 1626/7) declared Usulism a mistake. In relying on human reasoning, he wrote in *The Medinan Lessons* (*al-Fawa'id al-Madaniyya*), the fruit of several years of solitary meditation in the city of the Prophet, the Usulis had 'contradicted the reliably transmitted statements of the immaculate family [of the Prophet]'.[40] It was the inerrant statements (*akhbar*) of the spotless Imams, not the personal conjecture of fallible scholars, al-Astarabadi argued, which ought to be the basis of the law.[41]

Akhbarism, as al-Astarabadi's position became known, quickly spread through the Safavid lands. By the eighteenth century, it dominated the teaching of Shi'ism in the seminaries of Iran and the Iraqi shrine cities of Najaf and Karbala, so much so that the Usulis were forced to teach their rationalist method in secret.[42] Even those who didn't explicitly identify as Akhbaris came under its spell. The philosopher Mulla Sadra was sympathetic to its cause, while Muhammad Baqir al-Majlisi (*c.*1627–99), the Shaykh al-Islam of Isfahan, declared in the Akhbari spirit that the sayings of the Imams were 'the sole means of accessing the divine wisdom', and compiled a massive collection of each and every one of those sayings, proclaiming it the perfect tool to 'humble the despicable [Sunni] heretics'.[43]

Yet by the nineteenth century Usulism would be back in vogue. There were several possible reasons for this: the Persian plague of 1772–3 that killed many of the leading Akhbari scholars of the day; support for the Usulis from the Qajar dynasty, which, after the collapse of Safavid rule in 1722 and half a century of near anarchy, ruled Iran from 1785; the Akhbaris' inability to agree among themselves on key issues like whether the Usulis were to be classed as heretics; and, perhaps most importantly, the genius of the Usuli thinker al-Behbehani (*c.*1705–91/2), a Karbala-based scholar – celebrated by his fellow Shi'a as the 'renewer' of the twelfth century – who took the fight to the Akhbaris by asserting that reason could act, as the scholar of Shi'ism Robert Gleave has put it, as 'a short-cut to knowledge of

God's law' and training a generation of students in the methods of *ijtihad*.[44] Whatever the reason, the ultimate success of Usulism was perhaps representative of a broader trend. Despite the best efforts and undoubted successes of the revivalists, it was impossible to stamp out the rationalist strand in Islamic thought.

Chapter Eleven

FACING MODERNITY

Eighteenth-century Islamic revivalists like Ibn 'Abd al-Wahhab and Shah Wali Allah had been little concerned with Europe. For them, the impulse to reform had been spiritual decay within the Muslim community. The next generation of Muslim thinkers, however, could not so easily ignore the Western 'other'. In 1798, Napoleon Bonaparte landed at Alexandria, bringing with him the whole might of revolutionary France – not just soldiers and guns, but an arsenal of novel political concepts like 'freedom', 'equality', and 'the republic', and a squadron of scientists tasked with dissecting the history and geography, laws and customs, and flora and fauna of the colonized country.[1]

The Egyptians were shocked, appalled, and intrigued. In a memorable opening to his account of the year 1798, the historian al-Jabarti (1753–1825/6) described it as 'the first year of great apocalyptic battles, weighty events, unfortunate occurrences, shocking misfortunes, the multiplication of evils, one thing following another, continuous trials, the rupture of the age, the upheaval of the natural order and the overturning of custom, successive horrors, the change of conditions, the corruption of the administration, the arrival of destruction, the generalization of devastation, and the unsettling of effects.'[2]

A graduate of the Sunni college al-Azhar trained in Ash'ari theology, al-Jabarti sought an explanation for this calamity in the will of Allah. As Qur'an 11:117 makes clear, 'Your Lord would not destroy the cities unjustly, if their inhabitants were righteous.' But Allah worked through human beings, and in this instance He had blessed the Frankish conquerors with intellectual marvels and technological wonders. Visiting the Institute of Egypt, the sumptuous Cairo headquarters of Napoleon's scientific committee, al-Jabarti was pleasantly surprised to find a large, illustrated book on the life of the Prophet and 'many other Islamic books translated into their language'. He was impressed, too, by what he described as their 'extraordinary learning in the sciences, especially mathematics and linguistics, and the great effort' – the word he used was *ijtihad* – 'they put into studying languages and logic, to which they devote themselves day and night'. He marvelled as well at their astronomical instruments, at the precision of their portrait painters and engineers, at their strange chemical experiments, and many other things that 'perplexed the intellect'.[3]

The Napoleonic occupation would last less than three years. Yet its impact would be far-reaching. Muslim thinkers were now forced to face up to what they acknowledged as the 'backwardness' (*ta'akhkhur*) of the *umma* next to the technological and military might of Europe – a situation that was problematic not simply because it heralded a life of miserable subservience to outsiders, but, more fundamentally, because it seemed to run counter to the divine plan.

This problem of Muslim weakness vis-à-vis the West would define Islamic thought in the modern age. While Muslims would react in many different ways, perhaps the most far-reaching response was the one given by the Muslim modernists. They reacted to the rise of the West by embracing its scientific and intellectual achievements and reinterpreting Islam in the light of modern discoveries. In its true and original state, they believed, Islam was inherently rational, scientific, and modern; indeed, it was *the* religion of modernity, for weren't the sciences of the Europeans built on texts and theories that Muslims had transmitted to them in the Middle Ages? Yet something, they acknowledged, had gone wrong. For centuries, they alleged, Muslims had neglected the rational side of their faith in favour of a legalism built on 'blind emulation' – *taqlid* – and a Sufi mysticism that was fatalistic, irrational, and foreign. Only by recovering the spirit of reason, by opening themselves up to modern science and relying less on the traditions and institutions of the medieval past, could the Muslim community regain its former strength.

One of the first to voice this thesis was the Egyptian Rifaʻa Rafiʻ al-Tahtawi (1801–73). A graduate, like al-Jabarti, of al-Azhar, and a student of al-Jabarti's Francophile disciple Hasan al-ʻAttar (*c.*1776–1835), in 1826 al-Tahtawi was appointed *imam* to a study mission sent to France by Egypt's modernizing ruler Muhammad ʻAli (r. 1805–48). During his five years in Paris, al-Tahtawi came to see for himself the intellectual superiority of those he called 'the Franks'. While the Muslims had neglected the rational sciences, he explained, the 'sages' of England, France, and Austria had surpassed Aristotle, Plato, and Hippocrates in their wisdom and learning.[4] To recover their former position, Muslims needed to learn from the West, and to enable this they needed, first, to translate European scientific, literary, and philosophical books into Arabic, and, second, to adopt modern methods of education. In both respects, al-Tahtawi led by example. He translated books on minerals, mathematics, and hygiene – as well the Napoleonic Code and François Fénelon's *The Adventures of Telemachus* (1699) – into Arabic, directed the newly established School of Languages, and argued for the education of *all* Egyptians, girls as well as boys, making the point that if the Prophet's wives had been taught to read and write, then why shouldn't Egyptian girls?[5]

Others applied the modernist thesis to the political sphere. In an 1868 work, *The Straightest Path to Knowledge of the Conditions of Kingdoms (Aqwam al-masalik fi ma'rifat ahwal al-mamalik)*, Khayr al-Din al-Tunisi (1822/3–90), chief minister of Tunisia and later grand vizier of the Ottoman Empire, explained that the weakness of the Muslim world was a result of Muslims turning their backs on disciplines like economics and political science. This, he wrote, was a 'clear mistake, for if something emerges from elsewhere, and is correct and in agreement with the sources [of the Shari'a] … then there is no reason to reject it' – an echo, a thousand years on, of al-Kindi's famous defence of philosophy.[6] Modernization, he argued, would in fact only mean that Muslims were taking back what had been taken from them. Even European historians acknowledged that their civilization had only emerged from its Dark Ages by borrowing sciences cultivated in Muslim Baghdad and Cordoba, while there was little difference between the modern parliament and those councils of religious scholars and notables who had long advised Muslim sovereigns.[7]

In India, too, similar arguments could be heard. In 1858, in the wake of the so-called Indian Mutiny – the unsuccessful uprising against the British East India Company – the British crown had assumed direct control of the country. Aided by the boom in printing, the ease of travel on the newly constructed railways, the improvement in communications brought about by the invention of the telegraph and postal services, and the rise of Urdu as a common Muslim language, several reformist movements emerged in reaction to colonial rule. Among these were the Deobandis, Hanafi ulema who sought to recover Muslim strength by expunging 'innovations' in religious practice and reviving the traditional madrasa curriculum with the help of modern innovations like classrooms, a central library, fixed timetables, and regular exams; the Barelwis, who clung to Sufism, the cult of saints, and the belief in the special spiritual powers of the Prophet; the People of Hadith (*ahl-i Hadith*), who argued that the legal madhhabs should be abandoned and replaced with direct engagement with the Qur'an and Sunna; and the Ahmadis, who believed their leader, Mirza Ghulam Ahmad (*c.*1839–1908), to be the Messiah and perhaps even a prophet, and reinterpreted jihad to mean interreligious debate.[8]

Then there were the modernists. Their leader was Sayyid Ahmad Khan (1817–98). A former civil servant for the East India Company, Sayyid Ahmad believed that the key to reconciliation with the modern world was education. In 1869 he travelled to Britain, where he rented rooms in Bloomsbury, discussed the life of Muhammad with the historian Thomas Carlyle, and attended the last public reading given by Charles Dickens. 'All good things, spiritual and worldly, which should be found in man,' he wrote in a letter home, 'have been bestowed by the Almighty on Europe, and especially on England' – a fact which he deemed to be 'entirely due to the education of the men and women'.[9]

Believing that Muslims needed to be offered an education on the English model, in 1875 Sayyid Ahmad founded the Anglo-Muhammadan Oriental College at Aligarh. Situated eighty miles south of Delhi, Aligarh was modelled on an Oxford or Cambridge college. Dotted around its two main quads were student rooms, a library and debating chamber, a dining hall, and a mosque for communal worship. There were college gardens and a cricket pitch. Students – who, despite Sayyid Ahmad's admiration for the level of female education in England, were exclusively male – wore black gowns and Turkish fezzes and were expected to study and play and eat and pray at fixed times. Instruction was in English; the faculty was staffed by Cambridge-educated Englishmen as well as Indians; and the curriculum was weighted towards modern subjects like mathematics, the natural sciences, history, and English literature.[10] The overall aim was to fulfil the vision of Thomas Babington Macaulay, the Whig politician and historian, to create a 'class of persons, Indian in blood and colour, but English in taste, in opinions, in morals and in intellect'.[11]

To achieve this, Sayyid Ahmad thought, Islam itself needed to be reinterpreted. Presenting himself as the heir to Shah Wali Allah and the Wahhabis, he argued that Muslims needed to return to the Qur'an. Unlike those earlier revivalists, however, he believed that scripture should be interpreted in light of the findings of modern science, for there could be no conflict between 'God's word' (the Qur'an) and 'God's work' (the natural world).[12] Miracles had to be understood in the light of the laws of nature: when Moses led his people out of Egypt, the Red Sea had not actually parted; the Israelites had simply crossed over at a shallow point. Likewise, when the Qur'an described the creation of man, it foreshadowed the modern theory of evolution.[13] Hadiths of what Sayyid Ahmad called 'an extravagant and eccentric character' were similarly to be considered of doubtful authenticity, and Islamic law was to be reinterpreted in light of liberal ideas.[14] Thus, jihad was purely defensive; slavery was illegal; polygamy was condemned; lending at interest was permissible; and Muslims were allowed to dine with Christians or eat food that they'd slaughtered.[15] Throughout, the aim was to ward off the criticisms of Islam's opponents – particularly British orientalists – and to show, as Sayyid Ahmad put it in a letter to the Ottoman sultan, how 'the onward march of science and enlightenment is in every respect compatible with Islam'.[16]

These early modernists looked on Europe as a model and source of inspiration. Yet by the last quarter of the nineteenth century, the sense of weakness relative to the West had only grown stronger. The Tunisian, Egyptian, and Ottoman governments had fallen into heavy debts to European banks, and this had resulted in increased European meddling and, soon enough, in direct imperial rule, as the French – a colonial presence in Algeria since 1830 – occupied Tunisia in 1881 and Britain followed suit in Egypt a year later.

For the modernist thinker Jamal al-Din al-Afghani (1838/9– 97), the cause of these calamities was all too apparent. 'O, sons of the East,' he exhorted his coreligionists, 'don't you know that the power of the Westerners and their domination over you came about through their advance in learning and education, and your decline in these domains?'[17] Described by a sympathetic British contemporary as 'a wild man of genius', to his admirers al-Afghani was 'the Sage of the East', 'truth personified', and an embodiment of 'the transcendent prophetic spirit'.[18] His enemies, by contrast, charged him with unbelief, political subversion, even murder. An ascetic who ate little, slept even less, drank tea constantly, and had a fondness for cigars, he was a man of mystery and contradictions.[19] Though he claimed to be an Afghan and a Sunni, he was in fact a Shi'i from Iran. A perennial wanderer, his career took him to almost every major Muslim country, and everywhere he went he preached his modernist doctrine of intellectual reform and political revival. If Muslims could only reclaim the spirit of reason, he believed, the yoke of colonialism could be thrown off and the *umma* restored to its former glory.

Al-Afghani's early years found him in India, where he first became acquainted with the modern sciences; Afghanistan, where he was suspected by the British of being a Russian agent;[20] and Istanbul, where he courted controversy with a public lecture that appeared to place philosophy on a par with prophecy.[21] The most productive period of his career was the eight years between 1871 and 1879 that he spent in Cairo. There he became the intellectual mentor to a group of talented and ambitious young students, many of them connected to the illustrious Sunni college of al-Azhar but dissatisfied with what they saw as its stultified curriculum. In private lessons given at his home in the old Cairo souk, and nightly gatherings at the Busta Café – a hotbed of intellectual ferment – al-Afghani opened his young charges' eyes to Islamic philosophy and Western science, held forth on the depravities of the imperial powers, and urged his students to write for the newspapers that were then springing up all over the Egyptian capital.[22]

This was too much for the powers-that-be, and in 1879 al-Afghani was deported to India, where he launched a devastating critique of Sayyid Ahmad Khan. Though Sayyid Ahmad was a fellow modernist, he was also, in al-Afghani's eyes, a lackey for the British and a proponent of the atheistic philosophy of materialism. Like the medieval philosophers, al-Afghani believed that religion was conducive to a stable and harmonious social order, and so by undermining Muslims' faith in their religion Sayyid Ahmad had threatened the stability of the *umma* and exposed it to foreign exploitation; indeed, it was for this reason, al-Afghani alleged, that the British had financed his college at Aligarh.[23]

In 1883 the ever-restless al-Afghani arrived in Paris. In March of that year the prominent French orientalist Ernest Renan delivered a lecture at the Sorbonne in which he argued that the weakness of the Muslim world was the result of Islam's innate hostility to science. Al-Afghani's response revealed the same utilitarian view of religion as his attack on Sayyid Ahmad Khan. While conceding Renan's point that the Muslim religious authorities had invariably 'tried to stifle science', al-Afghani noted that the same was true of the Catholic Church, and also argued that religion was a necessary stepping-stone on the path to modernity.[24] After all, he suggested, it had been Martin Luther's Reformation that had set the West on its modern course.[25]

In addition to its contribution to social order and progress, there was another sense in which al-Afghani thought religion could be useful. Under the influence of the 'pan-Islamic' ideology that was being discussed in Ottoman circles, al-Afghani came to believe that the Islamic religion itself could be a weapon in the anti-imperialist struggle. From Paris, he and his chief disciple

Muhammad 'Abduh (1849–1905) founded *The Firmest Bond* (*al-'Urwa al-wuthqa*), a short-lived yet influential journal proposing Islamic unity as the solution to Muslim weakness.[26] This did not so much mean establishing a political union as achieving solidarity between Muslims of all kinds, Arab and Persian, Turkish and Indian, Sunni and Shi'a.[27] If Muslims everywhere recognized that Islam was their true 'nationality' and the Qur'an their true 'sultan', al-Afghani explained, they could repel the foreign powers and regain their strength and independence.[28]

Islam's power, al-Afghani insisted, derived from the fact that it was the best religion, which meant, in the first instance, the most rational. Islam, he explained in *The Refutation of the Materialists* (*al-Radd 'ala al-dahriyyin*), his polemic against Sayyid Ahmad Khan, had 'polished the intellect' with its highly rational doctrine of monotheism, 'purifying it of the defilement of delusions'. It was also the most egalitarian of the world's faiths: while the Hindus had their caste system, the Jews their idea of the Chosen People, and the Christians their priesthood, in Islam, people were distinguished 'only by intellect and virtue'. Indeed, in al-Afghani's view, Islam was practically unique in addressing the intellect, connecting human happiness to the intellectual life, and calling for the education of all people.[29] In this idealized, rationalist form, Islam was perfectly compatible with modernity; indeed, it was the religion of modernity *par excellence*.

This, in brief, was the Muslim modernist thesis. Ultimately, however, it was al-Afghani's disciple Muhammad 'Abduh who came closest to achieving that ideal balance between Islam and modernity that the modernists were seeking. Born in a small village in the Nile Delta, the young 'Abduh, initially repulsed by the rote learning of the local mosque-school, developed a passion for knowledge under the influence of his Sufi uncle Shaykh Darwish. In his late teens he went to study at al-Azhar, where again he was unimpressed by the standard of education and started to practise an increasingly ascetic form of Sufism. His life was then changed again by the arrival of another teacher, al-Afghani, who taught him how to read a book critically, and instructed him in *falsafa*, philosophical theology, and the modern sciences.[30] Under al-Afghani's influence, 'Abduh moved away from Sufism towards a more rational interpretation of Islam, composing a series of glosses on a major work of philosophical *kalam* and teaching books from that tradition to his fellow students at al-Azhar.[31] He also began to write for the popular press: an 1876 article in *al-Ahram* (The Pyramids), for instance, called for the teaching of the modern sciences and European history in order to learn the secrets of Western progress.[32]

In 1879 'Abduh was appointed lecturer in history at Dar al-'Ulum, a new college in Cairo for training teachers in the modern sciences. There he taught the *Introduction to History* (*al-Muqaddima*) of Ibn Khaldun, a favourite of the modernists for its analysis of the rise and fall of states and civilizations.[33] He was made editor, too, of the government paper *al-Waqa'i' al-Misriyya* (The Egyptian Events), using that platform to call again for educational reform and an end to outdated customs like polygamy.[34] He was a supporter of the 'Urabi Revolt, the proto-nationalist, military-led movement to depose the viceroy Tawfiq (r. 1879–92) and end British influence. When the revolt failed and Egypt was occupied, 'Abduh was banished from the country. In 1884 he was in Paris, where he worked on *The Firmest Bond* with al-Afghani. He spent some time, too, in England, visiting the Houses of Parliament and going to Brighton to see Herbert

Spencer, the thinker who coined the term 'the survival of the fittest'. After a period in Tunis, supposedly spent plotting on behalf of the Mahdist rebellion in Sudan, in 1885 he ended up in Beirut. There, 'Abduh launched himself into teaching, his great passion, delivering a series of lectures on theology that were later published as *The Treatise on Monotheism* (*Risalat al-tawhid*).

The essential message of those lectures was that Islam was a religion of reason. The Qur'an, he declared, 'spoke to the rational mind and alerted the intelligence'.[35] Where the other religions of the day had preached blind subservience to religious dogma, Islam had encouraged people to use their intellects.[36] It taught them that through their natural reason they could know the first principles of religion, such as the existence and unity of God (here 'Abduh rehearsed Ibn Sina's proof for God's existence), the basic features of prophecy, and the distinction between good and evil (a position which bore the mark of Maturidi influence).[37]

Yet some things, 'Abduh explained, were beyond the power of reason to comprehend. Human intelligence could not penetrate the essences of things – in particular, it was dangerous to speculate about the divine essence.[38] Nor was it able to know things like Allah's attributes of speech, hearing, and sight, or the reasons for the details of the ritual prayer. For these things, Allah had sent prophets to guide people to happiness in this life and the next.[39] Of these prophetic 'helpers', the greatest, undeniably, was Muhammad. Religion and human progress, 'Abduh insisted, had reached their 'culmination in Islam'.[40]

If this was the good news for 'Abduh's listeners, the bad news he delivered was that decline had set in early in the history of Islam. With the First Fitna, the rise of Shi'ism, the errors of the Mu'tazila, and the misguided Mihna, sectarian divisions and theological schisms had diverted the Muslim community from its true course. Though al-Ash'ari and other 'renewers' of the faith had mitigated some of the damage, Muslims, 'Abduh declared, had since 'evicted intellect from its rightful place'; hence the urgent need for reform.[41]

Back in Egypt in 1889 after he was pardoned by Tawfiq, 'Abduh set to work spreading this message of reform. He was appointed to a committee charged with reforming al-Azhar, where he also returned to teach, giving a series of lectures on the Qur'an in which he preached the same basic message as he had in Beirut. The Qur'an, he said, called on people to reflect rationally on the signs of Allah in the natural world, and taught that faith depended on knowledge, which was founded in turn on rational proof.[42] Where the intellect was insufficient, revelation offered guidance that was relevant 'for all times and places'.[43] The Qur'an's rulings on social issues – such as its prohibition of drinking, gambling, and prostitution – would, if implemented, lead inevitably to 'religious and societal flourishing'.[44] And its political guidance – such as its instruction to Muslims to fight the unbelievers with the same weapons that were used against them – provided for the worldly strength of the Muslim community.[45] Yet Muslims had neglected the Qur'anic message. Instead of following revelation and their God-given intellects, they had fallen into ignorance, and this explained their present weakness.[46]

As Chief Mufti of Egypt from 1899 until his death in 1905, 'Abduh had an opportunity to try to implement his version of Islam. Like many before him, his basic legal principle was the avoidance of blind *taqlid* in favour of rational *ijtihad*.[47] Like Shah Wali Allah, he condemned excessive attachment to a particular legal school. 'The Shari'a,' 'Abduh (who was himself a Hanafi) said, 'is not limited to the books of the Hanafis.'[48] When issuing a legal ruling, he would sometimes employ the relatively novel juristic technique known as *talfiq*, the 'patching together' of the teachings of the different madhhabs to utilize what worked best from each of them.[49] Of the almost 1,000 fatwas he issued in his capacity as Chief Mufti, the most famous were those where he tried to interpret the sacred law in accordance with the modern age, like the 1903 'Transvaal Fatwa', in which 'Abduh, preferring his own analysis of the relevant Qur'anic texts to centuries of juristic opinion, advised a group of Muslims living in South Africa that it was lawful for them to wear European hats and to eat meat slaughtered by Christians.[50]

In 'Abduh's thought, all the strands of Islamic modernism seemed to come together. Like al-Tahtawi and Sayyid Ahmad Khan he admired the West, learning French, reading Rousseau, Gibbon, and Tolstoy, and travelling to Europe whenever he could. Yet, under the influence of al-Afghani, he also loathed European interference in the Muslim world.[51] Like all the modernists, he taught that Islam was the religion of reason, and the Qur'an the most rational of scriptures. 'Our religion,' he declared, 'contains nothing that is contrary to modern civilization.'[52] Properly interpreted, he thought, the Qur'an could teach Muslims how to be liberal and modern, and so to recover their rightful place in the world.

Chapter Twelve

FROM MODERNISM
TO ISLAMISM

For some, the changes 'Abduh had advocated were too much, too fast. For others, they were not radical enough. Few had his ability to balance the traditional and the modern, the revolutionary and the conservative, and synthesize them into a harmonious whole. This meant that his ideas were almost bound to be extended in ways that, though apparently consistent with his basic principles, nevertheless failed to capture the essential spirit of his thought.

This, it seems fair to say, was the case with his closest disciple, Muhammad Rashid Rida (1865–1935). Born in Syrian Tripoli, as a young man Rida was awakened to the problems of Islam in the modern world by *The Firmest Bond*, the pan-Islamic journal that al-Afghani and 'Abduh had published from their Parisian exile. 'When I read its articles calling for Islamic unity,' he recalled, 'the return to the glory, power, and grandeur of Islam, the recovery of its lost territories, and the liberation of its peoples from foreign tyranny, it left such a mark on my heart that I entered a new stage of life.'[1]

That new stage was to begin in Cairo. Arriving in Egypt in

1897, Rida became 'Abduh's most trusted student. He threw himself into Islamic journalism, founding the reformist journal *The Islamic Lighthouse* (*al-Manar al-Islami*), which featured a serial of 'Abduh's lectures on the Qur'an alongside articles on political and religious subjects, and would gain subscribers in places as diverse as Russia, India, Bosnia, Sierra Leone, the United States, and Southeast Asia, as well as the traditional Islamic heartlands, helping to spread the reformers' message far and wide.[2]

Rida proclaimed that his views were in total alignment with those of his '*imam* and teacher'. Like 'Abduh, he believed that Islam was fundamentally a religion of reason, and that the Muslim world was weak because Muslims were, as he put it, 'ignorant of the true version of their religion'.[3] He called on them to abandon *taqlid* and return to the Qur'an and Sunna as understood by the *salaf al-salih* or 'pious ancestors'. He called for Islamic law to be interpreted in accordance with the demands of the age and the common good, justifying interest-bearing loans, for instance, on the grounds that Muslims had to be financially strong enough to ward off Western capitalists.[4] (Though lending at interest had once been condemned as usury by the Christian church, a more lenient attitude had prevailed in Europe from around 1400.[5]) He advocated a rationalist interpretation of scripture, proposing, like Sayyid Ahmad Khan, that Moses and the Israelites must have crossed the Red Sea at a low tide, just as Napoleon's army had done during the occupation of Egypt.[6] And he campaigned for reforming education on modern lines, setting up his own Islamic school in Cairo in 1912 for training a new generation of modernist ulema.

Nevertheless, the tone of Rida's writings was sharper than 'Abduh's, and the vision more exclusive. Inspired by Ibn Taymiyya, whom he celebrated as the greatest 'renewer' of the Middle

Ages, his criticisms of the still dominant medieval tradition were bitter and sweeping.[7] Muslims had been distracted from the Qur'an's true meaning, he complained in the introduction to his edition of 'Abduh's Qur'an commentary, by 'the debates of the theologians, the derivations of the grammarians, the deductions of the blindly imitative jurists, the allegorical interpretations of the Sufis, and the zealotry of the sects and legal schools'.[8] Dismayed by the continued colonial presence in the Muslim world and revolted by the industrial violence of the First World War, his attitude towards the West, too, was unambiguously hostile. 'The whole world of man,' he wrote, 'is in a state of misery due to these unjust, wicked, covetous states.'[9] Christian missionaries, he said, were 'zealots' who 'spat out the poison of their hostility in intellectual and political periodicals', preying on Muslim weakness.[10] And, like Ahmad Sirhindi and Ibn 'Abd al-Wahhab, he loathed Muslim minorities, dismissing Shi'ism as 'full of fairy tales and illegitimate innovations', and Mirza Ghulam Ahmad, the 'prophet' of the Ahmadis of India, as the Dajjal or Islamic anti-Christ.[11]

Rida was less progressive than his mentor, too, on gender issues. 'Abduh had argued that true Islam afforded women a high status, but that, in this as in so many other respects, Muslims had 'failed to follow the guidance of our religion'.[12] This argument had been carried forward by several of his acolytes, most notably the Egyptian judge Qasim Amin (1863–1908), who had argued in his 1899 book *The Liberation of Women* (*Tahrir al-mar'a*) that Egypt and the wider Muslim world could only be woken from their slumber if the status of women in Islamic society was improved in line with the original teachings of Islam.[13] Following him, feminist activists like Malak Hifni Nasif (1886–1918) and

Huda Sha'rawi (1879–1924) would campaign for improved education for women, the abolition of forced veiling, and an end to polygamy.[14] Rida, by contrast, argued in *A Call to the Gentle Sex* (*Nida' ila al-jins al-latif*) that women ought to be obedient and submissive to their husbands; that polygamy was defensible provided the husband could do justice to all of his wives; that 'Islam had given the man alone the right to initiate divorce'; and that a woman should not be alone with a man to whom she was not married or travel unaccompanied by her husband.[15]

Rida was also more insistent than 'Abduh on the political dimension of Islam. Islam, he wrote in the introduction to 'Abduh's Qur'an commentary, was 'a religion of sovereignty and power'; it was 'spiritual and societal, political and militant'.[16] The Qur'an was a 'book of practical guidance, not of art or theoretical knowledge'; it 'contained everything that man needed for religious, social, political, economic, and military reform'.[17] When Mustafa Kemal (Atatürk), the secularist founder of the Republic of Turkey, abolished the Ottoman sultanate in 1922, leaving only a spiritual caliphate which would itself be abolished two years later, Rida began to write and campaign for a revived caliphate, calling for the leadership of a religious scholar qualified to interpret the Shari'a in accordance with the needs of the age.[18] Here, as in other respects, his position was not necessarily representative of the wider 'Abduh movement. In 1925, the Islamic judge and 'Abduh-disciple 'Ali 'Abd al-Raziq (1888–1966) published a controversial book, *Islam and the Principles of Government* (*al-Islam wa-usul al-hukm*), in which he argued that the caliphate had no basis in Islam and that Muhammad had brought no political doctrine. Islam, 'Abd al-Raziq declared, was 'a message, not a government; a religion, not a state', and Muslims ought to be free to order their societies as they saw fit.[19] Stripped of his status as a member of the ulema, among those who rushed to condemn his tract was Rida, who accused 'Abd al-Raziq of making Islam 'prey to the savage colonialists'.[20]

In this way, 'Abduh's modernism was merged, in Rida's thought, into the new movement known as Salafism. A rigid and exclusivist reading of Islam, so named because of its adherents' reverence for the *salaf al-salih* – the 'pious predecessors' who had lived around Muhammad's time – Salafism was close, in its loathing of impious 'innovations', its high regard for Ibn Taymiyya, and its hostility to Shi'ism and other 'heresies', to the puritanical revivalism of Ibn 'Abd al-Wahhab. Later in his career, in fact, Rida would forge an increasingly close relationship with the Wahhabis of Arabia, celebrating the Saudi conquest of the Hijaz in 1925, and defending the Wahhabis as 'the most zealous followers [of Islam] among the Muslim peoples of this age'.[21] Ibn 'Abd al-Wahhab, he said, had been the 'renewer' of his time, and it was thanks to him that the books of Ibn Taymiyya were read again,[22] while 'Abd al-'Aziz ibn Sa'ud (1875–1953), the founder of the Kingdom of Saudi Arabia, was the best hope for the unification of the Muslim peoples.[23]

The impact of this development on the modernist movement was profound. Though there were others who would carry forward the liberal elements in 'Abduh's thought, it was Rida's Salafi version of 'Abduh's modernism, disseminated throughout the Muslim world through the *Islamic Lighthouse*, which would reverberate the loudest through twentieth-century Islamic thought.

★

Outside of Egypt, many Muslim thinkers were confronting the same sorts of questions as 'Abduh and his disciples, such as the appropriate stance to take towards the medieval heritage, the role of Islam in politics, and the relationship with the West. Some, like the Muhammadiyya movement in Indonesia, or, at the other end of the Muslim world, the Association of Algerian Muslim Ulema, came under the direct influence of the 'Abduh movement.[24] Others, like the South Asian philosopher-poet Muhammad Iqbal (1877–1938), pursued a more independent course. Described by the novelist E.M. Forster (the author of *A Passage to India*) as a genius, Iqbal was perhaps the most original thinker in twentieth-century Islam.[25] A native of the Punjab, as a young man he studied Hegelian philosophy at Trinity College, Cambridge, was called to the bar at Lincoln's Inn, and submitted a thesis to the University of Munich on *The Development of Metaphysics in Persia* (1908), an attempt to interpret Persian thought (both pre-Islamic and Islamic) in the language of modern philosophy.[26]

On his return to India, Iqbal pursued a career as a barrister and achieved renown as a poet in Urdu and Persian. In 1922, he was knighted for his services to literature. Later, he would become involved in the politics of the subcontinent: while chairing the annual congress of the Muslim League at Allahabad in 1930, he floated the idea that the four north-western provinces of British-ruled India be constituted into a separate Muslim state – an idea for which he would come to be regarded as the spiritual founder and patron saint of Pakistan.[27]

Iqbal described poetry as 'the heir of prophecy' and saw himself as 'the voice of the poet of Tomorrow'.[28] His starting point was that of all reformers. Why, he asks in his Urdu poem *The Complaint* (*Shikwa*) (1909), has Allah abandoned Muslims and bestowed

His blessings on the unbelievers?[29] The answer, as so often, is that they have abandoned Islam. In *The Response to the Complaint* (*Jawab-i shikwa*) (1913), Iqbal has Allah castigate the Muslims for their idleness and complacency, their constant quarrelling and 'philosophizing', their aping of 'alien ways and civilizations'.[30]

In *The Secrets of the Self* (*Asrar-i khudi*) (1915), a Persian poem styled on Rumi's *Mathnawi*, Iqbal explains the philosophical basis of these ills. Muslims have been tricked by 'pantheistic' Sufis into renouncing the world and denying their 'selves'.[31] True Islam, by contrast, is a religion of assertiveness and vigorous action, of individuality and self-affirmation.[32] Allah has created man to be His deputy on earth, and this means strengthening the 'self' (*khud*), embracing conquest and dominion, and striving to 'create a new world' in partnership with God.[33] But it also means giving oneself over to love, which is essential to Islam, and crucial, Iqbal thought, to the development of the individual self.[34] And the perfection of the self, he explains in the follow-up poem *The Mysteries of Selflessness* (*Rumuz-i bikhudi*) (1918), can only be attained in the context of the ideal community. This is not the nation, but the worldwide community of Muslims, which Allah had created to be the 'seal' of communities just as He had created Muhammad to be the seal of prophets.[35]

Iqbal's influences were eclectic. His philosophy of self-assertion contained something of the Sufi idea of the perfect man, and something of Friedrich Nietzsche's notion of the Übermensch – though he rued the fact that the 'German genius', as he called Nietzsche, had stopped at the first half of the Islamic testament of faith: 'There is no god'.[36] Iqbal's call for a revived and united Muslim community owed something to al-Afghani.[37] His struggle for the revival of Islam in India took inspiration from the Mughal Emperor Awrangzeb and Shah Wali Allah.[38] The title of his *Reconstruction of Religious Thought in Islam*, a series of lectures delivered in 1928 in which he called on his coreligionists 'to rethink the whole system of Islam without completely breaking with the past', alluded to al-Ghazali's *Revival of the Religious Sciences*.[39]

His greatest hero, however, was Rumi. In the *Javidnama* (1932), his most celebrated Persian poem, Iqbal tells of how 'the Sage of Rum' led him through the celestial spheres and into the divine presence.[40] The poem brings together all of Iqbal's characteristic ideas, many of them articulated by characters taken from the history of Islam and other world religions. The doctrine of self-affirmation is put into the mouths of Rumi, the Buddha, and Zoroaster.[41] Mankind is celebrated as the divine viceregent, whose station is 'loftier than the heavens'.[42] Love is presented as the way to 'make an assault on the Infinite' and to know God.[43] Contemporary Muslims are criticized for not following true Islam: Satan appears in the poem in the form of 'drunkard and mullah, philosopher and Sufi'.[44] The *umma* is held up as the ideal community, transcending race and nationality: 'Give up this talk of Syria, Palestine, Iraq,' Iqbal has al-Afghani say.[45] Communism and capitalism are dismissed as morally bankrupt ideologies, and the West condemned for its covetous and exploitative colonialism: 'I will take nothing from Europe except – a warning!'[46]

Yet, as ever in Iqbal's poetry, the anger and assertiveness are tempered by a mysticism of love. 'Religion is love,' his Rumi declares;[47] 'God is more manifest in love,' he has the Sufi martyr al-Hallaj say. 'Love is a better way than violence.'[48]

★

In their anti-imperialism, their insistence on the political nature of Islam, and their advocacy of pan-Islamic union, Rida and Iqbal paved the way for one of the most important developments in twentieth-century Islam. This was the rise of Islamism, the doctrine that Islam is a political ideology, comparable (and superior) to socialism, fascism, or capitalism – a comprehensive, self-sufficient 'system' for ordering the modern world.

The godfather of Islamism was the Egyptian primary school teacher Hasan al-Banna (1906–49), the founder, in 1928, of the Society of the Muslim Brothers (*Jama'at al-Ikhwan al-Muslimin*). Al-Banna famously described the Muslim Brotherhood as 'a Salafi message, a Sufi way, a Sunni truth, a political organization, an athletic group, a cultural-educational union, an economic company, and a social idea'.[49] He viewed the Society as the practical, activist extension of the reformist tradition of al-Afghani, 'Abduh, and Rida.[50] Like them, he started from the problem of Muslim weakness, adopting the characteristically Salafi view that decline in the *umma* had set in early, right after the passing of the 'rightly guided caliphs' in the mid-seventh century, and had reached its nadir in modern times. The problems, as he saw them, were self-evident: the increasing secular-liberal drift and pervasive moral degeneracy of newly independent Egypt, the dismantling of the caliphate, and the spread of Western imperialism, Zionism, and communism.[51]

The cure that al-Banna prescribed was the age-old solution of a return to 'true' Islam. Inspired by the Salafis, he advocated going back to the Qur'an, and seeing the Islamic scripture for the political manifesto that he believed it was. 'The Qur'an is our constitution,' went the slogan of the Muslim Brotherhood. Islam, al-Banna declared, inverting the famous formula of the secularist 'Ali 'Abd al-Raziq, was 'a faith and a ritual, a nation and a nationality, a religion and a state'.[52]

In al-Banna's view, this political religion was meant for all of humanity, regardless of nationality or skin colour; the ultimate goal of the Brotherhood was to establish what al-Banna called the Islamic 'system' (nizam) across the globe.[53] This was to be achieved, he instructed his followers, through 'learning, education, and jihad' – in that order.[54] Before any other action was taken, Muslims had to be called back to the moral teachings of Islam through missionary work. A coffee-house preacher in his youth, from 1939 al-Banna would lecture on Islam every Tuesday evening at the Brotherhood's Cairo headquarters.[55] Armed struggle would come later. Al-Banna described jihad as 'the first and most sacred of the Islamic duties', while the Brothers' slogan concluded with the words 'Jihad is our path; death on the path of Allah is our hope'.[56] From the mid-1930s, this call to jihad was centred on the anti-Zionist struggle, the Brotherhood leadership declaring 'the jihad for Palestine' to be a duty incumbent on every Muslim.[57]

The Brotherhood's preaching and activism achieved considerable success. By the late 1940s, it could boast 4,000 branches and somewhere between 300,000 and 600,000 members in Egypt, drawn from all social classes.[58] Its missionary activity and pro-Palestinian activism helped spread al-Banna's message, too, into neighbouring Muslim countries, turning the Brotherhood into an international organization.[59] This success, and the fact that al-Banna condoned the use of violence, unnerved the Egyptian authorities. In December 1948, the Brotherhood was dissolved on the charge of plotting the overthrow of the established order by terrorist means. After a young Muslim

Brother assassinated the prime minister in retaliation, al-Banna was himself assassinated on 12 February 1949.[60]

His Islamist ideas, however, could not be so easily killed off. Parallel to the rise of al-Banna and the Muslim Brotherhood in Egypt, the career of another Islamist mastermind was taking off in the Indian subcontinent. This was Abu'l-A'la Mawdudi (1903–79), the founder of the Jama'at-i Islami (Islamic Society), the Brotherhood's South Asian counterpart.

The son of a graduate of the modernist college at Aligarh, Mawdudi earned his living as a journalist. Early in his career he wrote in support of the Khilafat movement – an Indian campaign to preserve the Ottoman caliphate in the wake of the First World War – and authored a series of articles on the permissibility of aggressive jihad. In 1932, he acquired a journal named *The Interpreter of the Qur'an* (*Tarjuman al-Qur'an*), which became his mouthpiece, as the *Lighthouse* had been for Rida. In 1941 he founded the Jama'at-i Islami. His most important work, begun the following year and taking thirty years to complete, was a monumental Urdu translation and commentary on the Qur'an – a testament to this adoption of the Salafi principle that 'everyone who is duly lettered must have his own, direct access to the Holy Qur'an and the Sunna'.[61]

Like al-Banna, Mawdudi insisted that Islam was essentially political. 'The chief characteristic of Islam,' he wrote, 'is that it makes no distinction between the spiritual and the secular life.'[62] In Islam, Mawdudi said, drawing upon an idea developed by the Khilafat movement, sovereignty (*hakimiyya*) belonged to Allah alone.[63] When the Qur'an spoke of Allah as 'Lord' (*rabb*), this meant that only God had the right to issue rules and regulations, and that humans were charged with 'exclusive and total submission' to

Allah and His laws.[64] The first goal of the Jama'at, therefore, was to establish what Mawdudi called a 'divine government' (*hukumat-i ilahi*), a caliphate in which the Shari'a was rigorously applied.[65] When Allah's sovereignty was acknowledged, all lending at interest would be banned; gender segregation would be enforced and women barred from public life; the religious and political freedoms of non-Muslims would be limited; and apostasy from Islam – including joining the 'unbelieving' Ahmadi movement – would be punished by death.[66]

If this was Islam, then everything else was *jahiliyya*. Rooted in the Qur'an, the term *jahiliyya* had traditionally been used to denote the so-called 'period of ignorance' prior to the coming of Islam. Building on Ibn Taymiyya and Ibn 'Abd al-Wahhab, Mawdudi transformed the concept into a timeless condition, a state of mind whose essence was the failure to acknowledge the sovereignty of Allah, and which could be found just as easily among nominal Muslims as among unbelievers. 'A Muslim is not a Muslim,' he said, 'by appellation or birth, but by virtue of abiding by holy law.'[67] *Jahiliyya*, he insisted, had been present throughout all of Islamic history since the passing of the rightly guided caliphs. It was present, too, in the 'polytheistic' popular religious practices and beliefs of the Sufis and Shi'a. And it was present, finally, in all political ideologies – nationalism and socialism, communism and fascism – in which humans, not Allah, were sovereign.[68]

Though in practice Mawdudi was something of a pragmatist, in theory his goal, as his female disciple, the Jewish convert Maryam Jameelah (1934–2012) put it, was nothing less than 'a total revolutionary break, with the medieval past and its so-called Muslim society'.[69] It was in Egypt, among the Muslim Brothers languishing in Gamal 'Abdel Nasser's prison camps, that the latent radicalism of Mawdudi's Islamist ideology would be actualized. At the centre of this group was Sayyid Qutb (1906–66). A one-time secular literary critic and employee of the Ministry of Education, in the late 1940s Qutb – enraged by European imperialism, Zionism, and the plight of the Egyptian poor – turned to Islamism, arguing in *Social Justice in Islam* (*al-'Adala al-ijtima'iyya fi'l-Islam*) (1948) that Islam provided a comprehensive programme for 'worship and human relations, government and economic policy, legislation and moral guidance, belief and behaviour, this world and the world to come'.[70][71]

In 1948 Qutb went to the United States, where he developed a repulsion to what he saw as the spiritual and moral bankruptcy of the West. On his return, he wrote books with titles like *The Battle Between Islam and Capitalism* (*al-Ma'raka bayn al-islam wa'l-ra'smaliyya*) and *Our Battle with the Jews* (*Ma'rakatuna ma'a al-yahud*), in which he identified the enemies of Islam as Western imperialists, the Egyptian state which trod on the backs of the poor, ulema who 'sold themselves, not to God, or the nation, but to Satan', 'brown English' and 'American Muslims' (meaning Egyptians who had adopted Western ideas), Western orientalists who distorted Islam, communists who advocated the abandonment of religion, and, behind them all, the Jews.[72]

At the same time, Qutb drew increasingly close to the Muslim Brotherhood. In March 1953 – four years after al-Banna's assassination – he formally joined the Society, becoming head of its propaganda section and editor of its weekly journal. 'No other movement,' he wrote, 'can stand up to the Zionists and the colonialist Crusaders.'[73] Along with the rest of the Brotherhood, he supported the Free Officers' Revolution of July 1952, which brought the secular Arab nationalist, and erstwhile ally of the Brotherhood, Gamal 'Abdel Nasser to power. When Nasser clamped down on the Brotherhood in October 1954, however, Qutb was arrested and condemned to fifteen years' hard labour in the notorious Tura prison.[74]

There he devoted himself to writing what were increasingly hardline Islamist texts. He wrote and revised *In the Shade of the Qur'an* (*Fi zilal al-Qur'an*), a commentary on the sacred text that was at once intensely personal and radically political. Rejecting both the scholasticism of the traditional exegetes and theologians and the West-oriented modernism of the 'Abduh school, Qutb told of how he had been blessed to 'hear Allah speak to me through this Qur'an'.[75] This unmediated access to the divine word, he believed, had enabled him to return to what he called 'the pure Muslim way of thinking, to the pure Arab mentality'.[76]

Adopting the ideas and terminology of Mawdudi, whose work he had read in Arabic translation, Qutb argued that in its purest form the Qur'anic message was revolutionary and political. 'The Noble Qur'an was revealed to the heart of God's Messenger,' he explained, in order to 'bring forth a community, found a state, [and] organize a society'.[77] This society would function – as it had in Muhammad's time – according to the principle that Allah alone was sovereign. Any system that recognized the sovereignty of someone or something other than Allah was a system of unbelief, or as Qutb put it, borrowing again from Mawdudi, *jahiliyya*.[78] Between Islam and *jahiliyya*, he insisted, there was no middle ground. 'Whoever does not desire the rule (*hukm*) of Allah desires the rule of *jahiliyya*, and whoever rejects the Shari'a of Allah accepts the Shari'a of *jahiliyya* and lives in *jahiliyya*.'[79] This starkly dualistic vision, a repudiation of the traditional 'middle way' approach of Sunnism, led Qutb to the view that even so-called Muslim societies were sunk in *jahiliyya*. Indeed, he asserted, 'we must include in this category all the societies that now exist on earth!'[80]

In *Signposts on the Path (al-Ma'alim fi'l-tariq)* (1964), a short tract summarizing his most radical ideas, Qutb outlined the way in which *jahiliyya* could be destroyed and replaced with Islam. The model, as always, was Muhammad and his companions. Just as Muhammad and the first Muslims had left pagan Mecca for Medina, Muslims had to begin by separating themselves, in mind and spirit if not in body, from godless society.[81] Secular slogans like 'national liberation' and 'social reform' had to be abandoned, and replaced with the Islamic credo that there was no god but Allah.[82] In Qutb's view, as soon as three believers came together under this banner, an Islamic society or 'vanguard' (*jama'a*) would be born. It was then that the true battle with *jahiliyya* would begin. Establishing the government of Allah, Qutb warned, would not happen through debate and discourse. Violent jihad would be needed.[83]

In Qutb's mind, of course, the archetypal *jahili* society was contemporary Egypt, led by the secularist tyrant Nasser. *Signposts*, smuggled out of prison and committed to memory by radicalized Muslim Brothers, was a subversive text, which encouraged the violent overthrow of the established order and jihad against fellow Muslims. Nasser, therefore, could not leave it unanswered. In 1966 his answer came, in the form of Qutb's execution and burial in a secret, unmarked grave.

★

Islamism was not a phenomenon confined to the Sunni world. In March 1979, following the overthrow of the Pahlavi Shah, 98 per cent of voters in Shi'i Iran elected to replace the monarchy with an Islamic republic – a system, the second article of the country's new constitution proclaimed, whose basis was the characteristic Islamist doctrine of the 'exclusive sovereignty' (*hakimiyyat*) of Allah.[84]

The leader of the Islamic Revolution, and chief ideologue of Shi'i Islamism, was Ayatollah Khomeini. Born in the central Iranian town of Khomein in 1902 into a family of Shi'i ulema recently returned from northern India, Khomeini – unlike al-Banna, Mawdudi, and Qutb – was a professional religious scholar, educated in the seminaries of Qom. Drawn to the mystical philosophy of Ibn 'Arabi and Mulla Sadra as well as to Shi'i legal theory, as a young man he earned renown for his lectures on Islamic ethics, displaying an uncommon ability to harmonize a mystical reading of Islam with a political interpretation of the faith.[85] In 1943 his first published book appeared. Titled *The Unveiling of Secrets* (*Kashf al-asrar*), it already featured Islamist themes. 'The only government that reason accepts as legitimate and welcomes freely and happily,' he wrote, 'is the government of God.'[86]

By the early 1960s, Khomeini was widely recognized as an Ayatollah (literally, a 'sign of God') and *Marja' al-taqlid* (a 'source of emulation'), titles reserved for those at the very top of the scholarly hierarchy of Twelver Shi'ism. In 1963, in response to the Shah's so-called 'White Revolution', a US-inspired programme of political, social, and economic reform, the Ayatollah began to denounce the Iranian regime with remarkable frankness and intensity. Under the guidance of the United States and Israel,

Khomeini alleged, the government sought 'to bring about the total effacement of the ordinances of Islam', while the Shah himself, Khomeini thundered on Ashura, the anniversary of the tragedy of Karbala, was the latest incarnation of Yazid, the tyrannical murderer of Husayn.[87]

Khomeini was arrested, sparking what would become known as the 15th Khordad Uprising, the beginnings of the organized Islamic movement against the Shah. When, in October 1964, Khomeini denounced a new law granting US personnel stationed in Iran immunity from prosecution, he was exiled, first to Turkey, then to the Shi'i shrine city of Najaf in Iraq. He continued, however, to attack what he called Iran's 'regime of terror and thievery', its servitude to 'the pseudo-state of Israel' and the 'lords of the dollar', and its willingness to finance a lavish celebration of the 2,500th anniversary of the Iranian monarchy while ordinary Iranians languished in poverty and hunger.

This populist rhetoric – which echoed the Marxist version of Islam being developed around the same time by Khomeini's compatriot 'Ali Shari'ati (1933–77) – was intermingled with more theoretical reflections on the nature of Islam.[88] In early 1970, Khomeini delivered a series of lectures on Islamic government in which he presented his Islamist doctrine in its ideal form. The enemies of Islam – Jews and crusaders, imperialists and orientalists – Khomeini alleged, had distorted Muslims' view of their own religion. While they restricted Islam to a corpus of ritual law, allowing 'systems of unbelief' to take hold in Iran and other Muslim countries, Islam was in fact an essentially political religion, a 'complete social system' whose scripture was principally concerned with sociopolitical and economic questions. The foundation of this system was the principle that

Allah alone was sovereign. Islamic government was nothing other than the rule of divine law over men.[89]

So far, so typical of Islamist ideology. Yet, at the heart of Khomeini's theory of Islamic government was an idea that was distinctively Shi'i. This was the doctrine of *vilayat-i faqih*, 'the governance of the jurist'. With the occultation of the Twelfth Imam, Khomeini argued, the political authority of the Shi'i Imams had devolved to the *fuqaha'*, the experts in Islamic law. It was the religious scholars who were duty-bound to lead the people in the jihad against the infidel regimes, to work towards the establishment of an Islamic government, and, once that had been achieved, to govern the Islamic state.[90]

With the Islamic Revolution of 1979, Khomeini's vision of Islamic government was realized. 'During the Occultation of the Lord of the Age [the Twelfth Imam],' Iran's new constitution declared, 'the governance and leadership of the nation devolve upon the just and pious jurist (*faqih*) who is acquainted with the circumstances of his age.'[91] Yet though his doctrine of *vilayat-i faqih* was distinctively Shi'i, Khomeini's ultimate vision was non-sectarian. Calling on his followers to export the revolution beyond Iran, he dreamt of a united Muslim world, freed from the shackles of the United States ('the Great Satan') and its allies and proxies, most of all Israel and Britain ('the Little Satan'). Indeed, he went further. On Valentine's Day 1989, Khomeini issued a fatwa calling on Muslims to kill British Indian author Salman Rushdie, on the alleged grounds that the latter's novel *The Satanic Verses* had besmirched Islam, the Prophet, and the Qur'an.[92] The implication was clear: for Khomeini, as for all Islamists, the sovereignty of Allah extended throughout the world.[93]

ISLAM
TODAY

The history of Islamic thought is a story with multiple narratives, interwoven yet distinct, mutually influential yet competing. From Sufis to Salafis, Shafi'is to Shi'a, Mu'tazila to Muslim Brothers, Muslim thinkers have produced many different answers to the major questions relating to God and man, this life and the next.

Intellectually stimulating and significant in their own right, these competing currents have also set the contours of contemporary Islam. Amid the diversity of Islamic thought in the late twentieth and early twenty-first centuries, three broad tendencies can be said to define contemporary Islam.[1]

First, there is what might be called 'neo-traditional Islam', that version of the faith that seeks continuity with the traditional Islam of the legal madhhabs, the schools of theology, and the Sufi orders. Its spokesmen are ulema – graduates of institutions like the al-Azhar in Cairo or the traditional Shi'i seminaries of Iraq and Iran – and members of conservative organizations like Indonesia's Nahdlatul Ulama (The Revival of the Scholars). For them, Islam is a theological doctrine, a moral code, and a spiritual teaching. Though they believe in the continued applicability of the Shari'a to the modern age, they do not think that the practice of Islam is conditional upon the establishment of an Islamic government, advocating loyalty to the modern nation-state as long as it grants Muslims freedom of worship, and deeming patriotism an Islamic virtue.[2] They tend to be socially conservative, condemning in their mosque sermons, online fatwas, and televised lectures such supposedly corrupting practices as the mixing of the sexes, homosexuality, and provocative films and music.[3] They are jealous of the sanctity of the Qur'an and the Prophet, committed to the universal truth of Islam, and sensitive to Western criticisms of Islam's treatment of women and its allegedly inherent violence.[4] At the same time, they are willing to engage in religious dialogue with representatives of the West's Christian heritage, with whom they share a belief in the spiritual crisis of modernity, and stress Islam's inherent tolerance and moderation.[5]

Then there is liberal Islam.[6] An extension of the open-minded, West-facing strand of Islamic modernism, its advocates are invariably university academics, doctors, or lawyers. Committed secularists, for them Islam is a matter of individual conscience and personal belief, not a system for regulating society.[7] It is a religion of modern values like human rights, religious pluralism, and gender equality – values, they believe, which can be uncovered in the Qur'an if the sacred text is properly interpreted.[8] Advocating what the Egyptian liberal Muhammad Sa'id al-'Ashmawi (1932–2013) called 'the temporality of Qur'anic rulings' (*waqtiyyat al-ahkam al-qur'aniyya*), they seek to limit the applicability of the Qur'an's teachings on jihad and polygamy, slavery and gender segregation to the seventh century, and to contrast those historically specific rulings with the Qur'an's eternal liberal principles.[9] As well as the nineteenth- and twentieth-century Muslim modernists, they seek inspiration from those elements of the Islamic intellectual heritage (*turath*) that are often marginalized in modern Islam – like the rationalism of the Mu'tazila and Ibn Rushd, or the spirituality of Ibn 'Arabi and Rumi – with the aim of showing that their liberalism is not simply borrowed from the West, but native to the Islamic tradition.[10]

Finally, there are those who make the most headlines: the Salafis and Islamists. Salafis, as we have seen, are those who advocate a return to the Qur'an and Sunna and the Islam of the *salaf al-salih* or 'pious predecessors'. Heirs to Ibn Taymiyya and Ibn 'Abd al-Wahhab, their main concern is purity of practice and belief. This means conceiving of Allah just as He has described Himself in the Qur'an; ridding the Sunna of all inauthentic Hadiths (even when they appear in such canonical collections as those of Bukhari and Muslim);[11] dressing and speaking, eating and praying just as the Prophet and his companions did; and shunning reprehensible innovations (*bid'a*) like visiting the tombs of the 'friends of Allah'.[12] Opposed to both neo-traditional and liberal Islam – and hostile to Sufism, Shi'ism, and non-Islamic religions – the Salafis are not merely content to practise Islam correctly themselves, but also seek to purify others' religious practice and belief.

They differ among themselves, however, over how to go about this.[13] At one end of the spectrum are the so-called quietist Salafis, like the prominent Syro-Albanian Hadith scholar Nasir al-Din al-Albani (1914–99) and the Wahhabi religious establishment in Saudi Arabia, who eschew political activity in favour of what they call 'purification and education' (*al-tazkiya wa'l-tarbiya*).[14] Further along the spectrum are those Salafis who advocate changing society through political action. They include Islamist societies like the Muslim Brotherhood and its sister organizations, Salafi political parties like Egypt's Hizb an-Nour (Party of Light), and ulema connected to what has been called the 'Islamic awakening' (*al-sahwa al-islamiyya*), such as the Qatar-based, Muslim Brotherhood-affiliated cleric Yusuf al-Qaradawi (b. 1926), widely regarded as the most influential Sunni Muslim scholar alive today. Committed to advancing 'the Islamic solution' (*al-hall al-islami*) to all social and political problems, and bitterly hostile to secularism, Israel, and the West, they are generally willing to work within the established order, with the ultimate aim of replacing that order with an Islamic one.[15]

At the far end of the spectrum, finally, are Salafi-jihadis like al-Qaeda and ISIS (the Islamic State of Iraq and Syria). They advocate the revolutionary overthrow of the existing order through violent jihad, and its replacement with a global caliphate.[16] In their view, jihad is essential to Islamic piety and belief, an obligation binding on all Muslims, and, as the influential Palestinian jihadi ideologue 'Abdallah 'Azzam (1941–89) put it, 'the most excellent form of worship'.[17] They root this position in the Verse of the Sword and other militant Qur'anic verses and Hadiths, rejecting the notion that the 'greater jihad' is the spiritual struggle against one's own self.[18] Having grown out of the radical wing of the Muslim Brotherhood, the Salafi-jihadis regard themselves as heirs to Sayyid Qutb.[19] Like Qutb, they make belief in the exclusive sovereignty (*hakimiyya*) of Allah central to Islamic monotheism, and condemn all other political doctrines as *jahiliyya*.[20] Inspired by their reading of Ibn Taymiyya, they are strong advocates of *takfir* (pronouncing other Muslims unbelievers) and the principle of *al-wala' wa'l-bara'* ('loyalty' towards true believers, and the 'disavowal' of unbelievers).[21] They label secularist Muslims, the Shi'a, and rulers of Muslim countries as apostates, scholars who support the incumbent regimes as 'clerics of evil', democracy as 'the tribulation of this age', and the West as 'the Judeo-crusading alliance'.[22] All of these groups, they think, can and should be legitimately fought and killed.[23]

Though rooted in a certain interpretation of the Qur'an and Hadith, these jihadi views are not representative of broader Islamic opinion. Thinkers from across the Islamic spectrum – Sunnis and Shi'a, liberals and neo-traditionalists, Sufis and Wahhabis – have come out strongly against the Salafi-jihadis and their radical Islamist ideology, dismissing ideas like the *jahiliyya* of the present age and the sovereignty of Allah as a perversion of the teachings of Islam, denouncing members of jihadist groups like al-Qaeda and ISIS as heretics, and declaring the battle against them to be a holy struggle.[24] As for the Taliban, who as this book goes to press have just returned to power in Afghanistan, they represent a slightly different form of radical Islamism. Though they are close to al-Qaeda and share the Salafi-jihadis' commitment to jihad and deep hostility to Shi'ism and secularism, their militant puritanism is rooted not in Salafism but in the Deobandi tradition of South Asia, their name denoting their background as 'students' (*taliban*) of the Deobandi madrasas of southern Afghanistan and Pakistan.

The debates of the twenty-first century are just the latest instalment in an age-old struggle to define Islam. That struggle, of course, is one for Muslims themselves to resolve. As a wise scholar of Islam once wrote, 'Islam in the end must be what Muslims say it is.'[25] Yet such is the nature of our modern world that their interpretations, perhaps more than ever before, will affect almost everyone, everywhere. Insofar as those interpretations will inevitably be influenced by the views of their predecessors, it is clear that the history of Islamic thought matters, and that it matters to us all.

ACKNOWLEDGEMENTS

The journey towards writing this book began during my schooldays, when I started learning Arabic under the guidance of Haroon Shirwani. For sparking my passion for Arab-Islamic culture, I owe so much to Haroon. Around the same time, I was first exposed to the culture of the Persian world by Bijan Omrani, while Henry Proctor, Gareth Mann, and Andrew Robinson taught me how to write history.

I received my formal academic training in Arabic, Persian, and Islamic Studies at Oxford. I was very fortunate to be trained there in the rather old-fashioned approach of reading texts closely and slowly in the original languages. In Arabic, I was immensely lucky to be taught by Nadia Jamil, Otared Haider, Taj Kandoura, Geert Jan van Gelder, Mohamed-Salah Omri, and Clive Holes. In Persian, I benefited from the instruction of Pouneh Shabani-Jadidi, Sahba Shayani, Arezou Azad, and Dominic Brookshaw, and, informally, from the guidance of Ali Mir-Ansari and my good friend Ufuk Öztürk. Time spent at the Institut Français du Proche-Orient in Beirut and the Dehkhoda Institute in Tehran hugely improved my Arabic and Persian language skills, while the generosity of Adil Dajani and the British-Kuwaiti Friendship Society enabled formative trips to Morocco and Kuwait. Allison Shaw introduced me to Urdu with some memorable lessons at the Oxford Centre for Islamic Studies. In Islamic history, I learnt much from Nicola Clarke, Talal al-Azm, Marie Legendre, Robert Hoyland, and Nassima Neggaz. My study of the Islamic religion began under Christopher Melchert, a caring and inspirational tutor at Pembroke College. As the notes to this book show, I have remained highly indebted to his work. Later I studied Qur'an and Islamic theology and philosophy with Nicolai Sinai, another very kind and thoughtful teacher. My real teacher in the history of Islamic thought, however, has been Ron Nettler. From 2013 till the present day, Ron has guided me, on an almost weekly basis, through the great texts and trends of medieval and modern Islam. Though he, like the other teachers mentioned, bears no responsibility for its judgements and inevitable errors, this book is to a large extent the result of that guidance.

While writing my doctorate in Sufi thought I was extremely fortunate to be elected to an Examination Fellowship at All Souls College, Oxford. The fellowship provided the perfect opportunity to write a book like this; indeed, I feel sure that I wouldn't – and couldn't – have written it otherwise. My admiration for the Warden and Fellows of the college knows no bounds, and I thank them for their continued faith in me, and the college staff for their constant support for us all. I owe a particular debt of thanks to Sir Noel Malcolm, my academic advisor at the college, who has not only provided a model for how to write intellectual history but has also made several helpful suggestions for this project. Thanks as well to the Very Revd John Drury, whose virtual chapel services helped me get through during the difficult days of 'lockdown'. Beyond the college, I have benefited from conversations with my colleagues Bishop Michael Nazir-Ali, Christian Sahner, and Usaama al-Azami.

The idea for this book was Georgina Capel's. George has been a great enthusiast for the project from start to finish, and wonderfully helpful in getting it into the hands of two amazing publishers. At Head of Zeus and OUP, I have been lucky to have Neil Belton and Tim Bent as my editors. Their incisive observations have hugely improved the final product, while Matilda Singer has done a marvellous job in seeing the book through to publication.

Nothing, not least a project this ambitious, would be possible without my family. To my parents Richard and Helena, my eight wonderful siblings (Flo, Tuppy, Millie, Clara, Oki, Theo, Cecily, and Bea), my grandparents Jackie, Tony, Noel, and Carmel, my parents-in-law Marilena and Johannes, and my perfect wife Dyedra, I can only express my thanks and love.

Endnotes

Preface

1 Mahmud Shaltut, *al-Islam: 'aqida wa-shari'a* (Cairo, 1959), 7.

2 D.Z.H. Baneth, 'What did Muḥammad mean when he called his religion "Islam"?' (*Israel Oriental Studies*, 1971).

3 William Graham, 'Scripture' (*Encyclopedia of Religion*, 2005).

4 W.C. Smith, *Islam in Modern History* (Princeton, 1957), 17, n. 13; *idem*, 'Some Similarities and Differences between Christianity and Islam', in James Kritzeck & R. Bayly Winder (eds.), *The World of Islam* (London, 1959), 57–8.

5 S.D. Goitein, *Studies in Islamic History and Institutions* (Leiden, 1967), 8.

6 Miriam Meyerhoff, *Introducing Sociolinguistics* (London, 2011), 114–15.

7 Bryan Turner, *Weber and Islam* (London, 1974), 138.

8 Sachiko Murata & William C. Chittick, *The Vision of Islam* (London, 2006), 42.

9 Katib Çelebi, *The Balance of Truth* (London, 1957), 118.

10 Nasr Hamid Abu Zayd, 'Towards understanding the Qur'ān's worldview', in Gabriel S. Reynolds (ed.), *New Perspectives on the Qur'an* (London, 2011), 48.

11 Cf. Ignaz Goldziher, *Muslim Studies* (London, 1967), II:255.

12 Cf. Muhammad 'Abid al-Jabiri, *The Formation of Arab Reason* (London, 2011).

13 Marshall Hodgson, *The Venture of Islam* (Chicago, 1974), I:159.

14 Michael Cook, *Ancient Religions, Modern Politics* (Princeton, 2014), xi.

15 Noel Malcolm, *Useful Enemies* (Oxford, 2019), xiii.

1. The Word of Allah

1 Translations from the Qur'an are inspired by Yusuf Ali, *The Holy Qur'an* (Birmingham, 1946); N.J. Dawood, *The Koran* (London, 2014).

2 Cf. Sean Anthony, *Muhammad and the Empires of Faith* (Oakland, 2020), ch. 7.

3 William Montgomery Watt et al., 'Makka' (*Encyclopaedia of Islam, Second Edition* [hereafter *EI²*]); Maxime Rodinson, *Muhammad* (London, 1971), 38.

4 Nadia Jamil, *Ethics and Poetry in Sixth-Century Arabia* (Cambridge, 2017), 339.

5 Alan Jones, *Early Arabic Poetry* (Reading, 1992), I:69–70.
6 Robert Hoyland, 'The Jews of the Hijaz in the Qur'an and their Inscriptions', in Gabriel S. Reynolds (ed.), *The Qur'an in its Historical Context 2* (London, 2011).
7 Anthony, 19.
8 D.B. MacDonald, 'Ilāh' (*EI²*); Toshihiko Izutsu, *God and Man in the Koran* (Tokyo, 1964), 106.
9 M.J. Kister, '*Al-Taḥannuth*: an enquiry into the meaning of a term' (*Bulletin of the School of Oriental and African Studies*, 1968).
10 Ma'mar ibn Rashid, *The Expeditions* (New York, 2015), 10.
11 Ibn Ishaq, *al-Sira al-nabawiyya* (Beirut, 2004), 169.
12 Goldziher, *Muslim Studies*, I:243f.
13 Nicolai Sinai, *The Qur'an* (Edingburgh, 2017), 11.
14 Abu Zayd, 'Towards understanding', 47.
15 Angelika Neuwirth, 'Qur'anic Readings of the Psalms', in *eadem* et al. (eds.), *The Qur'ān in Context* (Leiden, 2010).
16 Al-Nisa'i, *Tafsir* (Beirut, 1990), II:570 (Q 112:1); al-Baydawi, *Anwar al-tanzil wa-asrar al-ta'wil* (Beirut, 1998), V:347 (Q 112:1).

17 Josef van Ess, *Theology and Society in the Second and Third Centuries of the Hijra* (Leiden, 2017–20), IV:407.
18 Gabriel S. Reynolds, *The Qur'ān & the Bible* (New Haven, 2018), 775.
19 Sinai, 143–53.
20 Daud Rahbar, *God of Justice* (Leiden, 1960), 40ff.
21 Toshihiko Izutsu, *Ethico-Religious Concepts in the Qur'ān* (Montreal, 1966), 119.
22 Goldziher, *Muslim Studies*, I:201–8; Izutsu, *God and Man*, 222–35.
23 Mohammed Arkoun, *Lectures du Coran* (Paris, 1982), 111.
24 Fred M. Donner, *Muhammad and the Believers* (Cambridge, Mass., 2010), 68–74.
25 Reynolds, *Qur'ān*, 146–7.
26 Al-Baydawi, IV:229–30 (Q 33:26).
27 Goitein, *Studies*, chs. 3–5.
28 Bernard Lewis, *The Jews of Islam* (Princeton, 1984), 14–16.
29 Donner, 83–4.
30 Muhammad Abdel Haleem, *Understanding the Qur'an* (London, 1999), 52–6.
31 Al-Baydawi, II:73 (Q 4:34); Ali, *Holy Qur'an*, 190.
32 Eric Ormsby, 'The Koran' (*Standpoint*, 2008).
33 Sinai, 202–5.

2. Heirs to the Prophets

1 van Ess, *Theology*, I:3; Anthony, 35.
2 F.E. Peters, *Muhammad and the Origins of Islam* (Albany, 1994), 255.
3 Patricia Crone, 'On the Meaning of the 'Abbasid Call to *al-Riḍā*',

in C.E. Bosworth et al. (eds.), *The Islamic World* (Princeton, NJ, 1997).
4 Hugh Kennedy, *The Prophet and the Age of the Caliphates* (London, 2016), 144.

5 Bernard Lewis, *The Political Language of Islam* (Chicago, 1988), 53–6; Patricia Crone, *Medieval Islamic Political Thought* (Edinburgh, 2004), 44–7.

6 Patricia Crone & Martin Hinds, *God's Caliph* (Cambridge, 1986), 26–8, 116–26; S.D. Goitein, 'The School of Oriental Studies', in W.M. Brinner & Moses Rischlin (eds.), *Like All the Nations?* (Albany, 1987), 171.

7 Hugh Kennedy, *The Caliphate* (London, 2016), 54, 11.

8 Norman Calder, 'The Significance of the Term *Imām* in Early Islamic Jurisprudence' (*Zeitschrift für Geschichte der Arabisch-Islamischen Wissenschaft*, 1984).

9 Crone & Hinds, 43–57.

10 Malik, *Muwatta'* (Tunis, 1863), 342.

11 Hamza Yusuf (tr.), *The Creed of Imam al-Ṭaḥāwī* (Berkeley, 2007), 54–5.

12 Al-Tabari, *The Reunification of the 'Abbāsid Caliphate* (Albany, 1987), 205–7.

13 Josef van Ess, *The Flowering of Muslim Theology* (Cambridge, Mass., 2006), 9.

14 Martin Hinds, 'Miḥna' (*EI²*).

15 van Ess, *Theology*, I:45ff.

16 Hodgson, *Venture*, I:316–17; Christopher Melchert, 'The Etiquette of Learning in the Early Islamic Study Circle', in Claude Gilliot (ed.), *Education and Learning in the Early Islamic Study Circle* (Abingdon, 2012), 44.

17 Noel Coulson, *A History of Islamic Law* (Edinburgh, 1964), 12; cf. Goitein, *Studies*, 127–8.

18 Ibn al-Nadim, *Fihrist* (New York, 1970), I:494.

19 Umar Abd-Allah, *Mālik and Medina* (Leiden, 2013), 33–4; Joseph Schacht, 'Mālik ibn Anas' (*EI²*).

20 Yasin Dutton, *The Origins of Islamic Law* (Richmond, 1999), 4.

21 Patricia Crone, 'Mawlā' (*EI²*); Goldziher, *Muslim Studies*, I:101ff.

22 Joseph Schacht, 'Aṣḥāb al-Ra'y' (*EI²*).

23 Joseph Schacht, *The Origins of Muhammadan Jurisprudence* (Oxford, 1950), 27–33, 269ff., 294ff.; idem, 'Abū Ḥanīfa' (*EI²*); idem, 'Abū Yūsuf' (*EI²*).

24 Eerik Dickinson, *The Development of Early Sunnite Ḥadīth Criticism* (Leiden, 2001), 2.

25 Fakhr al-Din al-Razi, *Manaqib al-Imam al-Shafi'i* (Cairo, 1986), 34–7; Eric Chaumont, 'al-<u>Sh</u>āfi'ī' (*EI²*).

26 Al-Razi, *Manaqib*, 51–2.

27 Robert Brunschwig, 'Polémiques autour du rite de Mālik' (Al-Andalus, 1950), 389.

28 Al-Razi, *Manaqib*, 54–5; al-Shafi'i, *Kitab al-Umm* (al-Mansura, 2001), VIII:513ff.

29 Al-Shafi'i, *al-Umm*, IX:57.

30 Al-Shafi'i, *The Epistle on Legal Theory* (New York, 2015), 64–5.

31 Schacht, *Origins*, 15–16, 135.

32 Al-Shafi'i, *al-Umm*, IX:67–8.

33 Schacht, *Origins*, 122–4; Yasin Dutton, *Original Islam* (Abingdon,

2007), 36; Wael Hallaq, *The Origins and Evolution of Islamic Law* (Cambridge, 2004), 117–18.

34 Al-Razi, *Manaqib*, 156; al-Shafi'i, *Epistle*, xv.

35 Christopher Melchert, *Ahmad ibn Hanbal* (Oxford, 2006), 1–6.

36 Al-Razi, *Manaqib*, 60ff.

37 Joseph Schacht, 'Ahl al-Ḥadīth' (*EI²*).

38 Goldziher, *Muslim Studies*, II:165.

39 Christopher Melchert, *The Formation of the Sunni Schools of Law* (Leiden, 1997), 25–6; *idem, Ahmad*, 73.

40 Melchert, *Ahmad*, 19.

41 *Ibid.*, 16; Thomas Arnold, *The Preaching of Islam* (London, 1913), 74.

42 Rudolf Otto, *The Idea of the Holy* (London, 1923); Hodgson, *Venture*, I:397.

43 Gershom Scholem, *Major Trends in Jewish Mysticism* (New York, 1974), 4; Christopher Melchert, 'Origins and Early Sufism', in Lloyd Ridgeon (ed.), *Cambridge Companion to Sufism* (Cambridge, 2014), 14.

44 Christopher Melchert, *Hadith, Piety, and Law* (Atlanta, 2015), 169–70.

45 Al-Kalabadhi, *Kitab al-Ta'arruf li-madhhab ahl al-tasawwuf* (Cairo, 1933), 5; al-Sarraj, *Kitab al-Luma'* (Leiden, 1913), 21; Ibn Khaldun,

The Muqaddimah (London, 1958), III:77.

46 Ibn Khaldun, III:76.

47 Al-Kalabadhi, 6; Melchert, 'Origins', 6, 11; Melchert, *Hadith*, 171; Alexander Knysh, *Sufism* (Princeton, 2018), 18, 20–21.

48 Melchert, 'Origins', 8.

49 'Attar, *The Tadhkiratu 'l-awliya'* (London, 1905–7), 59.

50 Al-Makki, *Qut al-qulub* (Cairo, 2001), 1067; Margaret Smith, *Rabi'a the Mystic and Her Fellow-Saints in Islam* (Cambridge, 1928), 102.

51 Al-Sarraj, *al-Luma'*, 391.

52 Al-Sarraj, *Pages from the Kitāb al-Luma'* (London, 1947), 5–6.

53 Al-Tustari, *Tafsir* (Cairo, 2004), 161; al-Sarraj, *al-Luma'*, 383–4.

54 Goiten, *Studies*, 228.

55 Christian Sahner, '"The Monasticism of My Community is Jihad"' (*Arabica*, 2017).

56 Al-Sarraj, *al-Luma'*, 5; al-Sulami, *Tabaqat al-sufiyya* (Cairo, 1986), 2.

57 Melchert, *Hadith*, 132.

58 Ali Abdel-Kader, *The Life, Personality and Writings of al-Junayd* (London, 1962), 30–1.

59 Melchert, *Hadith*, 133–7.

60 Al-Junayd, *Rasa'il* (Cairo, 1988), 58.

61 Al-Subki, *Tabaqat al-shafi'iyya al-kubra* (Cairo, 1964–76), II:263.

3. Defenders of Islam

1 Nancy Khalek, *Damascus after the Muslim Conquest* (New York, 2011); Michael Morony, *Iraq after the Muslim Conquest* (Princeton, 1984), pt. III.

2 Oleg Grabar, 'The Umayyad Dome of the Rock in Jerusalem' (*Ars Orientalis*, 1959), 53–5; *idem, The Formation of Islamic Art* (New Haven, 1987), 61–6.

3 Khalek, ch. 3; van Ess, *Theology*, I:15–21.

4 Bernard Lewis, *Islam* (Oxford, 1974), 219–23; Milka Levy-Rubin, *Non-Muslims in the Early Islamic Empire* (Cambridge, 2011).

5 Anthony, 42, 57.

6 St John of Damascus, *Writings* (New York, 1958), 153–60; Andrew Louth, *St John Damascene* (Oxford, 2002), 75–80; Daniel Sahas, *John of Damascus on Islam* (Leiden, 1972).

7 van Ess, *Flowering*, 2.

8 Josef van Ess, 'Mu'tazila' (*Encyclopedia of Religion*, 2005); Sarah Stroumsa, 'The Beginnings of the Mu'tazila Reconsidered' (*Jerusalem Studies in Arabic and Islam*, 1990).

9 Al-Ash'ari, *Kitab Maqalat al-islamiyyin* (Istanbul, 1929), 86.

10 *Ibid.*, 138; Michael Cook, *Early Muslim Dogma* (Cambridge, 1981).

11 Al-Shahrastani, *al-Milal wa'l-nihal* (London, 1842–6), 33.

12 van Ess, 'Mu'tazila'.

13 Al-Ash'ari, *Maqalat*, 188; al-Shahrastani, 30; Albert Nader, *Falsafat al-Mu'tazila* (Alexandria, 1950–1), I:46, 57.

14 Louis Gardet & Georges Anawati, *Introduction à la théologie musulmane* (Paris, 1948), 37; van Ess, *Theology*, I:31; Ignaz Goldziher, *Introduction to Islamic Theology and Law* (Princeton, 1981), 71.

15 William Montgomery Watt, *Free Will and Predestination in Early Islam* (London, 1948), 20ff.

16 *Ibid.*, 48–9.

17 van Ess, *Theology*, III:48ff.

18 George Hourani, *Islamic Rationalism* (Oxford, 1971), 10–11.

19 Al-Tabari, *The Zenith of the Marwānid House* (Albany, 1990), 207.

20 van Ess, *Flowering*, 31.

21 *Ibid.*, 5.

22 Ibn Khaldun, III:49.

23 van Ess, 'Mu'tazila'.

24 Richard Walzer, *L'éveil de la philosophie islamique* (Paris, 1971), 25; Sebastian Brock, 'From antagonism to assimilation', in *idem, Syriac Perspectives on Greek Learning* (London, 1984).

25 Dimitri Gutas, *Greek Thought, Arabic Culture* (London, 1998), 34–45.

26 Christopher Shields, 'Aristotle' (*Stanford Encyclopaedia of Philosophy*).

27 Christian Wildberg, 'Neoplatonism' (*Stanford Encyclopaedia of Philosophy*).

28 Gutas, 96–104.

29 Ibn Khaldun, III:249.

30 Cristina D'Ancona, 'Greek Sources in Arabic and Islamic Philosophy' (*Stanford Encyclopaedia of Philosophy*).

31 Paul Kraus, 'Plotin chez les Arabes' (*Bulletin de l'Institut d'Égypte*, 1941); Peter Adamson, *The Arabic Plotinus* (London, 2002).

32 Gutas, 130–1; Goitein, *Studies*, 236–7; Kennedy, *The Prophet*, 220.

33 Hugh Kennedy, *The Caliphate*, 147–8.

34 Gutas, 13; Goitein, *Studies*, 57.

35 Ibn Khallikan, *Kitab Wafayat al-a'yan* (Paris, 1842–71), I:478.

36 Ibn al-Nadim, 615; Peter Adamson, *al-Kindi* (New York, 2007), 4–6.

37 Sa'id al-Andalusi, *Kitab Tabaqat al-umam* (Beirut, 1912), 52.

38 Al-Kindi, *Rasa'il al-Kindi al-falsafiyya* (Cairo, 1950), I:97, 103.

39 *Ibid.*, 98.

40 *Ibid.*, 105.

41 Adamson, 74–105; Richard Walzer, *Greek into Arabic* (Oxford, 1962), 187–96; Herbert Davidson, *Proofs for Eternity, Creation, and the Existence of God* (New York, 1987), 106–16.

4. The Sunni Compromise

1 Tim Winter, *Understanding the Four Madhhabs* (1999) (http://www.masud.co.uk/ISLAM/ahm/newmadhh.htm).

2 Al-Ash'ari, *Maqalat*, 3.

3 Al-Shahrastani, 12.

4 Ibn al-Nadim, 436.

5 Al-Ash'ari, *Maqalat*, 458–9; Dickinson, 121–3.

6 H.A.R. Gibb, *Studies on the Civilization of Islam* (London, 1962), chs. 8–9.

7 Goldziher, *Muslim Studies*, II:ch. 8; Jonathan Brown, *Hadith* (Oxford, 2009); *idem*, *The Canonization of al-Bukhari and Muslim* (Leiden, 2007).

8 Ignaz Goldziher, *The Ẓāhirīs* (Leiden, 1971), 33, n. 56.

9 Al-Shirazi, *al-Luma'* (Bahrain, 2013), 82.

10 *Ibid.*, 82–3; Hodgson, *Venture*, I:338.

11 Melchert, *Formation*.

12 Ibn Khaldun, III:31.

13 Goldziher, *Ẓāhirīs*, 66; *idem*, *Muslim Studies*, II:78.

14 Yasin Dutton, "'Amal vs Hadith in Islamic Law' (*Islamic Law and Society*, 1996).

15 Ibn Rushd, *The Distinguished Jurist's Primer* (Reading, 2000), I:98–9.

16 Goldziher, *Muslim Studies*, II:173; George Makdisi, 'Autograph Diary of an Eleventh-Century Historian of Baghdād I' (*Bulletin of the School of Oriental and African Studies*, 1956), 13–16.

17 A.C.S. Peacock, *Early Seljūq History* (London, 2010), 110; R.W. Bulliet, 'The Political-Religious History of Nishapur in the Eleventh Century', in D.S. Richards (ed.), *Islamic Civilisation 950–1150* (Oxford, 1973), 80–5.

18 Melchert, *Formation*, 54ff.; Hallaq, *Origins and Evolution*, 127; *idem*, 'Was al-Shafi'i the Master Architect of Islamic Jurisprudence?' (*International Journal of Middle East Studies*, 1993), 598; George Makdisi, *The Rise of Colleges* (Edinburgh, 1981), 8–9.

19 Goldziher, *Ẓāhirīs*, 89ff.

20 Hodgson, *Venture*, I:333, n. 6.

21 George Makdisi, *Ibn 'Aqil* (Edinburgh, 1997), 21.

22 Edward Badeen, *Sunnitische Theologie in Osmanischer Zeit* (Würzburg, 2008), 78.

23 S.D. Goitein, *A Mediterranean Society* (Berkeley, 1967), II:5–6.

24 Schacht, *Origins*, 128, 258–9; Melchert, *Formation*, 74.

25 Ibn 'Asakir, *Tabyin kadhb al-muftari fima nusiba ila al-imam Abi 'l-Hasan al-Ash'ari* (Damascus, 1928), 40.

26 Al-Ash'ari, *al-Ibana 'an usul al-diyana* (Hyderabad, 1843), 8.

27 Ibn Khallikan, II:227; al-Ash'ari, *al-Ibana*, 5.

28 Al-Ash'ari, *The Theology of al-Ash'arī* (Beirut, 1953), 93.

29 *Ibid.*, 87.

30 Ibn al-Nadim, 451; Ibn Khallikan, II:228 [adapted].

31 Al-Ash'ari, *al-Ibana*, 24–5.

32 *Ibid.*, 13–23; Ibn Furak, *Mujarrad maqalat al-Ash'ari* (Beirut, 1987), 82.

33 Al-Ash'ari, *Theology*, 39.

34 Frank Griffel, *Al-Ghazālī's Philosophical Theology* (New York, 2009), 124–8.

35 Daniel Gimaret, *Théories de l'acte humain en théologie musulmane* (Paris, 1982), 79–85; Goitein, *Studies*, 248–9.

36 Hasan al-Shafi'i, *al-Madkhal ila dirasat 'ilm al-kalam* (Karachi, 1989), 80.

37 Sohaira Zaid Siddiqui, *Law and Politics under the 'Abbasids* (Cambridge, 2019), pt. 3.

38 Ibn Khallikan, II:671.

39 Ibn Khaldun, III:51, 13.

40 Georges Vajda, 'Le témoignage d'al-Māturīdī sur la doctrine des Manichéens, des Daysanites et des Marcionites' (*Arabica*, 1966); Ulrich Rudolph, *al-Māturīdī and the Development of Sunnī Theology in Samarqand* (Leiden, 2013), ch. 5.

41 Rudolph, 291–6.

42 George Hourani, *Reason and Tradition in Islamic Ethics* (Cambridge, 1985), ch. 5.

43 Rudolph, 231, 265, 297–8.

44 *Ibid.*, 304–8, 212; Wilferd Madelung, 'al-Māturidī' (*EI²*); Gimaret, 175ff.

45 Wilferd Madelung, 'The Spread of Māturīdism and the Turks', in *idem, Religious Schools and Sects in Medieval Islam* (London, 1985); Rudolph, 2–3, 7.

46 Hujwiri, *The Kashf al-mahjúb* (Leiden, 1911), 151.

47 Louis Massignon, *The Passion of al-Hallaj* (Princeton, 1982).

48 Al-Sarraj, *al-Luma'*, 15.

49 *Ibid.*, 103.

50 Al-Qushayri, *al-Risala al-Qushayriyya* (Beirut, 2001), 51.

51 Al-Sarraj, *al-Luma'*, 10.

52 Al-Sulami, 155; al-Qushayri, *al-Risala*, 50; al-Sarraj, *al-Luma'*, 10; al-Kalabadhi, 56.

53 Al-Sarraj, *al-Luma'*, 74, 81; al-Kalabadhi, 14–16, 18, 20, 23; al-Qushayri, *al-Risala*, 19, 20, 382; Hujwiri, 28–9.

54 Al-Sarraj, *al-Luma'*, 2.

55 *Ibid.*, 422–7; Hujwiri, 131, 260.

56 Al-Sarraj, *al-Luma'*, 23–4.

57 *Ibid.*, 72–92, 105–11; al-Tustari, 157–8 (Q 8:72); al-Qushayri, *Lata'if al-isharat* (Cairo, 2000), II:564 (Q 22:78).

58 Al-Sarraj, *al-Luma'*, 41–72; al-Kalabadhi, 61; al-Qushayri, *al-Risala*, 91–2.

59 Hujwiri, 210ff.

60 Al-Sarraj, *al-Luma'*, 267–300.

5. The Shi'i Vision

1 Al-Nu'mani, *Kitab al-Ghayba* (Qom, 2013), 69.

2 Najam Haider, *Shi'i Islam* (Cambridge, 2014), 36.

3 Goldziher, *Muslim Studies*, II:113; Haider, 34.

4 Etan Kohlberg, 'The Term *Muhaddath* in Twelver Shī'ism', in *Studia Orientalia Memoriae D.H. Baneth Dedicata* (Jerusalem, 1979).

5 Mohammad Ali Amir-Moezzi, *The Divine Guide in Early Shi'ism* (Albany, 1994), 16–17, 69–79; Said Amir Arjomand, 'The Crisis of the Imamate and the Institution of Occultation in Early Shi'ism' (*International Journal of Middle East Studies*, 1996), 497.

6 Amir-Moezzi, *Divine Guide*, 24.

7 *Ibid.*, 79–91; Etan Kohlberg, 'Some Notes on the Imāmite Attitude to the Qur'ān', in Samuel Stern et al. (eds.), *Islamic Philosophy and the Classical Tradition* (Oxford, 1972); Meir Bar-Asher, 'Variant Readings and Additions of the Imāmī-ši'a to the Quran' (*Israel Oriental Studies*, 1993).

8 Goldziher, *Introduction*, 72 (adapted).

9 Najam Haider, 'Zaydism: A Theological and Political Survey' (*Religion Compass*, 2010).

10 Al-Nawbakhti, *Firaq al-Shi'a* (Beirut: 2012), 114–15; Farhad Daftary, *The Ismā'īlīs* (Cambridge, 2007), 88–90.

11 Amir-Moezzi, *Divine Guide*, 113–14.

12 Etan Kohlberg, 'From Imāmiyya to Ithnā-'Ashariyya' (*Bulletin of the School of Oriental and African Studies*, 1976), 522; Ignaz Goldziher, *Abhandlungen zur arabische Philologie* (Leiden, 1896–9), II:lxiiff.; Ibn Babawayh, *Kamal al-din wa-tamam al-ni'ma* (Qom, 2008), I:134–5.

13 Al-Nu'mani, 68; Kohlberg, 'From Imāmiyya', 525–8; Said Amir Arjomand, 'The Consolation of Theology' (*The Journal of Religion*, 1996), 552.

14 Ibn Babawayh, I:435–6.

15 Al-Nu'mani, 145.

16 Said Amir Arjomand, *The Shadow of God and the Hidden Imam* (Chicago, 1984), 61–2.

17 Al-Mufid, *Tashih al-i'tiqadat* (Qom, 1992), 137.

18 Ibn Babawayh, I:70.

19 Hossein Modarressi Tabataba'i, *An Introduction to Shī'ī Law* (London, 1984), 5; Amir-Moezzi, *Divine Guide*, 158, n. 143.

20 Al-Mufid, *Tashih*, 68.

21 *Ibid.*, 70; Martin J. McDermott, *The Theology of al-Shaikh al-Mufīd* (Beirut, 1978), 315.

22 Wilferd Madelung, 'al-Mufid' (*EI²*); Devin Stewart, 'al-Sharīf al-Murtaḍā', in Ousama Arabi et al. (eds.), *Islamic Legal Thought* (Leiden, 2013); Mohammad Ali Amir-Moezzi, 'al-Ṭūsī' (*EI²*).

23 Al-Mufid, *Awa'il al-maqalat* (Qom, 1992), 51–2, 57–8; *idem, Tashih*, 42; Wilferd Madelung, 'Imamism and Muʿtazili Theology', in *Religious Schools*, 23; McDermott, pt. I.

24 Stewart, 'Al-Sharīf', 175.

25 Al-Mufid, *Awa'il*, 35ff.; Hussein Ali Abdulsater, *Shiʿi Doctrine, Muʿtazili Theology* (Edinburgh, 2017), 151–73; McDermott, pt. III.

26 Amir-Moezzi, *Divine Guide*, 12.

27 Madelung, 'Imāmism', 25; McDermott, 8, 284; Devin Stewart, *Islamic Legal Orthodoxy* (Salt Lake City, 1998), 228.

28 Stewart, 'Al-Sharīf', 177.

29 *Ibid.*, 184–5.

30 *Ibid.*, 178–9; Stewart, *Islamic Legal Orthodoxy*, esp. 128.

31 Paul Kraus, *Jabir ibn Hayyan* (Cairo, 1942), I:li–lii; Samuel M. Stern, 'Ismaʿilis and Qarmatians', in David Bryer et al. (eds.), *Studies in Early Ismāʿīlism* (Jerusalem, 1983); David Bryer, 'The Origins of the Druze Religion' (*Der Islam*, 1975), 52–3.

32 Yossef Rapoport & Emilie Savage-Smith, *Lost Maps of the Caliphs* (Oxford, 2018), 236–7.

33 Heinz Halm, 'The Ismaʿili Oath of Allegiance and the "Sessions of Wisdom" (*majālis al-ḥikma*) in Fatimid Times', in Farhad Daftary (ed.), *Medieval Ismaʿili History and Thought* (Cambridge, 1996), esp. 108–9.

34 Paul Kraus, 'Hebräische und Syrische Zitate in Ismāʿīlitischen Schriften' (*Der Islam*, 1931); Samuel M. Stern, 'Fatimid Propaganda among Jews According to the Testimony of Yefet b. ʿAlī the Karaite', in *Studies in Early Ismāʿīlism*.

35 Paul E. Walker, 'Fatimid Institutions of Learning' (*The American Research Center in Egypt*, 1997); *idem*, 'Ibn Killis' (*EI³*).

36 Al-Qadi al-Nuʿman, *Daʿaʿim al-islam* (Cairo, 1963), 2, 20–28; *idem, Disagreements of the Jurists* (New York, 2017), xxvi.

37 Al-Qadi al-Nuʿman, *Disagreements*, ch. 4.

38 Al-Qadi al-Nuʿman, *Daʿaʿim*, 272; Ismail K. Poonawalla, 'Al-Qāḍī al-Nuʿmān and Ismaʿili Jurisprudence', in *Medieval Ismaʿili History and Thought*, 118.

39 Al-Qadi al-Nuʿman, *Disagreements*, chs. 7–9, 12.

40 Wilferd Madelung, 'The Fatimids and the Qarmaṭis of Baḥrayn', in *Medieval Ismaʿili History and Thought*, 22.

41 George Makdisi, *Ibn ʿAqīl et la résurgence de l'islam traditionaliste au*

XIe siècle: (Ve siècle de l'Hégire) (Beirut, 1963), ch. 4, II.

42 Stewart, 'Al-Sharīf', 174, 178–9.

43 *Ibid.*, 186–7.

44 George Makdisi, 'The Sunni Revival', in *Islamic Civilisation*.

6. Rationalists and Radicals

1 van Ess, *Flowering*, 26–7.

2 Paul Kraus, 'Beiträge zur Islamischen Ketzergeschichte' (*Rivista degli studi orientali*, 1933/4); Sarah Stroumsa, *Freethinkers of Medieval Islam* (Leiden, 1999), 37–86.

3 Paul Kraus, 'Raziana I' (*Orientalia*, 1935), 306–7, 309, 322; Stroumsa, *Freethinkers*, 93ff.; Muhsin Mahdi, 'Remarks on al-Rāzī's Principles' (*Bulletin d'études orientales*, 1996).

4 R.A. Nicholson, *Studies in Islamic Poetry* (Cambridge, 1921), 136; al-Maʿarrī, *The Epistle of Forgiveness* (Abu Dhabi, 2014), II:84–7.

5 Goldziher, *Muslim Studies*, II:132, n. 4.

6 Ibn al-Nadim, I:420.

7 Dimitri Gutas, 'FĀRĀBĪ i. Biography' (*Encyclopaedia Iranica*)

8 Al-Farabi, *Ihsa' al-ʿulum* (Cairo, 1949), 53; Ibn Khaldun, III:253–5.

9 Richard Walzer, *Galen on Jews and Christians* (London, 1949), 15-16, 59.

10 Al-Farabi, *Ihsa' al-ʿulum*, 63–74; Alfarabi, 'The Enumeration of the Sciences', in Ralph Lerner & Muhsin Mahdi, *Medieval Political Philosophy* (Cornell, 1963).

45 D.S. Richards, 'Ṣalāḥ al-Dīn' (*EI²*); Daftary, *The Ismaʿilis*, 253; cf. Fozia Bora, 'Did Salāḥ al-Dīn Destroy the Fatimids' Books?' (*Journal of the Royal Asiatic Society of Great Britain & Ireland* 2015).

11 Muhsin Mahdi, *Alfarabi and the Foundation of Islamic Political Philosophy* (Chicago, 2001); Richard Walzer, 'Al-Fārābī's Theory of Prophecy and Diviniation' (*Journal of Hellenic Studies*, 1957); Alfarabi, 'The Political Regime', in *Medieval Political Philosophy*.

12 Goitein, *Mediterranean Society*, I:75–6.

13 Luis Xavier López-Farjeat, 'al-Farabi's Psychology and Epistemology' (*Stanford Encyclopaedia of Philosophy*).

14 Shlomo Pines, 'Translator's Introduction', in Maimonides, *The Guide of the Perplexed* (Chicago, 1963), I:lx.

15 Avicenna, *The Life of Ibn Sina* (Albany, 1974), 19–20, 36–8.

16 *Ibid.*, 24–5, 30–1.

17 Thérèse-Anne Druart, 'FĀRĀBĪ iii. Metaphysics' (*Encyclopaedia Iranica*).

18 Avicenna, *Life*, 32–7.

19 *Ibid.*, 55–7.

20 *Ibid.*, 64–6.

21 Peter Heath, *Allegory and Philosophy in Avicenna* (Philadelphia, 1992), 113; Robert Wisnovsky, *Avicenna's Metaphysics in Context* (London,

2003), 11, 135; Nadja Germann, 'Avicenna and Afterwards', in John Marenbon, *Oxford Handbook of Medieval Philosophy* (New York, 2012), 85; Lenn E. Goodman, *Avicenna* (London, 1992), 26.

22 Dimitri Gutas, *Avicenna and the Aristotelian Tradition* (Leiden, 2014), 179–201.

23 Herbert Davidson, *Alfarabi, Avicenna, & Averroes, on Intellect* (New York, 1992).

24 Gutas, *Avicenna*, 184.

25 Fazlur Rahman, *Prophecy in Islam* (London, 1958), 30–45; Avicenna, 'Healing', in *Medieval Political Philosophy*, 100–1.

26 Muhsin Mahdi, 'AVICENNA i. introductory note' (*Encyclopaedia Iranica*).

27 Ibn Khallikan, IV:442.

28 Shahab Ahmed, *What is Islam?* (Princeton, 2017), 13.

29 Wisnovsky, *Avicenna's Metaphysics*, 199.

30 Ibn Sina, *Kitab al-Najah* (Beirut, 1985), 261; Wisnovsky, *Avicenna's Metaphysics*, 252–3.

31 Ibn Sina, *al-Najah*, 271; *idem, al-Isharat wa'l-tanbihat* (Cairo, 1947–8), III:17ff.; Goodman, *Avicenna*, 97; Davidson, *Proofs*, 281ff.

32 Lydia Schumacher, *Early Franciscan Theology* (Cambridge, 2019), 111; Leon Roth, *Spinoza, Descartes, & Maimonides* (Oxford, 1924), 77–9.

33 Toby Mayer, 'Ibn Sīnā's "Burhān al-Siddīqīn"' (*Journal of Islamic Studies*, 2001), 18.

34 Robert Wisnovsky, 'One Aspect of the Avicennian Turn in Sunni Theology' (*Arabic Sciences and Philosophy*, 2004); Davidson, *Proofs*, 385–8;

35 Siddiqui, ch. 4; Griffel, *Al-Ghazālī's*, 29–30; Wisnovsky, 'One Aspect', 91.

36 Al-Ghazali, *The Incoherence of the Philosophers* (Provo, 1997); Griffel, *Al-Ghazālī's*, 103–5.

37 Salomon Munk, *Mélanges de philosophie Juive et Arabe* (Paris, 1859), 382.

38 Ibn Khaldun, III:246, 250.

39 *Ibid.*, III:51–2, 153.

40 Samuel M. Stern, 'The Early Ismāʿīlī Missionaries in North-West Persia and in Khurāsān and Transoxiana', in *Studies in Early Ismāʿīlism*, 219–21; Bryer, 'Origins', 57–8.

41 Paul E. Walker, *Early Philosophical Shiism* (Cambridge, 1993).

42 Ikhwan al-Safa', *Rasa'il* (Beirut, 1957), I:53; Seyyed Hossein Nasr, *An Introduction to Islamic Comsological Doctrines* (London, 1978), 46.

43 Nasr, *Introduction*, 77.

44 Stern, 'Isma'ilis', 298; Nasr, *Introduction*, 32; Ian Netton, *Muslim Neoplatonists* (London, 2002), 98ff.

45 Paul E. Walker, *Hamid al-Din al-Kirmani* (London, 1999); Bryer, 'Origins', 58.

46 Khalil Andani, 'Reconciling Religion and Philosophy', in Khaled el-Rouayheb & Sabine Schmidtke (eds.), *The Oxford Handbook of Islamic Philosophy* (Oxford, 2016).

47 Farhad Daftary, 'CARMATIANS' (*Encyclopaedia Iranica*).

48 Goldziher, *Muslim Studies*, I:43.

49 Madelung, 'The Fatimids and the Qarmaṭis'.

50 Paul E. Walker, *Caliph of Cairo* (Cairo, 2009).

51 Personal communication from Alexander Knysh.

52 Marshall Hodgson, 'Al-Darazī and Ḥamza in the Origin of the Druze Religion' (*Journal of the American Oriental Society*, 1962); Bryer, 'Origins'.

53 Farhad Daftary, 'al-Ṭayyibiyya' (*EI²*); A.A.A. Fyzee, 'Bohorās' (*EI²*).

54 Marshall Hodgson, *The Order of Assassins* (The Hague, 1955), pt. 1; Farhad Daftary, 'Ḥasan-i Ṣabbaḥ and the Origins of the Nizārī

Isma'ili Movement', in *Medieval Isma'ili History and Thought*.

55 Shahrastani, 150–2; Hodgson, *Order*, 54–8.

56 Hodgson, *Order*, 59.

57 Al-Ghazali, *Fada'ih al-batiniyya* (Cairo, 1964), 58–9.

58 *Ibid.*, 78–9.

59 *Ibid.*, 89.

60 *Ibid.*, 151.

61 Hodgson, *Order*, pt. 2; Farhad Daftary, *The Isma'īlīs* (Cambridge, 2007), chs. 6–7.

62 Ernest Gellner, *Muslim Society* (Cambridge, 1981), 63; Malise Ruthven, 'Aga Khan III and the Isma'ili Renaissance', in Peter B. Clarke (ed.), *New Trends and Developments in the World of Islam* (London, 1998).

7. Sufism Ascendant

1 Al-Ghazali, *al-Munqidh min al-dalal* (Beirut, 1968), 65–6, 69, 103–4.

2 *Ibid.*, 105.

3 Ibn al-Jubayr, *Rihla* (Beirut, 1983), 215.

4 Griffel, *Al-Ghazālī's*, ch. 1.

5 Al-Ghazali, *Munqidh*, 60, 69–70.

6 *Ibid.*, 106.

7 Al-Ghazali, *Ihya' 'ulum al-din* (Beirut, 2005), 8.

8 Eric Ormsby, *Ghazali* (Oxford, 2008), 120; al-Ghazali, *Ihya'*, 9; Kenneth Garden, *The First Islamic Reviver* (New York, 2013), 64–5.

9 Al-Ghazali, *Ihya'*, 148.

10 Al-Subki, VI:191, 204–5, 216; Ibn Khallikan, II:621.

11 William Montgomery Watt, *Muslim Intellectual* (Edinburgh, 1963), vii.

12 Ibn Khallikan, IV:449.

13 Mohamed Talbi, ''Iyāḍ b. Mūsā' (*EI²*).

14 Janine M. Safran, 'The politics of book burning in al-Andalus' (*Journal of Medieval Iberian Studies*, 2014), 155–62; Yousef Casewit, *The Mystics of al-Andalus* (Cambridge, 2017), 50–6; al-Subki, VI:217–9.

15 Goitein, *Mediterranean Society*, I:65.

16 Al-Marrakushi, *Al-Mu'jib fi talkhis akhbar al-Maghrib* (Leiden, 1881), 128; Ibn Abi Zar', *Le livre de Mohammed ibn Toumert mahdi des*

Almohades (Algiers, 1903), 38; Griffel, *Al-Ghazālī's*, 77.

17 Ibn Abi Zarʿ, 39–40; Ibn Khallikan, III:207.

18 Ibn Khaldun, I:471–2.

19 Ibn Abi Zarʿ, 39; Ibn Khallikan, III:205–6; Henri Laoust, 'Une fetwâ d'Ibn Taiymīya sur Ibn Tūmart' (*Bulletin de l'Institut français d'archéologie orientale*, 1960), 163.

20 Ibn Khaldun, I:472; al-Marrakushi, 166; Kennedy, *The Caliphate*, 319.

21 Laoust, 'Une fetwâ', 164.

22 Safran, 162–4.

23 Sarah Stroumsa, *Maimonides in His World* (Princeton, 2009), 56–61.

24 Griffel, *Al-Ghazālī's*, 78–9; *idem*, Ibn Tūmart's Rational Proof for God's Existence and Unity', in Maribel Fierro et al. (eds.), *Los almohades* (Madrid, 2015).

25 Al-Marrakushi, 172.

26 Ibn Tufayl, *Hayy ibn Yaqzān* (Chicago, 2009), 143.

27 *Ibid.*, 95.

28 *Ibid.*, 9ff.

29 *Ibid.*, 45, 95–6.

30 *Ibid.*, 156.

31 *Ibid.*, 164.

32 Al-Marrakushi, 172.

33 *Ibid.*, 178.

34 Peter Adamson & Matteo Giovanni, *Interpreting Averroes* (Cambridge, 2019), 1.

35 Averroes, *On the Harmony of Religion and Philosophy* (London, 1976), 50; Richard Taylor, '"Truth does not contradict truth"' (*Topoi*, 2000).

36 Averroes, *On the Harmony*, 53–4.

37 Averroes, *Tahafut*, 163, 252–5; Wisnovsky, *Avicenna's Metaphysics*, 240.

38 Ibn ʿArabi, *al-Futuhat al-Makkiyya* (Cairo, 1972), II:372–3.

39 Claude Addas, *The Quest for the Red Sulphur* (Cambridge, 1993).

40 Ibn ʿArabi, *Fusus al-hikam* (Cairo, 1946), 47; Ibn ʿArabi, *al-Futuhat*, I:215–30.

41 Toshihiko Izutsu, *Sufism and Taoism* (Berkeley, 1984), 152; Michael Ebstein, *Mysticism and Philosophy in al-Andalus* (Leiden, 2014).

42 William C. Chittick, 'Rūmī and *wahdat al-wujūd*', in Amin Banani et al. (eds.), *Poetry and Mysticism in Islam* (Cambridge, 1994).

43 Ibn ʿArabi, *Fusus*, 106.

44 *Ibid.*, 48–9.

45 Fitzroy Morrissey, *Sufism and the Perfect Human* (Abingdon, 2020).

46 Al-Qashani, *Muʿjam istilahat al-sufiyya* (Cairo, 1992), 174.

47 Addas, 87–8; Michel Chodkiewicz, *Seal of Saints* (Cambridge, 1999), 98.

48 Ibn ʿArabī, *Fusus*, 62–4.

49 Chodkiewicz, *Seal*, 128–146; Addas, 77–81.

50 Ibn ʿArabi, *Fusus*, 72, 192–6.

51 *Ibid.*, 178; William C. Chittick, *Imaginal Worlds* (Albany, 1993), 142.

52 Carl Ernst, *Sufism* (Boston, 2011), 183; Addas, 234–6.

53 Michel Chodkiewicz, *An Ocean Without Shore* (Albany, 1993), 20.

54 Shams al-Din Aflaki, *The Feats of the Knowers of God* (Leiden, 2013), 63.

55 Ahmet K. Karamustafa, 'Antinomian Sufism', in *Cambridge Companion to Sufism*.

56 Aflaki, 64, 425–7.

57 Franklin Lewis, *Rumi* (Oxford, 2008), 173.

58 *Ibid.*, 167.

59 *Ibid.*, 137.

60 *Ibid.*, 330.

61 *Ibid.*, ch. 11.

62 'Attar, *Kitab-i Mantiq al-Tayr* (Paris, 1857), 167.

63 Rumi, *The Mathnawi* (Leiden, 1925–40), I:1.

64 *Ibid.*, I:86.

65 *Ibid.*, I:3; Samuel M. Stern & Alexander Altmann, *Isaac Israeli* (London, 1958), 66.

66 Rumi, I:3.

67 *Ibid.*, I:246.

68 *Ibid.*, I:343.

69 Lewis, *Rumi*, 157–9.

70 Aflaki, 135.

71 *Ibid.*, 136; Lewis, *Rumi*, 37.

72 Ahmed, 310.

73 Armando Salvatore, *The Sociology of Islam* (Oxford, 2016), ch. 4.

74 Lewis, *Rumi*, 29; Fritz Meier, 'Dervish Dance', in *idem*, *Essays on Islamic Piety and Mysticism* (Leiden, 1999).

75 Aflaki, 65.

76 J. Spencer Trimingham, *The Sufi Orders* (Oxford, 1971).

8. Reason, Revelation, and Inspiration

1 Ibn Khaldun, III:52.

2 Ibn Khallikan, II:653.

3 Paul Kraus, 'Les "controverses" de Fakhr al-Dīn al-Rāzī' (*Bulletin d'Institut d'Égypte*, 1937), 188–9; Frank Griffel, 'On Fakhr al-Dīn al-Rāzī's Life and the Patronage He Received' (*Journal of Islamic Studies*, 2007).

4 Ayman Shihadeh, 'From al-Ghazālī to al-Rāzī' (*Arabic Sciences and Philosophy*, 2005), 163.

5 John McGinnis, 'Naṣīr al-Dīn al-Ṭūsī', in *Oxford Handbook of Islamic Philosophy*; Toby Mayer, 'Fakhr al-Dīn al-Rāzī's Critique of Ibn Sīnā's Argument for the Unity of God, and Naṣīr al-Dīn al-Ṭūsī's Defence', in Peter Adamson (ed.),

Classical Arabic Philosophy (London, 2007); Binyamin Abrahamov, 'Fakhr al-Dīn al-Rāzī on God's Knowledge of Particulars' (*Oriens*, 1992).

6 Ayman Shihadeh, 'Al-Rāzī's (d. 1210) Commentary on Avicenna's *Pointers*', in *Oxford Handbook of Islamic Philosophy*, 305; Ibn Khaldun, III:143; Shihadeh, 'From al-Ghazālī', 168, 173; *idem*, *The Teleological Ethics of Fakhr al-Dīn al-Rāzī* (Leiden, 2006), 116ff.

7 Shihadeh, *Teleological*, 40; Kraus, Les "controverses"', 204–5, 209–11.

8 Kraus, 'Les "controverses"', 190–1, 205.

9 Ibn Khallikan, II:653.

10 Gardet & Anawati, 162; Heidrun Eichner, 'Handbooks in the

Tradition of Later Eastern Ash'arism', in Sabine Schmidtke (ed.), *The Oxford Handbook of Islamic Theology* (Oxford, 2016), 499–503.

11 Alnoor Dhanani, '*Al-Mawāqif fī 'ilm al-kalām* by 'Aḍud al-dīn al-Ījī, and its commentaries', in *Oxford Handbook of Islamic Philosophy*; Eichner; Reza Pourjavady, 'The Legacy of 'Aḍud al-dīn al-Ījī', in Ayman Shihadeh & Jan Thiele (eds.), *Philosophical Theology in Islam* (Leiden, 2020).

12 George Lane, 'ṬUSI, NAṢIR-AL-DIN i. biography' (*Encyclopaedia Iranica*).

13 Hodgson, *Order*, 239ff.

14 Wilferd Madelung, 'Nasir al-Din Tusi's Ethics', in Richard Hovannisian (ed.), *Ethics in Islam* (Malibu, 1985).

15 Toby Mayer, 'On Existence and Its Causes' (Oxford, 2001), 195ff., 305–6.

16 Robert Wisnovsky, 'Towards a Genealogy of Avicennism' (*Oriens*, 2014), 323–5.

17 Robert Wisnovsky, 'Avicennism and exegetical practice in the early commentaries on the *Ishārāt*' (*Oriens*, 2013).

18 Robert Wisnovsky, 'On the Emergence of Maragha Avicennism' (*Oriens*, 2018), 303; idem, 'Avicenna's Islamic Reception', in Peter Adamson (ed.), *Interpreting Avicenna* (Cambridge, 2013), 194, 203.

19 Sabine Schmidtke, *The Theology of al-'Allāma al-Ḥillī (d. 726/1325)* (Berlin, 1991), esp. 99ff.

20 Robert Gleave, *Inevitable Doubt* (Leiden, 2000), 5.

21 Lewis, *Rumi*, 58.

22 *Ibid.*, 59; Mohammed Rustom, 'Ibn 'Arabī's Letter to Fakhr al-Dīn al-Rāzī (*Journal of Islamic Studies*, 2014).

23 Kraus, 'Les "controverses"'; Fathalla Kholeif, *A Study on Fakhr al-Dīn al-Rāzī and His Controversies* (Cambridge, 1966).

24 Alexander Knysh, *Ibn 'Arabi in the Later Islamic Tradition* (Albany, 1999), 148–9; Khaled El-Rouayheb, *Islamic Intellectual History in the Seventeenth Century* (Cambridge, 2015), 313–15.

25 Ibn Khaldun, III:52–3, 82ff., 153; James W. Morris, 'An Arab Machiavelli?' (*Harvard Middle Eastern and Islamic Review*, 2009).

26 Henri Laoust, 'Ibn Taymiyya' (*EI²*); idem, *Essai sur les doctrines sociales et politiques de Taḳī-d-Dīn Aḥmad b. Taimīya* (Paris, 1939), pt. I; Carl Sharif El-Tobgui, *Ibn Taymiyya on Reason and Revelation* (Leiden, 2019), ch. 2.

27 Ibn Taymiyya, *'Aqida* (Riyadh, 1999), 57.

28 Ibn Taymiyya, *Majmu'at al-rasa'il al-kubra* (Beirut, n.d.), I:49, 427; idem, *al-Fatwa al-Hamawiyya al-kubra* (Riyadh, 1998), 199.

29 Ibn Taymiyya, *Dar' ta'arud al-'aql wa'l-naql* (Riyahd, 1979–83), I:4ff.; idem, *Majmu'at al-rasa'il*, I:107, 175ff;

idem, Majmu'at al-fatawa (Medina, 2004), I:29–30; El-Tobgui, ch. 3.

30 Kholeif, 5.

31 Ibn Taymiyya, *al-Fatwa al-Hamawiyya*, 204.

32 Wisnovsky, 'On the emergence', 303.

33 Ibn Taymiyya, *Majmu'at al-fatawa*, XI:223.

34 Ibn Taymiyya, *Majmu'at al-rasa'il*, I:11.

35 Ibn Taymiyya, *Majmu'at al-fatawa*, XI:235.

36 Fritz Meier, 'The Cleanest about Predestination', in *Essays on Islamic Piety*, 320.

37 Ibn Taymiyya, *Majmu'at al-fatawa*, XI:241.

38 Muhammad Umar Memon, *Ibn Taimīya's Struggle Against Popular Religion* (The Hague, 1976).

39 Daniella Talmon-Heller, *Sacred Place and Sacred Time in the Medieval Islamic Middle East* (Edinburgh, 2020), ch. 13.

40 Ibn Battuta, *The Travels of Ibn Baṭṭūṭa* (Cambridge, 1958), I:135; Donald P. Little, 'Did Ibn Taymiyya have a screw loose?' (*Studia Islamica*, 1975).

41 Donald P. Little, 'The Historical and Historiographical Significance of the Detention of Ibn Taymiyya' (*International Journal of Middle East Studies*, 1973), 312–13.

42 Jon Hoover, 'Ibn Taymiyya between Moderation and Radicalism', in Ahmad Khan & Elisabeth Kendall (eds.), *Reclaiming Islamic Tradition* (Edinburgh, 2016); Gilles Kepel,

The Roots of Radical Islam (London, 2005), 200–206.

43 Khaled El-Rouayheb, 'From Ibn Hajar al-Haytami (d.1566) to Khayr al-Din al-Alusi (d.1899)', in Yossef Rapoport & Shahab Ahmed (eds.), *Ibn Taymiyya and His Times* (Oxford, 2010); Christopher Melchert, *Hadith*, ch. 16.

44 Ibn Taymiyya, *Majmu'at al-rasa'il*, I:103–4, 178ff.

45 *Ibid.*, I:29, 73–4.

46 Jon Hoover, *Ibn Taymiyya's Theodicy of Perpetual Optimism* (Leiden, 2007).

47 Binyamin Abrahamov, 'The Creation and Duration of Hell in Islamic Theology' (*Der Islam*, 2002), 95ff.

48 Shihadeh, 'From al-Ghazālī', 141.

49 Norman Calder, '*Tafsīr* from Ṭabarī to Ibn Kathīr', in G.R. Hawting et al. (eds.), *Approaches to the History of the Interpretation of the Qur'an* (Oxford, 1988), 110ff.; Muhsin Mahdi, *Ibn Khaldūn's Philosophy of History* (London, 1957), 30–31.

50 Wisnovsky, 'On the Emergence', 273–4; al-Iji, *Kitab al-Mawaqif* (Cairo, 1907/8), 3–5.

51 Hodgson, *Venture*, II:210ff.; Madelung, 'Nasir al-Din Tusi's', 101.

52 Ibn Taymiyya, *Majmu'at al-fatawa*, XI:240, 245; Robert Irwin, *Ibn Khaldun* (Princeton, 2018), 89.

53 Constance Padwick, *Muslim Devotions* (London, 1961); Annemarie Schimmel, *And Muhammad is His Messenger* (Chapel Hill, 1985), ch. 10.

54 Ibn al-Naqib, *Reliance of the Traveller* (Evanston, 1991), 862.

9. The Age of Empire

1 Ross E. Dunn, *The Adventures of Ibn Battuta* (London, 1986).

2 Goldziher, *Muslim Studies*, II:245; Éric Geoffroy, 'al-Suyūṭī' (*EI²*).

3 Halik Inalcik, 'The Emergence of the Ottomans', in P.M. Holt et al. (eds.), *The Cambridge History of Islam* (Cambridge, 1977), 296.

4 Paul Wittek, *The Rise of the Ottoman Empire* (London, 1938); Bernard Lewis, *The Muslim Discovery of Europe* (London, 1982), 29.

5 Halil Inalcik, 'Istanbul: An Islamic City', in *idem*, *Essays in Ottoman History* (Istanbul, 1998), 252.

6 Evliya Çelebi, *Narrative of travels in Europe, Asia, and Africa in the seventeenth century* (London, 1834–50), I:58–9; Gülru Necipoğlu, 'The Life of an Imperial Monument', in Robert Mark & Ahmet Çakmak (eds.), *Hagia Sophia from the Age of Justinian to the Present* (Cambridge, 1992), 202.

7 Gülru Necipoğlu, 'The Süleymaniye Complex in Istanbul' (*Muqarnas*, 1985), esp. 99–106.

8 Inalcik, 'Istanbul', 253; Robert Dankoff, *An Ottoman Mentality* (Leiden, 2004), 9; Halil Inalcik, 'The Rise of the Ottoman Empire', in *Cambridge History of Islam*, 320–2; Colin Imber, 'The Ottoman empire (tenth/sixteenth century)', in Maribel Fierro (ed.), *The New*

Cambridge History of Islam Volume 2 (Cambridge, 2010), 350.

9 Madeline Zilfi, 'The Ottoman ulema', in Suraiya Faroqhi (ed.), *The Cambridge History of Turkey* (Cambridge, 2006), esp. 212–4; Gilles Veinstein, 'Religious institutions, policies and lives', in *Cambridge History of Turkey*, esp. 326–32.

10 Richard Repp, *The Müfti of Istanbul* (London, 1986), 193.

11 *Ibid.*, xix, 115–16, 284.

12 Imber, 'Ottoman Empire', 362; Elyse Semerdjian, *'Off the Straight Path'* (Syracuse, 2008), 51–3; Eugenia Kermeli, 'Ebusuud Efendi', in David Thomas & John Chesworth (eds.), *Christian-Muslim Relations, Volume 7* (Leiden, 2015), 718.

13 Repp, 211.

14 Imber, 'Ottoman Empire', 345; Veinstein, 'Religious institutions', 331.

15 Halil Inalcik, 'Islam in the Ottoman Empire', in *Essays in Ottoman History*, 231; Rudolph Peters, 'What does it mean to be an official madhhab?', in Peri Bearman et al. (eds.), *The Islamic School of Law* (Cambridge, Mass., 2005), 151; Guy Burak, *The Second Formation of Islamic Law*

ENDNOTES

(Cambridge, 2015), 11–12; Imber, 'Ottoman Empire', 362.

16 Bruce Masters, 'Ottoman Policies Toward Syria in the 17th and 18th Centuries', in Thomas Philipp (ed.), *The Syrian Land in the 18th and 19th Century* (Stuttgart, 1992), 17; Semiramis Çavuşoğlu, 'The Kadizadeli Movement' (Princeton, 1990), 114; Elizabeth Sirriyeh, *Sufi Visionary of Ottoman Damascus* (London, 2005), 5.

17 Colin Imber, *Ebu's-su'ud* (Edinburgh, 1997), ch. 5.

18 M. Sait Özervali, 'Theology in Ottoman Lands', in *Oxford Handbook of Islamic Theology*, 568; Badeen, 21.

19 Ayman Shihadeh, 'Khojazāda on al-Ghazālī's Criticism of the Philosophers' Proof of the Existence of God', in *Proceedings of the International Symposium on Khojazada* (Bursa, 2011); Muhammet Fatih Kılıç, 'An Analysis of the Section on Causality in Khojazāda's *Tahāfut*' (*Nazariyat*, 2016).

20 Özervali, 575; Badeen, 19.

21 Katib Çelebi, 21.

22 Inalcik, 'Emergence', 269; Cemal Kafadar, *Between Two Worlds* (Berkeley, 1995), 13, 15; Karamustafa, 115ff.

23 John Kingsley Birge, *The Bektashi Order of Dervishes* (London, 1937), 132.

24 H.A.R. Gibb & Harold Bowen, *Islamic Society and the West* (London,

1957), II:76; Diana Le Gall, *A Culture of Sufism* (Albany, 2005).

25 Timothy Winter, 'Ibn Kemāl (d. 940/1534) on Ibn 'Arabī's Hagiology', in Ayman Shihadeh (ed.), *Sufism and Theology* (Edinburgh, 2007), 138, 140, 148; Ahmed Zildzic, 'Friend and Foe' (Berkeley, 2012), 136–7.

26 Al-Bosnawi, *Sharḥ al-Fuṣūṣ 'alā lisān ahl al-lubb wa'l-khuṣūṣ* (Chester Beatty Library, MS 3474), 4; Hamid Algar, 'The Literature of the Bosnian Muslims' (*The Muslim News*, 25 Nov. 1994), 4.

27 Sirriyeh, 19.

28 Gottfried Hagen, 'Ottoman Understandings of the World in the Seventeenth Century', in *Ottoman Mentality*, 216; al-Bosnawi, 3.

29 Hüseyin Yılmaz, *Caliphate Redefined* (Princeton, 2018).

30 Michel M. Mazzaoui, *The Origins of the Safawids* (Wiesbaden, 1972).

31 Vladimir Minorsky, 'The Poetry of Shāh Ismā'īl I' (*Bulletin of the School of Oriental and African Studies*, 1942), 1026a; Arjomand, *Shadow of God*, 82.

32 Abbas Amanat, *Iran* (New Haven, 2017), 33.

33 Baha' al-Din 'Amili, *Haza kitab-i Jami'-i 'Abbasi* (n.p., 1855), 1.

34 Rula Abisaab, 'Bahā' al-Dīn al-'Āmili', in David Thomas & John A. Chesworth (eds.), *Christian-Muslim Relations Volume 10* (Leiden, 2017), 509–14.

35 Kashifi, *Rawdat al-shuhada'* (Lucknow, 1873), 1.

36 Babak Rahimi, *Theater state and the formation of early modern public sphere in Iran* (Leiden, 2012), 224.

37 Rula Jurdi Abisaab, *Converting Persia* (London, 2004), 27.

38 Rahimi, 225.

39 Arjomand, *Shadow of God*, 112ff.

40 Dankoff, 41, 67.

41 Repp, 220, n. 71.

42 Abdurrahman Atçil, 'Ottoman Religious Rulings Concerning the Safavids', in Hani Khafipour (ed.), *The Empires of the Near East and India* (New York, 2019), 101.

43 Azmi Bishara, *Sectarianism Without Sects* (London, 2021), ch. 3.

44 Sajjad Rizvi, 'ISFAHAN SCHOOL OF PHILOSOPHY' (*Encyclopaedia Iranica*).

45 Etan Kohlberg, 'BAHĀ'-AL-DĪN 'ĀMELĪ' (*Encyclopaedia Iranica*).

46 John Walbridge, *The Wisdom of the Mystic East* (Albany, 2001).

47 Sajjad Rizvi, 'Mir Dāmād in India' (*Journal of the American Oriental Society*, 2011), 11–15; Andrew Newman, 'DĀMĀD, MĪR' (*Encyclopaedia Iranica*).

48 Fazlur Rahman, *The Philosophy of Mulla Sadra* (Albany, 1975), 10; Toshihiko Izutsu & Mehdi Muhaqqiq, *The Metaphysics of Sabzavārī* (Delmar, 1977), 7–8; Sajjad Rizvi, *Mullā Ṣadrā and Metaphysics* (London, 2009), 4; idem, 'Mulla Sadra' (*Stanford Encyclopedia of Philosophy*).

49 Rahman, *Philosophy*, 11, 28; Izutsu & Muhaqqiq, 8–10.

50 Izutsu & Muhaqqiq, 10; Rizvi, *Mullā Ṣadrā*, 44–5.

51 Rahman, *Philosophy*, 35, 111; Rizvi, *Mullā Ṣadrā*, 29.

52 Mulla Sadra, *al-Hikma al-muta'aliyya fi'l-asfar al-'aqliyya al-arba'a* (Beirut, 1981), I:13; Rizvi, *Mullā Ṣadrā*, 30.

53 Rizvi, *Mullā Ṣadrā*, 138–40.

54 Mulla Sadra, I:5–6.

55 James W. Morris, *The Wisdom of the Throne* (Princeton, 1981), 46–7.

56 Izutsu & Muhaqqiq, 1; Morris, *Wisdom*, 49; Roy Mottahedeh, *The Mantle of the Prophet* (New York, 1985), 135–44; Alexander Knysh, '"Irfan" Revisited' (*Middle East Journal*, 1992).

57 Stephen Dale, *Babur* (Cambridge, 2018), 17.

58 John F. Richards, *The Mughal Empire* (Cambridge, 1993), 1.

59 Annemarie Schimmel, *Pain and Grace* (Leiden, 1976), 4; Dale, *Babur*, 9–10.

60 Babur, *Baburnama* (London, 1922), I:283; Dale, 14.

61 Richard Eaton, *India in the Persianate Age* (London, 2019), 234; Richards, 31; Abu'l-Fazl, *Akbarnama* (Calcutta, 1897–1921), II:502–8, III:63; Lewis, *Rumi*, 470.

62 Schimmel, *Pain and Grace*, 5; William C. Chittick, 'Notes on Ibn al-'Arabī's Influence in the Subcontinent' (*The Muslim World*, 1992); Gregory A. Lipton, 'Muḥibb Allāh Ilāhābādī's

ENDNOTES

Taswiya Contextualized', in Denis
Hermann & Fabrizio Speziale
(eds.), *Muslim Cultures in the Indo-
Iranian World During the Early-Modern
and Modern Periods* (Berlin, 2010).

63 Babur, I:76.

64 Asad Q. Ahmed & Reza
Pourjavady, 'Theology in the
Indian Subcontinent', in *Oxford
Handbook of Islamic Theology*,
611–12; G.M. Wickens, 'AKLĀQ-E
JALĀLĪ' (*Encyclopaedia Iranica*).

65 Sajjad Rizvi, 'MIR
FENDERESKI' (*Encyclopaedia
Iranica*); Francis Robinson,
'Ottomans-Safavids-Mughals'
(*Journal of Islamic Studies*, 1997);
Rizvi, 'Mir Dāmād'.

66 Richards, 30, 34–5.

67 Abu'l-Fazl, III:364ff.; Ahmed &
Pourjavady, 609.

68 Al-Bada'uni, *Muntakhab al-tawarikh*
(1989–1925), II:278–80; Azfar
Moin, *The Millennial Sovereign* (New
York, 2012), 139.

69 Eaton, 238.

70 Abu'l-Fazl, I:15ff.

71 Richards, 45–8; Moin.

72 Richards, 40; al-Bada'uni, II:316.

73 Richards, 101–2; Corinne Lefèvre,
'Messianism, Rationalism, and

Inner-Asian Connections' (*The
Indian Economic and Social History
Review*, 2017).

74 Richards, 122, 148.

75 *Ibid.*, 124–6; Wayne E. Begley, 'The
Myth of the Taj Mahal and a New
Theory of its Symbolic Meaning'
(*The Art Bulletin*, 1979).

76 Annemarie Schimmel, *The Empire
of the Great Mughals* (London, 2004),
107.

77 Munis D. Faruqui, 'Dara Shukoh,
Vedanta, and Imperial Succession
in Mughal India', in Vasudha
Dalmia & Munis D. Faruqui (eds.),
Religious Interactions in Mughal India
(New Delhi, 2014).

78 *Ibid.*, 32.

79 Richards, 152.

80 *Ibid.*, 153; Eaton, 445, n. 75.

81 Richards, 173–7.

82 Alan Guenther, 'Hanafi Fiqh in
Mughal India', in Richard Eaton
(ed.), *India's Islamic Traditions* (New
Delhi, 2003).

83 *Al-Fatawa 'Alamgiriyya* (Bulaq, 1892),
I:2; I:121ff.; V:353.

84 Hodgson, *Venture*, III:82.

85 Jawaharlal Nehru, *Glimpses of World
History* (New Delhi, 1980), 314.

10. Decline and Revival

1 Arnold.

2 Hasan Kafi, *Usul al-hikam* (Amman,
1986), 18.

3 Katib Çelebi, 146–7.

4 Dankoff, 113–14.

5 Katib Çelebi, 128–31.

6 Mehmed Birgivi, *al-Tariqa al-
Muhammadiyya* (Damascus, 2011),
30.

7 Hagen, 244–6; Katharina A.
Ivanyi, *Virtue, Piety, and the Law*
(Leiden, 2020).

8 Madeline Zilfi, 'The Kadizadelis' (*Journal of Near Eastern Studies*, 1986); Çavuşoğlu.

9 Katib Çelebi, 51.

10 *Ibid.*, 29, 108–9.

11 Çavuşoğlu, 142–8.

12 El-Rouayheb, *Islamic Intellectual History*, 272–311.

13 Michael Cook, 'On the Origins of Wahhābism' (*Journal of the Royal Asiatic Society*, 1992), 192; Ibn Bishr, *'Unwan al-majd fi tarikh Najd* (Riyadh, 1982), I:36.

14 Ibn 'Abd al-Wahhab, *Kitab al-Tawhid* (Egypt, 2008), 103.

15 *Ibid.*, 62.

16 Ibn 'Abd al-Wahhab, *Risala fi'l-radd 'ala al-rafida* (Cairo, 2006), 75ff., 109.

17 Cook, 'Origins', 174.

18 Ibn Ghannam, *Tarikh Najd* (Cairo, 1994), 87; Ibn Bishr, 42.

19 Zakariyya Kurşun, *Al-'Uthmaniyyun wa-Al Su'ud fi'l-arshif al-'Uthmani* (Beirut, 2005), 36, 38, 89, 105, 108.

20 Yohanan Friedmann, *Shaykh Ahmad Sirhindī* (Montreal, 1971), esp. 14, 59ff., 73.

21 Jahangir, *The Jahangirnama* (New York, 1999), 304.

22 El-Rouayheb, *Islamic Intellectual History*, 260–61.

23 Arthur F. Buehler, 'Ahmad Sirhindi's Ruminations', in *Empires of the Near East*, 162.

24 J.M.S. Baljon, *Religion and Thought of Shāh Walī Allāh Dihlawī* (Leiden, 1986), 13–14.

25 *Ibid.*, 13.

26 *Ibid.*, 105–6.

27 Shah Wali Allah, *The Conclusive Argument from God* (Leiden, 1996), 8.

28 Baljon, *Religion and Thought*, 13.

29 *Ibid.*, 77.

30 *Ibid.*, 79.

31 Marcia Hermansen, 'Shāh Walī Allāh of Delhi's Hujjat Allāh al-bāligha' (*Studia Islamica*, 1986), 145.

32 Baljon, *Religion and Thought*, 90.

33 Friedmann, *Shaykh Ahmad Sirhindī*, 103; Baljon, *Religion and Thought*, 29–30.

34 Muhammad U. Faruque, 'Sufism contra Shariah?' (*Journal of Sufi Studies*, 2016).

35 Baljon, *Religion and Thought*, 85–6.

36 *Ibid.*, 87; Aziz Ahmad, 'Political and Religious Ideas of Shah Wali-Ullah of Delhi' (*Muslim World*, 1962), 22.

37 Muhammad Khalid Masud, 'al-Dihlawī, Shāh Walī Allāh' (*EI³*).

38 John O. Voll, 'A History of the Khatmiyya Tariqa in the Sudan' (Ann Arbor, 1971); R.S. O'Fahey, *Enigmatic Saint* (London, 1990); R.S. O'Fahey & Bernd Radtke, 'Neo-Sufism Reconsidered' (*Der Islam*, 1993); Mark Sedgwick, *Saints and Sons* (Leiden, 2005).

39 Gleave, *Inevitable Doubt*, 106; idem, *Scripturalist Islam* (Leiden, 2007), 1–30.

40 Al-Astarabadi, *al-Fawa'id al-Madaniyya* (Qom, 1964), 28, 77.

41 Gleave, *Scripturalist Islam*, ch. 3.

42 Hamid Algar, *Religion and State in Iran, 1785–1906* (Berkeley, 1969),

35; Gleave, *Inevitable Doubt*, 9; *idem*, *Scripturalist Islam*, 8.

43 Morris, 47–8; Rainer Brunner, 'MAJLESI' (*Encyclopaedia Iranica*);

Etan Kohlberg, 'BEHĀR AL-ANWĀR' (*Encyclopaedia Iranica*).

44 Gleave, *Inevitable Doubt*, 218; *idem*, *Scripturalist Islam*, 303–5.

11. Facing Modernity

1 Ibrahim Abu-Lughod, *The Arab Rediscovery of Europe* (Princeton, 1963).

2 Al-Jabarti, *'Aja'ib al-athar* (Cairo, 1998), III:1.

3 *Ibid.*, III:57ff.

4 Al-Tahtawi, *An Imam in Paris* (London, 2011), 111–13, 130.

5 Albert Hourani, *Arabic Thought in the Liberal Age* (Cambridge, 2013), 68ff.; al-Tahtawi, *al-Murshid al-amin li'l-banat wa'l-banin* (Cairo, 1872), 67.

6 Khayr al-Din, *Aqwam al-masalik fi ma'rifat ahwal al-mamalik* (Tunis, 1867), 5.

7 *Ibid.*, 22–3; Hourani, *Arabic Thought*, 92–3.

8 Aziz Ahmad, *Islamic Modernism in India and Pakistan, 1857–1964* (London, 1967); Barbara D. Metcalf, *Islamic Revival in British India* (Princeton, 1982); Usha Sanyal, *Ahmad Riza Khan Barelwi* (Oxford, 2005); Yohanan Friedmann, *Prophecy Continuous* (Berkeley, 1989).

9 G.F.I. Graham, *The Life and Work of Syed Ahmed Khan* (Edinbrugh, 1885), 185.

10 David Lelyveld, *Aligarh's First Generation* (Princeton, 1978).

11 Thomas Babington Macaulay, *Speeches* (London, 1935), 359.

12 Christian W. Troll, *Sayyid Ahmad Khan* (New Delhi, 1978), 317.

13 J.M.S. Baljon, *The Reforms and Religious Ideas of Sir Sayyid Ahmad Khan* (Lahore, 1958), 63, 73–5, 107, 120; Martin Riexinger, 'Responses of South Asian Muslims to the Theory of Evolution' (*Die Welt des Islams*, 2009), 217–19.

14 Sayyid Ahmad Khan, 'Essay on the Mohammedan Theological Literature', 6–9, 'Essay on Mohammedan Traditions', in *idem*, *Essays on the Life of Mohammed* (London, 1870).

15 Sayyid Ahmad Khan, 'Essay on the question whether Islam has been beneficial or injurious to human society in general', in *Essays*; Ahmad, *Islamic Modernism*, 50ff.; Baljon, *Reforms*, 36ff.

16 Graham, 114.

17 Nikkie Keddie, *Sayyid Jamāl al-Dīn "al-Afghānī"* (Berkeley, 1972), 107.

18 Wilfrid Scawen Blunt, *Secret History of the English Occupation of Egypt* (New York, 1922), 76; Keddie, 8; Muhammad Rashid Rida, *Tarikh al-ustadh al-imam* (Cairo, 1906–31), I:ix.

19 Edward Granville Browne, *The Persian Revolution of 1905–1909* (Cambridge, 1910), 13.

20 Keddie, 51.

21 *Ibid.*, 69.

22 *Ibid.*, 144; Hourani, *Arabic Thought*, 109; Rida, *Tarikh*, I:x.

23 Al-Afghani, *al-Radd 'ala al-dahriyyin* (Egypt, 1902), 17–27; Keddie, 171–81, 393–4; Hourani, *Arabic Thought*, 124–9.

24 Keddie, 193.

25 Al-Afghani, *al-Radd*, 64–5; Keddie, 179, 391–2; Hourani, *Arabic Thought*, 122.

26 Al-Afghani, *al-Radd*, 68–9.

27 Sylvia Haim, *Arab Nationalism* (Berkeley, 1962), 15.

28 Al-Afghani & Muhammad 'Abduh, *al-A'mal al-kamila* (Tehran, 2000), I:133, 137.

29 Al-Afghani, *al-Radd*, 62–9; al-Afghani & 'Abduh, *al-A'mal*, I:132.

30 Charles C. Adams, *Islam and Modernism in Egypt* (London, 1933), 34.

31 *Ibid.*, 42; Keddie, 90; Wisnovsky, 'Avicenna's Islamic Reception', 191–2; 210–13.

32 H.A.R. Gibb, *Modern Trends in Islam* (Chicago, 1974), 39.

33 Irwin, 190.

34 Adams, *Islam*, 50.

35 'Abduh, *The Theology of Unity* (London, 1966), 30.

36 *Ibid.*, 126–8.

37 *Ibid.*, 44, 45ff., 65–75; Malcolm H. Kerr, *Islamic Reform* (Berkeley, 1966), 126–7.

38 'Abduh, *Theology*, 53–6.

39 *Ibid.*, 65–75, ch. 7.

40 *Ibid.*, 132.

41 *Ibid.*, 32–9.

42 Muhammad 'Abduh & Muhammad Rashid Rida, *Tafsir al-Manar* (Cairo, 1947), II:63–4 (Q 2:164), II:111 (Q 2:177); Ignaz Goldziher, *Die Richtungen der islamischen Koranauslegung* (Leiden, 1920), 352–3.

43 'Abduh & Rida, I:1.

44 *Ibid.*, II:321ff. (Q 2:220); Adams, *Islam*, 111, 172; Goldziher, *Richtungen*, 344.

45 Goldziher, *Richtungen*, 354.

46 'Abduh & Rida, I:12.

47 Hourani, *Arabic Thought*, 141.

48 Goldziher, *Richtungen*, 330.

49 Hourani, *Arabic Thought*, 152–3.

50 Charles C. Adams, 'Muhammad 'Abduh and the Transvaal Fatwa', in *The Macdonald Presentation Volume* (Princeton, 1933); Jakob Skovgaard-Petersen, *Defining Islam for the Egyptian State* (Leiden, 1997), 120ff.

51 Adams, *Islam*, 65–6; Hourani, *Arabic Thought*, 137–8.

52 Goldziher, *Richtungen*, 325.

12. From Modernism to Islamism

1 'Abduh & Rida, I:11.

2 Umar Riyad, *Islamic Reformism and Christianity* (Leiden, 2009), 6.

3 Muhammad Rashid Rida, *al-Wahy al-Muhammadi* (Beirut, 1984/5), 62.

4 Hourani, *Arabic Thought*, 238; Malcolm H. Kerr, 'Rashid Rida

ENDNOTES

and Islamic Legal Reform' (*The Muslim World*, 1960), pt. 2, 174.

5 Ian Harper & Lachlan Smirl, 'Usury', in Paul Oslington (ed.), *The Oxford Handbook of Christianity and Economics* (Oxford, 2014), 564–7.

6 Muhammad Rashid Rida, *Shubuhat al-Nasara wa-hujaj al-Islam* (Cairo, 1946/7), 6–7; Simon A. Wood, *Christian Criticisms, Islamic Proofs* (London, 2012), 79–80.

7 Rida, *Tarikh*, I:*jim*.

8 Rida & 'Abduh, I:7.

9 Rida, *al-Wahy*, 60.

10 Rida, *Shubuhat, jim*; Wood, 69.

11 Hourani, *Arabic Thought*, 231; Rida, *al-Wahy*, 64; Henri Lauzière, *The Making of Salafism* (New York, 2015), 84–5.

12 Adams, *Islam*, 152; Muhammad Rashid Rida, *Nida ila al-jins al-latif* (Cairo, 1932), 18.

13 Qasim Amin, *Tahrir al-Mar'a* (Cairo, 1899).

14 Bahithat al-Badiya, 'A Lecture in the Club of the Umma Party', in Charles Kurzman (ed.), *Modernist Islam, 1840–1940* (New York, 2002); Susanne Bräckelmann, *"Wir sind die Hälfte der Welt!"* (Würzburg, 2004); Margot Badran, 'The feminist vision in the writings of three turn-of-the-century Egyptian women' (*Bulletin of the British Society for Middle Eastern Studies*, 1988); eadem, *Feminists, Islam, and Nation* (Princeton, 1995).

15 Rida, *Nida*, 28, 37–48, 98, 110; Hourani, *Arabic Thought*, 238–9.

16 'Abduh & Rida, I:11.

17 Rida, *al-Wahy*, 210, 68.

18 Kerr, 'Rashid Rida', pt. 1, 101; pt. 2, 171, 173; Goldziher, *Richtungen*, 334–5; Adams, *Islam*, 194, 266; Hourani, *Arabic Thought*, 156, 240.

19 'Abd al-Raziq, *al-Islam wa-usul al-hukm* (Cairo, 1925), bk. 2, ch. 3.

20 Rida, 'Al-Islām wa-uṣūl al-ḥukm' (*al-Manar*, 1925), 100.

21 Rida, *al-Wahhabiyyun wa'l-Hijaz* (Cairo, 1925), 6.

22 Rida, Tarikh, I:*jim*; idem, *al-Wahhabiyyun wa'l-Hijaz*, 6.

23 Hourani, *Arabic Thought*, 231; Kenneth Cragg, *Counsels in Contemporary Islam* (Edinburgh, 1965), 45.

24 Fauzan Saleh, *Modern trends in Islamic theological discourse in 20th century Indonesia* (Leiden, 2001), 83–5; Carool Kersten, *A History of Islam in Indonesia* (Leiden, 2018), 109–15; Laoust, *Essai*, 538–9; Gibb, *Modern Trends*, 36; Ali Merad, 'Ibn Bādīs' (*EI²*).

25 E.M. Forster, *Two Cheers for Democracy* (London, 1951), 298.

26 Muhammad Iqbal, *The Development of Metaphysics in Persia* (London, 1908), xi.

27 Muhammad Iqbal, *The Mysteries of Selflessness* (London, 1953), x; Cragg, 59.

28 Muhammad Iqbal, *Javid-nama* (London, 1966), 45; *idem, The Secrets of the Self* (London, 1920), 4.

29 Muhammad Iqbal, *Shikwa and Jawab-i Shikwa* (Delhi, 1981), esp. 41, 44–5.

30 *Ibid.*, esp. 69, 71, 74, 76, 77, 81.

31 Iqbal, *Secrets*, chs. VI–VII.

32 Iqbal, *Shikwa*, 96; *idem, Secrets*, xviii.

33 Iqbal, *Secrets*, esp. xvi–xxxi, 48, 79–84, 90, 103.

34 *Ibid.*, 43, 116; *idem, Mysteries*, 24.

35 Iqbal, *Mysteries*, 1, 5, 13, 20, 32–3, 55.

36 Iqbal, *Javid-nama*, 111–13; *idem, The Reconstruction of Religious Thought in Islam* (Stanford, 2013), 154.

37 Iqbal, *Javid-nama*, 54ff.; *idem, Reconstruction*, 78.

38 Iqbal, *Mysteries*, 17–18; *idem, Reconstruction*, 78.

39 Iqbal, *Reconstruction*, 78; Annemarie Schimmel, 'IQBAL, MUHAMMAD' (*Encyclopaedia Iranica*).

40 Iqbal, *Javid-nama*, 44.

41 *Ibid.*, 29, 46, 48.

42 *Ibid.*, 59–61.

43 *Ibid.*, 26, 32, 57.

44 *Ibid.*, 103.

45 *Ibid.*, 55.

46 *Ibid.*, 57, 62.

47 *Ibid.*, 89.

48 *Ibid.*, 101.

49 Richard P. Mitchell, *The Society of the Muslim Brothers* (London, 1969), 14.

50 *Ibid.*, 326.

51 *Ibid.*, ch. viii; Gudrun Krämer, *Hasan al-Banna* (Oxford, 2010), 97–9.

52 Mitchell, 232–3.

53 Al-Banna, *Da'watuna fi tawr jadid* (Cairo, 1954), 5–6.

54 Mitchell, 214.

55 *Ibid.*, 188–9.

56 Al-Banna, 'Al-Jihad fi sabil Allah', 1, in *Majmu'at maqalat li'l-ustadh al-shahid Hasan al-Banna'* (https://archive.org/details/ maqalatealbana/mode/2up); Mitchell, 205–8; Krämer, 66, 101–4.

57 Israel Gershoni, 'The Muslim Brothers and the Arab Revolt in Palestine, 1936–1939' (*Middle Eastern Studies*, 1986), 384.

58 Mitchell, 328.

59 Krämer, 48.

60 Mitchell, 58–71.

61 Seyyed Vali Reza Nasr, *Mawdudi and the Ideologization of Islam* (New York, 1996), 135.

62 *Ibid.*, 80.

63 Muhammad Qasim Zaman, *Islam in Pakistan* (Princeton, 2018), ch. 4.

64 Nasr, *Mawdudi*, 57–8.

65 Zaman, 151.

66 Jan-Peter Hartung, *A System of Life* (London, 2020), 140–55.

67 Nasr, *Mawdudi*, 64.

68 Hartung, 68–9.

69 Nasr, *Mawdudi*, 111.

70 John Calvert, *Sayyid Qutb and the Origins of Radical Islam* (New York, 2013), ch. 3.

71 William E. Shepard, 'The Development of the Thought of Sayyid Quṭb as Reflected in Earlier and Later Editions of "Social Justice in Islam"' (*Die Welt des Islams*, 1992), 219.

72 Calvert, ch. 4; Ronald L. Nettler, *Past Trials and Present Tribulations* (Oxford, 1987).

73 Calvert, 186.

74 Fawaz Gerges, *Making the Arab World* (Princeton, 2018).

75 Olivier Carré, 'Aux sources des frères musulumans radicaux' (*Arabica*, 1985), 262–3; Sayyid Quṭb, *Fi Zilal al-Qur'an* (Cairo, 1968), I:1.

76 Carré, 267.

77 Ronald L. Nettler, 'Guidelines for the Islamic Community' (*Journal of Political Ideologies*, 1996), 187.

78 Zaman, 139.

79 William E. Shepard, 'Sayyid Qutb's Doctrine of Jahiliyya' (*International Journal of Middle East Studies*, 2003), 524.

80 Kepel, *Roots*, 46.

81 *Ibid.*, 52–3.

82 Shepard, 'Sayyid Qutb's', 530.

83 Carré, 277.

84 Hamid Algar (tr.), *The Constitution of the Islamic Republic of Iran* (Berkeley, 1980).

85 Hamid Algar, 'Imam Khomeini: A Short Biography', in Abdar Rahman Koya (ed.), *Imam Khomeini* (Kuala Lumpur, 2009).

86 Ruhollah Khomeini, *Islam and Revolution* (Berkeley, 1981), 170.

87 *Ibid.*, 175, 177.

88 *Ibid.*, 189, 191–2, 198, 200–208; Cook, *Ancient Religions*, 183.

89 Khomeini, *Islam*, 43, 28, 55–6.

90 *Ibid.*, 116, 126.

91 Algar, *Constitution*.

92 Ruhollah Khomeini, 'Fatwa against Salman Rushdie' (https://irandataportal.syr.edu/fatwa-against-salman-rushdie).

93 Gilles Kepel, *Away from Chaos* (New York, 2020), 36.

Islam Today

1 Cf. William E. Shepard, 'Islam and Ideology' (*International Journal of Middle East Studies*, 1987).

2 'Ali Gomaa, *al-Fatawa* (https://draligomaa.com) – 'Hal al-intima' ila al-watan yatanafi ma'a al-intima' ila al-Islam?'; al-Sistani, *al-Istifta'at* (https://www.sistani.org/arabic/qa/) – 'al-Bilad al-islamiyya'.

3 Gomaa, *al-Fatawa* – 'Qiyamat al-mar'a bi-khutbat al-jum'a wa-imamat al-muslimin', 'Hal yajib 'ala al-mar'a an tartadi al-niqab?'; Ahmad Al-Tayyib, *Ahl al-Sunna wa'l-jama'a* (Cairo, 2019), 8; al-Sistani, *al-Istifta'at* – 'al-Aflam', 'al-Internet', 'Ikhtilat al-jinsayn', 'al-Tilifizyun', 'Ru'yat al-aflam', 'al-Nazar ila al-suwar wa'l-aflam al-khali'a'.

ENDNOTES

4 Gomaa, *al-Fatawa* – 'Ma hukm man yudannis aw yazdari al-mushaf al-sharif?', 'Hal fasad al-muslimin yatarattab 'alayhi fasad al-'alam?', 'Ma haqiqat ta'addud al-zawjat fi'l-Islam?', 'Kayf yarudd al-Muslim 'ala shubhat man za'ama anna al-Islam zalama al-mar'a fi qadiyat al-mawarith?'; 'Open Letter to His Holiness Pope Benedict XVI' (https://www.bc.edu/content/dam/files/research_sites/cjl/texts/cjrelations/news/openletter-8238DA.pdf).

5 *A Common Word* (https://www.acommonword.com/); 'Human Fraternity for world peace and living together' (https://www.ohchr.org/Documents/Press/humanfraternity.pdf); Muhammad Hussein Fadlallah, *Mafahim wa-qadaya* (http://arabic.bayynat.org.lb/ListingBooksPage.aspx?id=25166) – 'al-Hiwar'.

6 Nettler et al., *Islam and Modernity*; Katajun Amirpur, *New Thinking in Islam* (London, 2015).

7 Ronald L. Nettler, 'Islam, Politics, and Democracy', in Ronald L. Nettler & David Marquand (eds.), *Religion and Democracy* (Oxford, 2000).

8 Mohamed Talbi, *Li-yatma'inna qalbi* (Tunis, 2007), 12.

9 Muhammad al-'Ashmawi, *al-Islam al-siyasi* (Cairo, 1996), 66; Suha Taji-Farouki (ed.), *Modern Muslim Intellectuals and the Qur'an* (Oxford, 2004).

10 Anke von Kugelgen, 'A Call for Rationalism' (*Alif*, 1996); Mohamed Abed Al-Jabri, *Introduction à la critique de la raison arabe* (Paris, 1994); 'Abdolkarim Soroush, *Siratha-yi mustaqim* (Tehran, 1998); Nasr Hamid Abu Zayd, *Hakadha takallama Ibn 'Arabi* (Cairo, 2004).

11 Brown, *Canonization*, 322–3.

12 Bernard Haykal, 'On the Nature of Salafi Thought and Action', in Roel Meijer (ed.), *Global Salafism* (New York, 2013), 35.

13 Quintan Wiktorowicz, 'Anatomy of the Salafi Movement' (*Studies in Conflict and Terrorism*, 2006).

14 *Ibid.*, 217; Haykal, 47, 49; Stéphane Lacroix, 'Between Revolution and Apoliticism', in *Global Salafism*, 69; Brown, *Canonization*, 323.

15 Hazem Kandil, *Inside the Brotherhood* (Cambridge, 2015); Martyn Frampton, *The Muslim Brotherhood and the West* (Cambridge, Mass., 2018), ch. 8; Frank Griffel, 'What do we mean by "Salafi"?' (*Die Welt des Islams*, 2015); Stéphane Lacroix, *Awakening Islam* (Cambridge, Mass., 2011); Bettina Gräf & Jakob Skovgaard-Petersen (eds.), *Global Mufti* (London, 2009); Sagi Polka, *Shaykh Yūsuf al-Qaradāwī* (Syracuse, 2019).

16 Haykal, 55.

17 *Ibid.*, 53; Shiraz Maher, *Salafi-Jihadism*, 34; Thomas Hegghammer, *The Caravan* (Cambridge, 2020), 293.

18 Maher, 32; Polka, 216;
    Hegghammer, 293.

19 Kepel, *Roots*; Gerges, 145–6;
    Hartung, 214; Polka, 16.

20 Maher, ch. 11; Polka, 155–6.

21 Maher, chs. 4–5, 6–7.

22 Polka, 35; Haykal, 55; Osama
    Bin Laden, 'Declaration of Jihad
    against the Americans Occupying
    the Land of the Two Holy
    Sanctuaries', in Gilles Kepel &
    Jean-Pierre Milelli (eds.), *Al Qaeda
    in its Own Words* (Cambridge, Mass.,
    2008), 47.

23 Maher, ch. 3.

24 Al-Tayyib, 15; Afifi al-Akiti,
    'Defending the Transgressed by
    Censuring the Reckless Against the

    Killing of Civilians' (Hellenthal,
    2005); 'Chechnya Conference
    – Who are the Ahl al-Sunna?'
    (https://chechnyaconference.org/
    material/chechnya-conference-
    statement-english.pdf); 'The
    Makkah Declaration' (https://
    www.oic-oci.org/docdown/?docI
    D=4498&refID=1251); al-Sistani,
    'Ma warada fi khutbat al-jum'a
    li-mumaththil al-marja'iyya
    al-diniyya al-'ulya fi Karbala,
    al-muqaddasa al-Shaykh 'Abd
    al-Mahdi al-Karbala'i fi 14
    Sha'ban 1435 / 13/6/2014'
    (https://www.sistani.org/arabic/
    archive/24918/).

25 Cragg, 12; cf. Ahmed, 269–70.

Index

INDEX

Sunna (prophetic custom)
3, 31, 37–9, 59–60,
64–5, 82
Almohads and 115–6
innovations from *see*
bid'a
Islamic modernism
and 189
Islamic revivalism and
137, 164, 169, 178
philosophy and 101–2
Salafism and 137
Shi'ism and 79
Sufism and 43, 71, 129
ulema as interpreters
of 39, 82
Sunnism 29, 57–73, 78–9,
81–2, 85–90
four sources of the law
(*usul al-fiqh*) 39, 59–60
philosophical theology
and 102, 133, 140
Safavids and 151
Surat al-Ikhlas (The
Chapter of Sincerity)
12–13
al-Suyuti 142
Syria 8, 29, 51, 63, 80,
83, 92, 126, 152, 165,
188, 195
centre of Umayyad
caliphate 29
Christians of 8, 45–7
Druze in 106
Mamluk sultanate
in 136
Muslim conquest of 29
Nizari strongholds
in 107
Ottoman conquest
of 143

al-Taftazani, Sa'd al-Din
135
Tahmasp, Shah 149
al-Tahtawi, Rifa'a Rafi'
176–7, 187

Taj Mahal 159
Taliban 210
ta'lim ('authoritative
instruction') 107–10
taqlid (blind emulation of
authority) 65, 101, 112,
115, 170, 176, 186, 189
tariqas (Sufi orders) 130,
151, 155, 168, 171
Tawfiq of Egypt 184, 186
Timurid Empire 154
Torah 10, 19, 20, 38
translation movement
52–5, 121
al-Tunisi, Khayr al-Din
177
al-Tusi, Nasir al-Din
133–4, 140
al-Tusi, Shaykh al-Ta'ifa
80, 88–9

ulema (Muslim scholars)
33, 39, 43, 50, 79–81,
114–15, 120, 144–5,
147, 158, 165–6, 178,
189, 206
'Umar II, caliph 29,
39, 46
'Umar, Second Caliph
28, 29, 31, 34, 58, 75,
151
Umayyad Caliphate 29,
34, 45–6, 76
umma (Muslim
community) 57, 60,
168, 175, 181, 182,
195, 196
'the unbelievers' (*al-
kafirun*) 17–18, 88, 163,
194, 199
arguments of 93
Nizaris labelled as 109
other Muslims labelled
as (takfir) 209–10
philosophers labelled
as 98, 102, 147
punishment of 26, 125

sinners labelled as 47,
75, 139, 166–7
war with 12, 166, 186
Safavids and 151
'Urabi Revolt 184
Usulism 135, 171–3
'Uthman, Third Caliph
11, 29, 58, 75, 151

Verse of the Sword (*ayat
al-sayf*) 22–3, 209
Verse of Piety (*ayat al-birr*)
25
vilayat-i faqih ('the
governance of the
jurist') 205

Wahhabism 166–7, 171,
179, 192, 208–9
Walad, Baha' al-Din 126
walaya ('sainthood,
spiritual authority')
72–3, 87, 108, 124, 141,
170, 208
Wali Allah, Shah 168–71,
174, 179, 186, 195
al-Walid I, caliph 46
al-Walid II, caliph 30
Wasil ibn 'Ata' 48
al-Wathiq, caliph 31

Yathrib (*now* Medina)
8, 11
Yazid, caliph 76, 150–1,
204
Yusuf ibn Tashfin,
Almoravid leader 114

Zahirism 62–3, 115, 125
zandaqa (heresy) 91
Zayd ibn 'Ali 76
Zionism 196, 197, 200
Zoroastrianism 40, 45